The Tudor privy council

Dorothy Meads Gladish

THE TUDOR PRIVY COUNCIL,

BY

DOROTHY M. GLADISH.

————o————

RETFORD :

PRINTED AT THE OFFICE OF "THE RETFORD, GAINSBOROUGH AND WORKSOP TIMES."

1915.

ERRATA.

p. 2, l. 5, for " 1448 " read " 1443."
p. 9, l. 8, after " transcripts " read " in."
p. 13, l. 16, for " other " read " others."
p. 14, l. 36, for " VI." read " VII."
p. 18, l. 22, for " or " read " of."
p. 20, l. 42, for " courses " read " causes."
p. 21, note (1), after " L. and P." read " Vol. XIII."
p. 29, l. 7, for " Northmapton " read " Northampton."
p. 29, l. 17, for " Cheyne " read " Cheyney."
p. 29, l. 21, for " save " read " serve."
p. 34, l. 34, after " but " read " the."
p. 34, note (6), for " Grenville " read " Grenvelle."
p. 41, note (16), for " Serinia " read " Scrinia."
p. 42, l. 7, for " David " read " Daniel."
p. 43, l. 24, for " years " read " year."
p. 45, l. 29, for " Nnole " read " Knole."
p. 45, l. 35, for " Hallingbury, Morley," read " Hallingbury Morley."
p. 46, l. 9, for " Palce " read " Place."
p. 55, l. 5, for " ime " read " time."
p. 55, l. 35, for " met " read " mete."
p. 59, l. 2, after " regularly " read " as the King's advisers. At the same time there were men of lower rank who were needed for their knowledge of the law and abilities in administration. To this outer circle of advisers, who were regularly "
p. 59, l. 3, for " to " read " the."
p. 60, l. 9, for " 1489 " read " 1589."
p. 60, l. 20, for " Privy " read " King's."
p. 60, l. 36, for " squires " read " Squires."
p. 62, l. 18, for " fortori " read " fortiori."
p. 66, l. 3, for " excellent " read " excellence."
p. 66, l. 27, for " Throne " read " throne."
p. 70, l. 1, after " testy " read " so as."
p. 70, l. 2, after " presence " read " (2)."
p. 70, l. 7, after " received " read " opinion."
p. 70, l. 30, for " VI." read " VII."
p. 72, l. 15, omit " (7)."
p. 72, for " Ibid." in Notes (2) and (3), read " L. and P."
p. 75, l. 14, omit " or ordinary errors."
p. 76, l. 4, for " received " read " reserved."
p. 78, l. 26, omit " (1)."
p. 80, l. 38, for " unveil " read " reveal."
p. 81, l. 32, for " £2,000 " read " £20,000."
p. 82, l. 28, for " 1451 " read " 1541."
p. 82, l. 31, for " borning " read " burning."
p. 82, note (2), for " 217 " read " 227."
p. 87, l. 10, omit " (2)."
p. 100, l. 7, for " petoronells of " read " petronells by."
p. 104, note (4), before " 25 Sept., 1556 " read " A.P.C."
p. 108, l. 26, for " III." read " C."
p. 111, for references (1), (2), (3), (4), read notes (5), (6), (7), (8) respectively.
p. 112, l. 17, for " Ilfracombe " read " Melcombe."
p. 112, l. 33, for " even " read " ever."
p. 114, l. 38, for " Roger " read " Rogers."
p. 115, for references (2), (4), (5), read notes (1), (2), (4) respectively.
p. 116, for reference (1) read note (5) on p. 115.
p. 117, l. 26, for " years " read " year."
p. 119, note (5), for " I." read " II."
p. 121, l. 10, for reference (5) read (3).
p. 121, l. 14, for " Harlings " read " Harling."
p. 123, l. 40, for " other " read " others."
p. 123, for lines 44 and 45, read thus: " semi-ecclesiastical offences. Wherever they had jurisdiction, however, their action was always under the supervision of the Central Council, of which the Commissioners were often "
p. 124, l. 32, for " full " read " sharp."
p. 125, l. 30, for " prohibition " read " prohibitions."
p. 126, l. 12, for " is " read " its."
p. 126, l. 37, for " expectation " read " expedition."
p. 129, l. 13, for " to " read " of."
p. 132, l. 13, for " s." read " c."
p. 134, l. 3, for " 1504 " read " 1540."
p. 139, l. 16, for " Daubney " read " Daubeney."

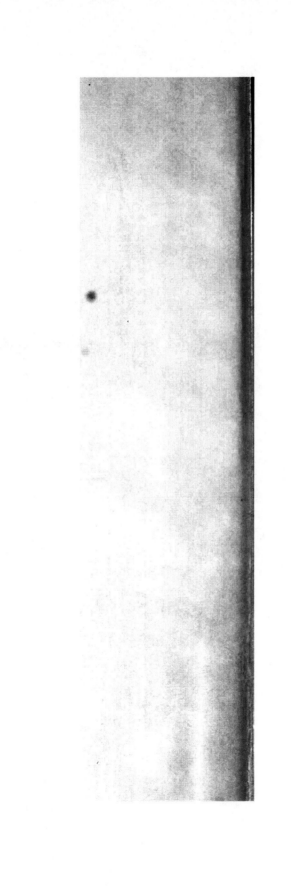

Contents.

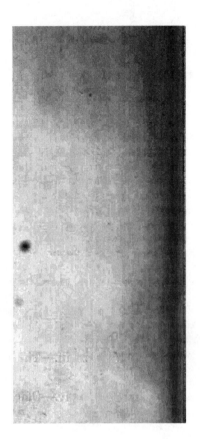

I.--THE COUNCIL IN PRE-TUDOR DAYS.

—————— :0 :——————

DURING the minority of Henry III. there appeared for the first time a Council which
included the great officers of state, a body with constitution and powers as yet
ill-defined. In addition to such departmental duties as any of them might discharge,
the members of this Council had the duty and responsibility of advising the King, of
acting with him, and of being always in immediate attendance upon him. They formed
a body distinct from the larger deliberative assembly, the Magnum Concilium, from the
more frequently summoned assembly of magnates, and from the judicial and financial
staff which transacted the business of the courts of the Chancery and the Exchequer.

By the middle of the thirteenth century this body had assumed so definite a
form that the mode of its selection formed an important feature in the Provisions
of Oxford. From the reign of Henry III. it had, as an assembly, acquired a corporate
character; its members were sworn as councillors of the Crown; in it general questions
of policy were discussed, and prepared if necessary for the estates of the realm; finally
it became the medium through which the King, himself irresponsible, performed acts of
State: it was in short, as Anson calls it, the Continual Council. (1)

The minority of Richard II. was the time when the powers of this Council were
defined as being practically co-extensive with the Prerogative, but, with his reign, the
Council's period of growth closed. Before Richard's accession the character of English
institutions had become permanently fixed. The vagueness which marked the constitution
of the Curia Regis had passed away; the law courts had become distinct bodies, and the
Court of Chancery, though closely connected with the Council until a later period, was
rapidly tending to become a separate Court of Equity. The Great Councils, though still
frequently convoked, had surrendered their most important functions to Parliament, and
the Council itself had become the same body which, in constitution and powers, it remained for at least a century.

The Council's proceedings were probably first accurately recorded when its existence as a separate institution was for the first time distinctly recognised; the earliest
extant records of its proceedings date from the reign of Richard II. From 1386 for a
period of about seventy years it is possible to gain from these records precise information on many points, and it is clear from them that what the Council was under Richard
II., such it was in all essential respects under Henry VI. Its influence varied greatly
during the period 1386-1460 (at which time the records fail until 1540), but not its
character. These minutes of the Council possess peculiar value because they exhibit that
body under such diverse circumstances; it is shown as influenced " by the tyranny and
caprice of Richard; by the crafty astuteness of Bolingbroke; by the vigour and success
of the victor of Agincourt, and by the piety and imbecility of his son." (2)

The members of the Council were appointed for a year, and usually re-appointed
at its expiration; they were bound to attend meetings, and, if the value of money in the
fifteenth century be taken into account, were highly paid for their services. (3)   The
Chancellor and Treasurer were accustomed to receive salaries for their attendance at the
Council Board. Salaries were generally in the form of assignments of the King's revenue,

(1) Anson: " Law and Custom of the Constitution," II. Pt. I. pp. 62--63.
(2) Dicey, p. 26.
(3) Nicholas—" Proceedings and Ordinances of the Privy Council " I. p. v.;
     III. p. xix., p. 154.

2

payable annually so long as one should remain in the Council; they were offered for the first time on a consistent plan in the reign of Richard II., but the plan did not continue for any length of time, being a heavy burden on the available resources of the Crown. The Commons attempted with moderate success to control the appointment of the Council between 1377-1422; after that date their efforts ceased. An ordinance made in 1443 (1) ~~1448~~ marks the highest point which the authority of the Council as contrasted with that of the King ever reached. Under the guise of a series of formal rules concerning the presentation of petitions, this ordinance practically ensured that every grant of the Crown should, from the moment of its presentation as a petition to the time when it was formally issued as a royal writ, be under the notice of the King's ministers. Moreover, when a petition had been granted and signed by the King, and sent to the Keeper of the Privy Seal to be forwarded thence to the Lord Chancellor, it was ordered that if the Keeper of the Privy Seal " thinks that the bills received by him under the signet contain matters of great weight, he is to refer them to the Council, who may refer them to the King again." (2) It is true that after a few years this ordinance was disregarded, but it is nevertheless worthy of note.

For the first time during the reign of Henry VI. the Council assumed the title of the ' Privy Council ' instead of ' the Council.' It might be conjectured that the alteration in name marked a change in character, but nowhere is its exact nature clearly described. Before the Wars of the Roses commenced, the Council towered above every other constitutional authority. Under the House of Lancaster it overshadowed Crown, Parliament, and people, composed as it was of great feudal lords, whose mission it was to see that the royal policy was framed on lines approved by the baronage. In the early part of the fifteenth century it included men of business of no great birth or estate, as well as the great lords. The business of the Council covered the whole field of executive action. A study of the Privy Council records from the beginning of the fifteenth century to their cessation in 1460 gives the student a picture of the daily occupation of the rulers of the Middle Ages, colourless and omitting much, but yet having the advantage of being true. The time of the Council was taken up by an infinite number of trivial cases. At one moment it settled questions of policy; at another took measures for the provision of funds by which the work of administration might be carried on; at another it is seen reviewing minute accounts, communicating with aliens or merchants, or interfering for the preservation of the King's peace. It is impossible to comprise the administrative functions of the Council under any definite number of heads. In modern days, legislative and judicial, administrative and political functions have been separated from each other to an extent which would have seemed unnatural to the statesmen of the fifteenth century. Indefinity and fluidity are the marked characteristics not of the organisation of the Council only, but of all medieval institutions, and even when the process of differentiation had gone so far that a well-marked sphere was assigned to one institution, it was sure to continue to deal with questions which modern opinion would regard as belonging to some other department. The Council was a body which had to do with all departments alike. (3) The governmental functions which it exercised were those of assistants and advisers of the King in matters which, it was agreed, fell outside the liberties of the subject, such as military service and the right to leave the country. (4) Dicey brings under four heads the administrative labours of the Council. (5)

(1) Dicey, p. 39, says that the date is " a little uncertain," and gives it as 1422. Anson, II. Pt. I. p. 159, gives it as 1443, as does Gretton " King's Government," p. 36.
(2) Nicholas: "P. and O. of Privy Council" VI. p. clxxxvii and pp. 316—320.
(3) Tout, in review on Baldwin: " King's Council " E.H.R., Jan., 1915.
(4) Steele: Proclamations p. lxxiv.
(5) D. p. 51 75.

First, its management of the finances. The whole of the royal expenditure, public and private, was laid before it, and it was consulted as to the best methods of raising and spending the revenue.

Secondly, its dealings with aliens and with trade. In theory and in fact foreigners in England were under the arbitrary rule of the monarch. They came naturally within the Council's province, for the Council's power was nothing but the King's prerogative exercised through his officers, and aliens had no legal rights except those accorded by special concessions or particular treaties between England and their country. Besides issuing regulations by Proclamation concerning aliens, the Council saw to the execution of the statutes made by Parliament concerning foreign merchants; many particular powers were conferred on the Council by Parliament in this way, especially during the Tudor period. (1) The Council appears, moreover, to have been at liberty to relax the operation of statutes. It interfered irregularly and capriciously with the general course of trade, and no prerogative was more cherished or more constantly exercised by the Council than the privilege of appointing certain places as staples. Innumerable statutes limited freedom of commercial intercourse between different parts of England as well as between England and foreign countries, and the operation of these acts was rendered more or less stringent at the will of the Council. It exercised, too, the privileges of impressing labourers, soldiers and sailors, of erecting Guilds, or of depriving corporate bodies of their privileges. Such exertions of authority are noted in order that it may be understood how the rule of the Tudors, while differing in essential respects from that of Henry VI., could and did preserve in many ways the form of medieval government.

Thirdly, its relations with the Church. The ecclesiastical powers and the Council came frequently into contact, but there is little in the minutes of the Council which concerns the Church, although cases of heresy and sorcery came before it.

Fourthly, its work as preserver of the peace. The Crown's prerogative of preserving the peace was exercised as a matter of course through the Council. The ordinary law courts aimed at the same object, but the course of law was slow, expensive, and frequently impeded by the very violence which it was called upon to repress. Instances of the Council's interference on behalf of justice abound, and it is here that, to use modern expressions, its executive and judicial functions become confused. The minutes of the Council represent that body as pre-eminently the executive organ of government, although it must not be forgotten that, before the Tudors, the Council, although advising executive action, did not itself directly discharge executive functions. This want of executive authority involved of necessity some limitation to conciliar action. The Council might give advice and the King might take it, but the executive measures necessary to carry out that advice were, before Tudor times at least, seldom the act of the Council. (2) Attention has been drawn, however, almost exclusively to the character of the Council as a law court, the causes of this one-sided view of the Council's position being found in the immense extension of its judicial powers under the Tudors and in the prominence which this branch of its authority obtained in Parliamentary petitions.

(1) Statutes at Large: 21 H. 8 c. 16; 22 H. 8 c. 8.
(2) Tout: Review of Baldwin: " King's Council," E.H.R., Jan., 1915.

4

As early as 1355 a select body of councillors sat for judicial business in a room called the Star Chamber, while new forms of writ infringing the common law, such as *sub poena* and *certis de causis* were invented by John de Waltham, who became Master of the Rolls in 1381. (1) Parliament, however, resisted this extension of the Council's jurisdiction, and in 1390 the Council admitted that cases concerning the common law should be sent before the judges. In 1423 it reserved to itself cases " of too great might on the one side and too great unmight on the other "; in 1426 it added to the reservation " other reasonable cause," and these received Parliamentary sanction in 1429, while 31 H. 6 c. 2 legalised the issure of writs of privy seal summoning before the King or his Council offenders in cases of " great riots, extortions and oppressions." Thus, when the public peace was disturbed, the Council took measures to preserve order, and the government which suppressed the riot became identified with the court which tried the rioters, in this way going beyond the limits prescribed to the action of a modern government. Whenever the law courts were likely to prove inefficient, either from defect of legal authority to give judgment or from lack of power necessary to carry their decisions into effect, then the Council stepped in by summoning before it both defendant and plaintiff. Persons who after invoking the arbitration of the Judges on a matter of dispute refused to abide by their decisions, were summarily brought before the Council.

Such a tribunal was no doubt efficient, but its action was irregular and arbitrary, and as early as Edward III. the Commons had remonstrated against it. But though they attacked this use of the Council's power, they were ready enough in the fifteenth century to leave the Council a field of action whenever men needed to be coerced. The act of 1453 was so similar to that of 1487 that it, too, might well have created in the minds of the lawyers of the 17th century the erroneous opinion (2) regarding the foundation of the Court of Star Chamber. In a state of society where noble lords opposed the decisions of the courts of justice and " maintained and cherished " robbers, pillagers and ravishers of women, men turned with hope to the King and his Council who gave justice, arbitrary it might be, but yet efficacious, and at least professed to prefer the cause of the poor and weak. The constant jealousy of the Commons prevented this most important function of the Council from overstepping the bounds of justice and superseding the common law courts: not until the disorders of Henry VI.'s reign had sapped the authority of the Council was a considerable part of its powers assumed by the Court of Chancery. An inquiry into the legality of the judicial power of the Council has a real meaning only when made concerning the authority exercised by the Council under the Tudors, while an examination of the minutes of the Council under the Lancastrians will reveal precedents for many of the acts of the Council during that period.

In all these functions of the Council we can trace its relationship to the Great Council, especially in the claim of the peers to be present at these judicial sittings, even in Stuart times. (3) After the year 1460 there is no record of the proceedings of the Council remaining to us until 1540. There is either a great gap in the Council records, as Harris Nicholas thinks (4), or else there has been a material loss of records once existent—a problem which will be discussed later.

(1) Pollard: " The Reign of Henry VII. from Contemporary Sources," p. xxxviii.
(2) Ibid.
(3) Hudson: Star Chamber II. Collectanea Juridica, p. 25.
(4) P. and O.: VII., p. iii.

Direct records of the Council of Edward IV. are almost entirely lacking. A few fragments exist, mainly in the form of warrants with endorsements " per consilium " for letters under the privy seal, and likewise under the great seal, but of these administrative orders the quantity during the Yorkist period stands, in contrast to that during the Lancastrian, in the ratio of less than one to twenty, and during the first year of Edward IV.'s reign not one in a hundred of these warrants was passed by the authority of the Council. This lack of records may be due merely to an accident, but " it is no mere accident, however, that all collateral sources, such as the rolls of Parliament, the statute rolls, patent rolls, issue rolls of the Exchequer, the Year Books and other familiar collections are almost equally silent. The same sources are filled with references to the Court of Chancery which was obviously growing and making itself felt in every direction. But everything tends to strengthen the impression that for a number of years immediately following the revolution of 1460—1, the activities and responsibilities of the Council, while not entirely suspended, were reduced to a minimum." (1) Is Baldwin correct in arguing the reduced activity of the Council under the Yorkist Kings from the negative argument of the absence of conciliar records? He goes on, however, to support what he calls " the evidence of facts " by the " argument of motive." Under the Lancastrians the Council had been, like Parliament, an instrument of the nobility, and it had been identified with all the failures and weakness of that régime. To a considerable extent it had been used to exploit the power of the Crown to the profit of individual lords. Already in the later years of Henry VI. the disintegration of the Council was as complete as that of Parliament, and in his policy of restoring the rights of the Crown it was clearly not the intention of Edward IV. to maintain the Council on the old lines. In this respect he departed from his father's policy of 1453—55. A Council in form there was, as there was a Parliament, but the one body was changed in character as much as the other.

In the inauguration and settlement of the new government, the formation of a Council was mysteriously left in the background. Probably no list or large number of appointments was made at any time, but men were retained or employed as needed. Very few lords were to be found in the King's Council except those who held the great offices of State. Among these remained a few of the servants of Henry VI., but a larger number were new creations and promotions made by Edward. Archbishop Bourchier was paid £200 for attending the Council; John Tiptoft, Earl of Worcester, the Constable, 200 marks; the King's Chamberlain, William Hastings, was given £200 for his salary in the seventh year of Edward's reign, and the following year was assigned £100 " for his costs in attending the King's person and the Council," while the King's Butler, Chancellor, and Treasurer continued to receive their salaries of £200 and 200 marks: otherwise, salaries for attendance at the Council were given only in exceptional cases. It is equally noteworthy that neither the King nor any great lord attended the Council with any degree of frequency. (2)

In the absence of a fixed body of lords, a considerable number of knights and squires was a feature of Edward's Council; already we have signs of the later Tudor bourgeois body. Most of these men were office-holders especially in the King's household, e.g., Sir John Say, Speaker of the House of Commons, 1463; Sir John Fog, Treasurer of the Household; Sir John Scott, Comptroller, and others whose status it would be difficult to determine. Still more marked is the tendency already visible in the later years of Henry

(1) Baldwin: " King's Council," pp. 421—422.
(2) Ibid, p. 423.

VI.'s reign, and apparent throughout the Tudor period, to extend the title of 'Councillor' to more than a score of doctors of law, clerks, and other minor men of the court. This reversion to a body of officials, more marked than under Richard II., and the absence of great lords from the Council led in time to protests very similar to that of the Northern rebels in 1536. In 1469, the Duke of Clarence, the Archbishop of York, and the Earl of Warwick reminded the King of what had happened to Edward II., Richard II., and Henry VI.: "First where the said Kings estranged the great lords of their blood from their secret Council, and were not advised by them, and taking about them other not of their blood, and inclining only to their counsel, rule, and advice, the which persons take not respect nor consideration to the will of the said princes, nor to the commonweal of this land, but only to their singular lucre and enriching of themselves and their blood, as well as in their great possessions as in goods; by the which the said princes were so impoverished that they had not sufficient of livelihood nor of goods, whereby they might keep and maintain their honourable estate and ordinary charges within this realm." (1)

Sir John Fortescue traced all the misfortunes of England to the influence of irregular and irresponsible Councillors; he thought the King's business suffered from the inattention of the great lords, engrossed in their own affairs and in the advancement of their families and dependants. (2) It is difficult to define the Council of Edward IV., for there were on the one hand certain nobles of undoubted political influence, and, at the other extreme, scores who were called 'King's Councillors.' Baldwin repudiates the suggestion that these men of inferior rank were not strictly members of the Privy Council but stood to it in the relation of assessors, as being based on an old fallacy that the King's Council must needs be a definite and homogenerous body, and that beyond this there might be a council of different composition. Even in Edward IV.'s day, he asserts, no such view of the matter was yet conceived; the king's council whether called 'privy' or 'great' still remained a diversified body with all the anomalies of the past, and was designed to include not lords only, but men of every estate and kind of service. Moreover, when the business transacted by the Council comes to be considered, it is still more evident why the attendance and services of official and professional members were required. Sometimes a sitting of the Council was held, at which only one or two lords were present besides half a dozen or more doctors and clerks. There was no reluctance to place the names of these men on record, but in later times, as under the Tudors after 1540, 'ordinary councillors' were not so recognised.

The actual conduct of the government under Edward IV. is in strong contrast to the methods of the Lancastrians. "Instead of a ruling and guiding council it was at every step an emphasis of the royal authority." (3) Grants of the Crown were made in the name of the King with the consent or concurrence of the Council seldom expressed. Few letters under the great seal were attested "per consilium." (4) When the Council was consulted it appears to have been rather with reference to technical forms than to the policy involved. Among the statutes of the realm, none of the new acts appear to have been draughted by the Council or entrusted to it for execution.

Still, the King needed the Council, and royal acts are often stated in the form "rex de avisamento sui consilii voluit et mandavit," while the King in granting letters under the great seal frequently commanded the Chancellor either viva voce or by his

(1) Camden Society, 1839, f. 47, "Chronicle of first 13 years of Edward IV."
(2) "Governance of England," p. 145 (edit. Plummer).
(3) Baldwin, p. 426.
(4) The persistent "s" in this word is noteworthy.

signet "in the presence of the Council." On September 7th, 1469, an event clearly revealed that a distinction already existed between the Councillors attending the King wherever he went, and that part of the Council which remained behind at Westminster, a distinction still more marked, as will be seen later, during the reign of Henry VIII. (1) Already the former appear as the King's real advisers, while the latter are hardly more than an administrative board composed mainly of officials and doctors of law. The "Council with the King" was then, as always, the real consultative council, for the primary duty of the Council was to follow the King and to give him advice when asked to do so. From the reign of Edward I. onwards it was usual, when the King went abroad, for part of the council to attend him while part remained behind to assist with the regency.

Although the corporate action of the Council was now greatly reduced, it still had much to do, and individual Councillors were never more active in the King's service; clerks were employed incessantly in carrying messages, while greater men were sent on diplomatic missions. In the later years of Henry VI., the Council had almost ceased to exercise its judicial functions, and for the first eight years of Edward IV.'s reign, although the country was harried by the depredations of rebels and rioters, cases were generally given for trial to special assizes or else brought to the Court of Chancery. And this is true not only as regards criminal jurisdiction, but all kinds of litigation. Suitors generally ceased to address complaints to the King or his Council; they went instead to the Chancellor, and it seemed as though the entire jurisdiction of the Council, including cases of violence and maintenance, as well as equitable cases concerning property, would be diverted to him. But the jurisdiction of the Council was by no means abandoned or entirely superseded, for the Chancellor did not succeed so well with criminal as with civil cases, for which he was better equipped; the great evils of the time demanded a more vigorous authority.

About 1468 the tide turned in favour of the revival of the Council's authority; commissions of arrest were almost exclusively to bring offenders before the Council, and the records of several cases found on the rolls show that the normal functions of the Council were gradually being resumed. (2) But as regards rioters, its administration was anything but vigorous and efficient, and there is no instance in the period of a great offender being actually punished. The lords of the Council were themselves too much involved in illegal practices to discountenance the same in others, so that instead of effective punishment there were incomprehensible delays, pardons of outlawry and attempts at reconciliation; apparently the Council preferred to deal with these cases as little as possible.

Certain changes of procedure also appear in these years, denoting a break, to a certain extent, with older traditions. The King, even in judicial work, becomes much more prominent than before; the signet is used for the purpose of summoning the parties; on one occasion the King himself gave judgment. (3) Greater prominence, too, was given to the Chancellor when petitions were addressed to him as a means of approach to the Council, and there was apparently great confusion in the minds of suitors whether it was the Council or the Chancellor's Court which they were seeking (4), but by the end of the reign cases heard by the Council in the Star Chamber are more clearly in evidence.

Under Richard III. the same tendencies in the Council are still more definitely marked. Even less than his brother was Richard able to command the regular services of a body of nobles in his government, but this deficiency of lords was made up by the

(1) L. and P., XVI., 141, 1246, 1261; also A.P.C., vol. iv.
(2) Baldwin, p. 431.
(3) Calendar of Patent Rolls, 20 Edw. IV., 218.
(4) Baldwin, p. 433.

appointment of a number of professional men, some of whom were retained with annuities for life. It cannot be said that the Council was allowed any initiative or discretionary power in the control of the government, but it was fully awake to its responsibilities in the judicial field. Suitors in considerable number were seeking the remedies afforded by the Council. In the first year of the reign two clerks were appointed, one of whom, John Harrington, expressly " for his good service before the lords and others of the Council, especially in the custody, registration and expedition of bills, requests and supplications of poor persons." (1) Unfortunately little has been left for posterity from the custody and registration of these bills, but, as his successor a hundred years later explained, "And the time also when he served was in division between the two Houses of Lancaster and York, by which means the Acts of the Council were not so exactly kept and conserved as they are now." (2)

Throughout the middle ages from the very beginning, the King's Council had been a body vaguely outlined, uncertain in composition, undefined in function and unrestricted in scope of authority. Just previous to the accession of Henry VII. its outlines appear gradually with greater clearness. In the midst of a prevailing tendency to specialize, it had never lost its elemental freedom of action. Attempts had been made from time to time in Parliament to limit its powers, and also to a lesser extent to permit or assign certain functions to it, but these acts were never comprehensive in their scope nor was the conduct of the Council ever seriously affected by them. Inevitably the Council fell into certain customary lines of action, until it created, before the middle of the Tudor period, a jurisdiction and procedure distinctively its own, although it never became entangled in its own rules of action. Owing to the unsettled character of the Council there had been a ceaseless conflict as to which of the two dominant interests it should actually represent. The King wished to fill his Council with household officers and personal dependants, while the desire of the magnates and of Parliament, more in accordance with feudal traditions, was that it should be composed of a select number of bishops and barons. Never during the middle ages had the parliamentary plan of a Council been successful for more than a brief period of time, although supported by every legislative device, for there was always the same difficulty—the reluctance of the lords to serve with any degree of constancy. Not until after the accession of the Tudors was the problem fairly settled. As a result of the civil wars the strength of the older nobility was broken and a body of lords bound by various ties of interest was gradually reared in the service of the monarchy. In the Middle Ages, too, the duties of those councillors in attendance upon the King and of those who remained behind at Westminster were never satisfactorily fixed; consequently there was an inevitable sacrifice of one set of duties or the other.

Such, then, was the Council which the first Tudor found ready to his hand. What little evidence we have of its powers and work under the two Yorkist Kings would seem to show it as fallen somewhat in prestige but a strong organisation still, for its governmental power was almost untouched, although its judicial power was delegated, its legislative power confined to the making of executive orders, and its advisory powers almost a nullity. The Tudors singled it out from amongst all other institutions to be their instrument for the establishment and extension of their system of rule in England, and, to render it equal to the task, they developed and strengthened it " till it grew into a powerful body fit to gather and hold all the threads of administration and diplomacy." (3)

(1) Calendar of Patent Rolls I. Rich. III., 413.
(2) Leadam: Selden Society XII. Court of Requests, lxxxiv.
(3) " Privy Council under the Tudors," p. 1.

II.—THE PRIVY COUNCIL OF HENRY VII.

—————— :o: ——————

TO treat of the Privy Council during that crucial period when it was being reorganised by Henry VII. and his son is extremely difficult. The formal record of its proceedings between 1460 and 1540, if indeed any such was ever kept, is lost to us, and we are therefore driven to rely largely upon indirect evidence, especially for the composition of the Privy Council during these years.

But we have what is in some ways an approach to a minute book of the Council, the "Liber Intrationum," (1) the original of which has been lost; copies had fortunately been made, however, and a number of transcripts incomplete and fragmentary form exist. Four-fifths of the contents consist of a register of prosecutions and suits such as commonly belong to the tribunal of the Star Chamber, and these were plainly the main consideration of the Council, but judicial business was by no means separated from general administrative work for all were apparently entered in the same register at this period. The "Liber Intrationum" apparently consisted of a number of extracts taken, perhaps, from the Council Register for the purpose of illustrating the history of the Court of Star Chamber. It was a record of the business transacted by the Council when sitting in the Star Chamber.

Miss Scofield asserts "From the nature of the business shewn to have been transacted in the Star Chamber during the first two years of Henry VII.'s reign, and the number and character of those present at the meetings at which business was transacted, it is impossible to believe the entries in the 'Liber Intrationum' were anything but the meetings of the King's Council." (2) She is probably at fault in basing her conjecture upon the number and character of those present. Whenever the names of those who sat in the Star Chamber are recorded, they prove conclusively that those particular sittings were not assemblies of the King's Council as such, but were meetings of the King's Council in the Court of Star Chamber, together with the judges and others who with the Council itself composed that Court, and moreover the character of the business transacted at those meetings serves to show that as yet it was not departmentalised into purely Privy Council and purely Star Chamber business. Also, the presence of the King himself was recorded, which was never done in the minutes of the Privy Council proper. (3) The mistake may have arisen from the erroneous idea that Henry VII. had no fixed body of Privy Councillors, an opinion which will be dealt with hereafter. Some of the entries in the "Liber Intrationum" record the business transacted by the Privy Council alone sitting in the Star Chamber as the Privy Council of the King. There was very close connection between the Court of Star Chamber and the Privy Council at this period; the business of the two institutions was almost indistinguishable in kind, and, if the Liber Intrationum was made from the Council Register, seems to have been recorded in the same book. There is another set of records printed by Sir Julius Cæsar in 1597 to explain the history of the Court of Requests. All else concerning Henry's Council has to be gleaned from indirect sources. The reign of Henry VII. is at first sight one of the most uninteresting reigns in English history, but in reality it is one of equal fascination and value, for it completed the foundations, laid in the Lancastrian period, for the edifice of conciliar government raised by the Tudors.

(1) Add. MSS. vol. 4521 f. 104, also Harleian MSS. 297 f. 1.—Brit. Mus.
(2) Scofield: Star Chamber, p. 6.
(3) A.P.C. passim.

It is difficult to give a correct answer to the question: Had Henry VII a fixed body of councillors? It has been said that from the documents accessible it is difficult to distinguish between the King's Council and the Great Council in this reign; that it is impossible to compile a list of Councillors, and that there is small evidence of any control or even advice given to the Crown by any definite body, except the advice given by the Judges and other Lords of Parliament on constitutional questions and reported in the Year Books. It is also maintained that Henry "retained" certain councillors and sought their advice as individuals rather than as councillors (for we read of this or that Councillor being influential with the King), without being under any obligation to consult them as a body, and that the definite organisation of the Privy Council dates like that of so many other forces in the constitution from the reign of Henry VIII. (1)

This opinion is based upon the impression that the King's Council was, as it had been in the Middle Ages, a diversified body designed to include not the lords only, but men of every estate and kind of business, and that the term "councillor" could be used interchangeably with "one of the Privy Council." Moreover, it leaves out of consideration the Wars of the Roses and the subsequent Yorkist dynasty under which the composition of the Council was revolutionised. It is difficult to compile a list of Councillors because we lack records of the names of those present at Council meetings, those recorded in the Liber Intrationum being of the Council sitting in the Court of Star Chamber. Besides the Council, as the records show, there sat also in the Court of Star Chamber men whom Sir Thomas Smith later described as "other lords and barons which be not of the Privy Council and be in the town, and the judges of England." (2) Consequently the record of attendance in the Star Chamber under Henry VII is not to be regarded as furnishing exact information as to the personnel of his Privy Council, though it may assist us considerably. As to advice, it was always recognised that it was the duty of the King's Council to give advice either individually or collectively when called upon to do so, but the King was not bound to take that advice nor did he consider himself bound to ask advice or consult his Council. It is possible that under the Lancastrians a strong and independent Council had been able to modify this last rule; obviously, too, it would not apply during minorities. Under the Tudors, however, it certainly was not in force. The more abundant records of the reign of Henry VIII. illustrate that point in striking fashion, as will be seen later.

Henry VII. was the first English monarch for more than a century to find himself without the support of an influential party among the peers at his accession. But he wanted ability as well as loyalty, and he formed his Privy Council from the class below the peerage. Part of it was no doubt drawn from the supporters who had gathered round him at Rennes and from the Councillors of Edward IV. It was soon constituted; on 17th September, 1485, Henry entered London, and by 30th September the Privy Council was at work and a Clerk of the Council appointed. (3) On Dec. 5th, 1485, Rymer (4) records a commission to John Arundel, Dean of Exeter, Sir Richard Edgecombe, Comptroller of the Household, and John Bladiswell, (5) Clerk to the Council, to reduce the inhabitants of Calais, Guisnes, and the marches to obedience. The other Clerk of the Council in Henry's reign was Robert Rydon, who on 23rd September, 1490, is recorded as receiving together with Richard Malewe, President of Magdalen College, Oxford, a commission to deliver to the King and Queen of Castile Henry's ratification of his treaty with the Duchess of Brittany. (6) Evidently the Clerks of Henry's Council held no insignificant position.

(1) Pollard: Reign of Henry VII. from Contemporary Sources. Appendix I. p. 314, vol. III.

(2) Commonwealth of England 1565, Book 3 c. 4.

(3) Materials for a History of Henry VII. Rolls Series I. 154, 339

(4) Rymer: Foedera vol. II.

(5) Pollard gives his name as Baldeswell. Henry VII., vol. 3, p. 318.

(6) Rymer: Foedera. vol. II.

Henry is reputed to have been very successful in raising up a class of nobles who would be serviceable to him, though Perkin Warbeck's proclamation (1) gives the names of those who were considered by men outside the court to have most influence with the King: "Putting apart all well disposed nobles he hath none in favour and trust about his person but Bishop Fox, Smith, Bray, Lovell, Oliver King, Sir Charles Somerset, David Owen, Rysley, Sir James Turberville, Tyler, Robert Lytton, Guildeford, Chumley, Empson, James Hobert, John Cutte, Garth, Hansy, Wyat, and such others, caitiffs and villeins of simple birth which by subtle inventions and pilling of the people have been the principal finders, occasioners, and counsellors of the misrule and mischief reigning in England." (2) The charge of having "caitiff and villein" councillors was a stock complaint against the Tudor monarchs, and was evidently put forward by Perkin that it might by chance touch a sympathetic chord in noble breasts.

Henry was not long upon the throne before he gave many indications that he wished to raise himself above the aristocratic factions which had been the curse of England in the past. (4) He formed his Council not so much from the nobility as from such men as Morton Bishop of Ely (who became his Chancellor in 1486 in succession to John Alcock, Bishop of Worcester), Warham, Archbishop of Canterbury, who in turn become Lord Chancellor, Richard Fox, Lord Privy Seal (3), Sir Reginald Bray, Chancellor of the Duchy of Lancaster, Sir Richard Edgecombe, Comptroller of the Household, Sir John Dynham, Lord High Treasurer, and Sir Edward Poynings. His Secretaries were Oliver King, who had been French Secretary to Edward IV. (5), and Stephen Frion. The Queen Dowager was imprisoned on the outbreak of Simnel's rebellion, says Bacon, by a "close counsel without any legal proceeding upon far-fetched pretences." There were, indeed, some noble names among the list of Henry's Privy Councillors: the Earl of Oxford, hereditary

(1) B. M. Birch MSS. 4160.

(2) It is impossible to investigate fully how far this charge against Henry of having "caitiffs and villeins of simple birth" as his counsellors was true, for many, such as David Owen, Rysley, Tyler, Robert Lytton, John Cutte, Garth, and Hansy are unknown men. Of the others, Fox's station in life before he was employed by the Earl of Richmond at Paris seems unknown. William Smith, late Bishop of Lincoln, was at any rate educated in a noble family. Sir Reginald Bray had been receiver-general and steward of the household to the King's step-father, Henry, Earl of Stafford. Chumley may have been the Sir Richard Cholmeley who was made a member of Henry VIII.'s Privy Council in 1513 (S. P. Dom. H 8, 1. 5762). Sir Thomas Lovell was related to Francis, first Viscount Lovell. Oliver King may not have been well-born we do not know, but he had been French secretary to Edward IV. and a canon of Windsor. Somerset was the bastard son of Henry Beaufort, third Duke of Somerset. Sir Richard Guildford had lands in Sussex at Guildford Level. Richard Empson sat for Northamptonshire in the Parliament of 1491, and was made Speaker, although he was not knighted until 1504. James Hobart was a friend of John Paston and Attorney-General 1486—1507, although we know nothing of his birth. Sir Henry Wyatt appears to have been a well-born courtier. It is significant that Dudley is not mentioned here. Warbeck's examples do not altogether prove his charge.

(3) In 1487. John Gunthorpe was appointed by Richard III. in 1483 (D.N.B.), and seems to have been continued in the office by Henry until Richard Fox was appointed.

(4) For a list of Henry VII.'s Councillors, see Appendix I.

(5) Pollard says he surrendered the office when he became Bishop of Exeter in 1492 (H. VII., vol. III. p. 317). King was not made Bishop of Exeter till 1493 (D.N.B. and Le Neve).

Great Chamberlain of England, the Duke of Bedford, Henry's uncle, and the Earl of Derby, who was given the office of Constable pro hac vice in 1487 (1); but the chief characteristic of the Council was the large preponderence in it of hardened and tested middle class ability. Such were the veteran John Morton, Bishop of Ely, who had served at Towton and was summoned from exile in Flanders; Richard Fox, son of a Lincolnshire yeoman, a priest and doctor of the canon law, who had been of service in Paris to Henry when still Earl of Richmond; " vigilant men and secret, and such as kept watch with him upon all men else." (2) Sir Reginald Bray, diplomatist, soldier and architect, has left in the delicate tracery of Henry VII.'s Chapel a permanent memorial to his taste. Another Councillor, a Devon squire, Richard Edgecombe, had raised troops to join the Duke of Buckingham's rebellion in 1484, and had paid the common penalty of ill-success and become a proscript and an exile until there came a knighthood on Bosworth field. Sir Richard Guildford, another exile in Brittany, also became one of Henry's councillors; he was made one of the Chamberlains of the receipt of the Exchequer, Master of the Ordnance and the Armoury, and he became one of the King's most valued servants. It was a Council of useful talents rather than ornamental names, and largely composed of men whose " loyalty had been tried and whose spirit had been tested by the searching wind of adverse fortune." (3) A point was made of having the members of the Council sworn and admitted with due formality. On one occasion in the fourteenth year, there is a record of eight lords being introduced and sworn " to the Council of our Lord King," the Duke of Buckingham, the Earls of Northumberland, Shrewsbury, and Essex, Lords Burgavenny, Dacre, Grey de Wilton, and Hastings. On the 12th November of the same year occurs the entry " Dominus de Dudley est iuratus et admissus consilio Regio." (4) These facts are of importance as tending to dispose of the theory that Henry had no definite Council.

There were few of Henry's Councillors who did not hold office, either of State or of the Household; they were chosen from Churchmen, lawyers, and soldiers; and if we except his own relations the only members of the nobility who occupied high place were the Earls of Oxford and Surrey. Talent and loyalty superseded the factious influence of splendid lineage; Henry was continuing Edward IV.'s policy of introducing new men devoted to the business of official life and of no great weight in the country, and paving the way for the official bourgeois Council of his successors. The men who helped Henry in the task of Government had risen from lowly stations, like Morton, Fox, and Warham, by mere force of intellect and character through the avenue of the Church, or, like Dudley, were talented and serviceable lawyers. " The nobility was fast becoming a nobility of the court required to glitter at tournaments and festivals rather than contribute to the deliberations of the Council board." (5) " He established in his house a grave council of wise and politic men by whose judgment, order, and determination the people might be governed according to justice and equity, and that all causes might be finished and ended there without great bearing or expense in long suit. And for hearing and deciding these causes justly and speedily he swore of his council divers noble and

(1) These nobles had all rendered good service to one cause or another, and were probably included for that reason: the Earl of Oxford for long service to the Lancastrian cause, and Derby for more recent services.

(2) Bacon: History of Henry VII., ed. J. R. Lumby, p. 19.

(3) Fisher: Political History of England VI., 6.

(4) Add. MSS. vol. 4521 f. 113.

(5) Fisher: Political History of England VI., 124.

discreet persons who for their policy, wit, and singular gravity, were highly esteemed and renowned, whose names follow: Jasper Duke of Bedford, John Earl of Oxford, Thomas Stanley Earl of Derby, John Bishop of Ely, Sir William Stanley Lord Chamberlain of his Household, Sir Robert Willoughby, Lord Brooke, Lord Steward of his Household, Giles Lord Daubeney, John Lord Denham, after made Treasurer of England, Sir Reginald Bray, Sir John Cheney, Sir Richard Guildford, Sir Richard Tunstall, Sir Richard Edgecombe, Sir Thomas Lovell, Sir Edward Poynings, Sir John Risley with divers other wise men, which, as time required, he called to his counsayll and service now one and now another." (1) Hall in this extract apparently recognises Henry's Privy Councillor as a select body, and, moreover, he mentions others whom Henry called to the aid of himself and his Council, such men as the law officers of the Crown and the Judges of the several Courts who aided the Council when it sat, for instance, in the Court of the Star Chamber. Three concentric groups of councillors were coming to be defined for the first time under Henry VII.; first the King's privy council, then the ordinary council (which will be dealt with later) served by a less influential body of professional men, while beyond those again were the justices and "others of the council," a phrase constantly recurring in the official documents of the Tudor period, and which has been boldly suggested as meaning nothing more or less than the whole of what we should call Henry's civil service.

From the accession of Henry VII. the history of the Council is the history of the monarchy. The Council was, however, a variable factor; its real power was constantly changing. Under a strong King it was really no check upon his will; he could appoint and dismiss it; he was not obliged to take or even ask for its advice. Under the Tudors the Council ceased to be any restraint upon the King; its power increased, but that merely signified an increase in the power of the Crown. It was strong against all others but weak against the King, for it was but an assembly of the King's servants whom he appointed and dismissed at pleasure.

Henry VII. was his own first minister; Bacon says that in his greatest business he consulted none except Morton and Fox. De Puebla wrote in 1500 concerning negotiations for an alliance with Spain: "There are many counsellors in the Privy Council who have taken no part in the former negotiations and know nothing of the matter."(2) Throughout the Spanish and Venetian dispatches, Henry's Council and Privy Councillors are constantly mentioned: in 1498 "the counsellors and many other great dignitaries of the realm were called into the room," and in 1504 the marriage of the Queen of Naples is reported by De Puebla as much approved by the King and his Privy Council. (3) Though not without serious blemishes, Henry VII.'s government was free from some of the peculiar failings of autocracy; there were no court favourites, no jealousy of able men, no megalomania. The King's eye was all pervading; nothing was too small for his attention. Vergil says, "He allowed no one to usurp his authority, saying that he wished to rule, not to be ruled." The influence of the King's mother is reputed to have been very strong, as also is that of one or two of Henry's Councillors: "the persons who have the greatest influence in England are the mother of the King, the Chancelor, Master Bray, the Bishop of Durham, Master Ludel who is treasurer, the Bishop of London and the Lord Chancellor." (4) Morton's death in 1500 is said to have removed a wholesome influence which saved the King from unpopular courses, though Morton himself survived the worst blot on Henry's reign, the judicial murder of Warwick, and lived to incur "the great disdain and great hatred of the commons of the land."(5) The death of Sir Reginald Bray

(1) Hall's Chronicle (London, 1809), p. 424.
(2) Spanish Calendar I., 268.
(3) Ibid: 204, 419.
(4) Ibid: 204 (1498). It is noteworthy that Fox is not included.
(5) Kingsford: Chronicles of London, p. 232.

in 1503 cannot have influenced the King's conduct, for no Councillor exercised any appreciable control over Henry's policy. To trustworthy men like Warham and Fox Henry gave his official confidence, " that confidence which a self-confident autocrat can afford to give to men whose interests are the same as his own "; but he had also another set of ministers like Dudley and his satellite Empson whom he used as tools, " responsible tools to be used as long as they wer useful, but to be held responsible the moment their use was over and the outcry they provoked became more noxious than the ends they served were advantageous." (1) Fox is the most familiar figure during the close of the reign, but it is to Oxford that Flemish and Spanish diplomatists are represented as ascribing the greatest influence. This is due in part at any rate to editorial error. When Puebla (2) says, " The King of England has no confidential advisers; the Lord Great Chamberlain who is of his blood is however more in his confidence than any other person," there is manifest confusion between Oxford, who was Lord Great Chamberlain and Sir Charles Somerset. Lord Herbert, the illegitimate son of Henry's cousin, the third Duke of Somerset, appointed Chamberlain of the Household in 1505. (3) Henry, besides being his own first minister, chafed against the slightest attempt on the part of his Council to control him. He is said to have had great confidence and trust in De Puebla. There are indications that he entrusted to him more than he would confide to any other ambassador, and that there was not a single Englishman who shared the confidence of the King to so great an extent.

In 1500 Henry is represented as giving a very sharp order to his Council concerning a proposed treaty with Spain (4); they were to cease " disputing about words and to confer only on the material portion of the treaty." Henry could not have been controlled to any great extent by his Council, especially in the latter half of his reign, or he would never have been allowed to employ such men as Empson and Dudley for measures which men like Archbishop Warham and the Earl of Surrey could certainly not have approved, but which they appear to have been helpless to prevent, and against which they dared not remonstrate. Moreover, the King must have dealt directly with the subordinate officials in his service without much concert with his nominal ministers.

Henry found it necessary to create a new officer in his Council, that of the Lord President of the King's Council. This new office was different from that of Chancellor, Treasurer, or Keeper of the Privy Seal, in that it was not the head of an existing department, but was created solely for the purposes of the Council. The development of the office is very obscure; no trace of it has been found before 1496. Sir Thomas Lovell is said to have become Treasurer of the Household and President of the Council in, 1502. (5) Henry VII. describes Richard Fitzjames, Bishop of Chichester, as " Councillor and President of our Council " in 1506, whom he asserts he has appointed in the place of William, late Bishop of London, recently deceased. (6) The " Italian Relation " (7) refers to the President of the Council as one of the regular officers of State. The President is first mentioned in 1497, when he is seen taking the place of the Keeper of the Privy Seal in the proceedings of the Court of Requests, " coram Presidente Consilii Domini Regis." (8) Fitzjames' name occurs in the records of that Court as holding the office 1499—1500. The King would preside at Council meetings when he was present; in his absence this would probably devolve upon the Lord President, but of his duties and emoluments we know nothing. The creation of the office, however, tells strongly in favour of an organised Privy Council.

(1) Stubbs: Lectures on Medieval and Modern History, p. 248.
(2) Spanish Calendar, 5th Oct., 1507.
(3) Pollard: Henry VII., I. p. xxvii.   (4) Spanish Cal., 16th June, 1500.
(5) D.N.B. xxxiv. 126, which latter statement Pollard says (Henry VII. vol. 3, p. 316) is probably inaccurate.
(6) Venetian Calendar I., 876.
(7) Probable date 1499.
(8) Cæsar, p. 14.

Of the time and place of meeting of Henry's Council we know nothing, except the assertion of Lambard (1) that he had seen it registered that Henry VII. sat in judgment with his Council in the Star Chamber twelve times during the first two years of his reign. Most of these sittings of the King and his Council in the Court of Star Chamber are recorded in the Liber Intrationum also; and as they are for the first two years of Henry's reign they prove fairly conclusively that the Court of Star Chamber was not established by the unreasonably famous Act of 1487.

The Council took up its work from the beginning of the reign with great energy; the Liber Intrationum records it as sitting in the Star Chamber as often as four times a week during term. What little we can learn of actual Council business from the fifth part of the contents of this Book of Entries which deals with it, reveals the Council proposing to send a diplomatic commission to Calais to treat with the Emperor concerning trade relations between England and the Netherlands, 10th July, 1486, and later in the year considering a bull from the Pope and a proposal of peace with Scotland. In the sixth year, ambassadors from France appeared before the Council, Friday, 17th June, but, on being required to declare their intention and the cause of their coming, refused and asked to be taken into the King's presence. In the twentieth year Commissioners were appointed to provide for the "reformation of idle people and vagabonds, and the enormity of apparel, as well by great lords and gentlemen and other mean persons, the excess of meats and drinks and costly fare." The swearing in of members of the Council, and certain military indentures are also noted. That the records are concerned mainly with judicial business denotes that there was as yet very close connection between the Court of Star Chamber and the King's Privy Council; both, as we have remarked previously, seem to have had their records entered into the same book, and not until 1494 did the Court of Star Chamber acquire special distinction. (2)

It is not a matter for surprise that the chief work of the Council at the beginning of Henry VII.'s reign was judicial. Regard for law and order did not increase as the fifteenth century wore on; it seemed to be the determination of men of all classes to have their will with or without law. The latter was indeed regarded mainly as a means of oppression, and its elastic condition rendered it the facile instrument of chicanery and force. Machiavelli ascribed the political evils of the time to weakness of will, but he had in mind the impotence of the State. The will of the individual was strong enough, but it was anarchic and insubordinate, and the great political need of the time was the subjection of the over-mighty subject, the restraint of individual greed and irresponsible power by the will of the community in the interests of law and order. (3) Thus there is little novelty or originality in Henry's legislation or in his methods of government, because the issue was essentially one between order and disorder, the government being necessarily on th side of the former. Hence the statute of 1487, later known as Pro Camera Stellata, propounded nothing new. It was designed merely to make a statement of policy as well as certain definitions and extensions of the Council's jurisdiction which otherwise might be doubtful. One of the preliminary steps leading up to this Act was an ordinance made 10th July, 1486, on the subject of riots made by servants of lords. (4) "It is concluded

(1) Archeion, p. 139. According to Harl. MSS. 6811, Art. 2, this statement of Lambard's is true (Scofield: Star Chamber, p. 5.)

(2) Paston Letters, 1494. Sir T. Tyng to Sir J. Paston: "Sir, there hath been so great counsel for the King's matters, that my Lord Chancellor kept not the Star Chamber these eight days, but one day at London on Saint Leonard's Day."

(3) See Pollard, Henry VII. I., p. xxiii.

(4) Addit. MSS. 4521 f. 106., cited Scofield, p. xiii.

and agreed that every Lord and gent [leman], if any of his servants make a riot or other excess, the master of the same trespasser shall have in commandment to bring forth the same servant, and if he so do not abide such direction and punition as by the King and his Council shall be thought convenient, and over that if the same riot or excess, by cause or occasion of any quarrel or displeasure conveying the master of him that so exceedeth, the same master shall answer for the same excess or such wise as shall be thought to the King and his said Council expedient." 3 H. vii. c. 1 constituted a committee of the Council, consisting of the Chancellor, Treasurer, the Lord Privy Seal or any two of them with a spiritual and a temporal peer from the council, and the chief justices of the courts of King's bench and common pleas or other two judges to deal with cases of livery and maintenance, misconduct of sheriffs and other specified offences against law and order. They could, moreover, inflict statutory penalties on offenders " in like manner and form as they should or ought to be punished if they were thereof convict after the due order of law." There is, however, no record of any case under the Act where a duly constituted session of the Council did enforce a statutory penalty. The Act created no new offences or new jurisdiction; it merely specified certain misdemeanours which the circumstances of the time had brought into prominence, entrusted certain persons with the exercise of powers which the Council had always possessed, and legalised procedure by writs of subpoena and Privy Seal. The jurisdiction thus exercised was that of the King's Council, and the Act of 1487 merely improved upon a very similar act of 1453. It extended the number of offences with which the Council was by consent of Parliament henceforward competent to deal, and, in all cases covered by the statutory jurisdiction, it made legal the ancient practice of examining defendants on oath. In 1529 the Lord President was added to the seven mentioned in 3 H. vii. c. 1. The statute was designed to emphasise the jurisdiction exercised by the Council in order to meet the exigencies of a time of great unrest. When the country had begun to recover from the anarchy of Lancastrian and Yorkist weak government and civil war, these powers were no longer necessary. But the Star Chamber proper was by that time organised to exercise this and much of the other jurisdiction of the Privy Council. It could claim to fulfil in its composition the requirements of the statute of 1487, and there are certainly no records of any case under the Act in which a duly constituted session of the Council enforced a statutory penalty. A separate court was never established in virtue of 3 H. vii. c. 1. The assertion that, though the statutes of 3 H. vii. c. 1 and 21 H. viii. c. 20 were never strictly pursued, and were considered merely declatory of the authority of the Council yet they " virtually created the Court of Star Chamber as it existed under the Tudors," (1) is probably correct. Hitherto the Privy Council and the Court of Star Chamber had had practically no separate existence, but from this time Star Chamber proceedings became more technical and settled, new offices were gradually instituted, and the Court began to appear as a definite tribunal, exercising the inherent jurisdiction of the Crown and Council. In the 16th century the jurisdiction of the Court was extended far beyond the offences mentioned in the Act of 1487, to cases of forgery, perjury, contempt of proclamations, frauds, duels —in short, it exercised a very comprehensive penal jurisdiction. In Henry VII.'s reign, however, the administrative Council was in the habit of using the Star Chamber for its deliberations upon political affairs, (2) and hence confusion has arisen between the Council sitting as a part of the Court of Star Chamber and the Council sitting as the advisers of the King.

(1) Palgrave: Original Authority of the King's Council, p. 98.
(2) Leadam: Star Chamber; Vol. I., p. xxxviii., Selden Society.

By the end of Henry VII.'s reign the Council had entirely changed its position with regard to the Crown. It had ceased to be any check upon the King's will, and had sunk into being only a body of officials. No change of outward form had been necessary to effect this alteration. Henry VII. exercised no right which did not belong in theory to Richard II. None the less, he and his successor carried out a revolution. The admission to the Privy Council of numerous Commoners changed the nature of the whole body. Before Henry's death, the Council which, as Bacon says, at the opening of the reign " intermeddled too much with *Meum* and *Tuum*, for it was a very Court of Justice," was exercising very wide judicial powers. Empson and Dudley, who seem to have acted as a sort of sub-committee of the Privy Council, although only Dudley belonged to that body, were charged with habitually indicting guiltless persons of crimes, and when true bills were found, with extorting great fines and ransoms to stop further procedure. Pardons for outlawry were invariably purchased from them, and juries who returned verdicts for defendants in Crown prosecutions were heavily fined. (1) The Council was reputed to have supported these exactions, and to have been accustomed to send letters to judges dictating verdicts, although these last were supposed to be the work of juries. All objections to Henry's government were, however, more than outweighed by the pressing need of a strong hand at the helm, a need which was more than supplied by the system of government of the first Tudor and his successor.

(1) D.N.B.: Dudley.

III. THE PRIVY COUNCILS OF HENRY VIII. AND HIS CHILDREN, AND THEIR COMPOSITION.

———— :0 :————

HENRY VIII., on coming to the Throne in 1509, " did for respect of his own surety and the good government of his people, prudently (by the advice of his grand-mother, the Countess of Richmond and Derby) elect and choose forth of the most wise and grave personages to be of his Privy Council, namely such as he knew to be of his father's right dear and familiar friends, whose names were as followeth, William Warham Archbishop of Canterbury and Chancellor of England,* Richard Fox Bishop of Win-chester.* Thomas Howard Earl of Surrey and Treasurer of England,* George Talbot Earl of Shrewsbury and Lord Steward of the King's Household, Charles Somerset Lord Cham-berlain,* Sir Thomas Lovell, Sir Henry Wyatt, Dr. Thomas Ruthall,* and Sir Edward Poynings." (1) Sir Henry Marny and Sir Thomas Darcy also appear to have been sworn. (2) There were thus eleven in all. Henry VII. had consulted about fourteen privy councillors. (3) To style these holders of office at the beginning of his reign " great officers of State," who ex-officio exercised influence or control over the public administra-tion, would be to use the term " State " somewhat loosely, for some were feudal, others household dignitaries. Long before Henry's death, however, such hereditary offices as those of Constable and Marshall had sunk into insignificance and the flooding of the Council by nobles had ceased. In the Councils of the first Henry and his son the nobles never held undisputed sway. The officials formed a party less numerous but much better organised than the peers and their adherents. As a political force they were of recent origin, but Henry VII. had fully realised the impossibility of establishing a strong and durable government without having at his command a body of men thoroughly versed in all the acts of administration, owing obedience to no one but the King, and wholly devoted to him. Before he died he brought together a large number of able and energetic civil servants. Henry VIII. sacrificed a few of the most hated of his father's ministers (4), such as Empson and Dudley, but he was clever enough to know the value of the bureaucracy which Henry VII had left behind him, and he was careful not to disorganise so admirable an instrument for strong and efficient rule. Under Fox, and subsequently under Wolsey, the body of officials was strengthened and made even more effective. During the tenure of office of Wolsey and Cromwell, individual Privy Councillors and office-holders were

(*) The asterisk denotes Henry VII.'s executors. They had been of his Privy Council.

(1) Holinshed's Chronicle: III., p. 799.

(2) See Henry's reply to the Northern Rebels, L. and P. IX., 957.

(3) See lists in Hall's Chronicle, p. 424. and "A Chronicle of the Kings of England," by Sir Richard Baker, p. 237.

(4) L. and P.: I., 1004. Their victims had been " without any ground or matter of truth by the undue means of certain of the Council of our said late father, thereunto driven contrary to law, reason and good conscience, to the manifest charge and peril of the soul of our said late father."

overshadowed, as they were under Edward VI. by Somerset and Northumberland, and under Mary by Cardinal Pole and King Philip himself. The reigns of the minor Edward VI. and the religious fanatic Mary do not furnish true pictures of the Tudor system of government by Council, because under those sovereigns the Privy Council had lost its vital element, a strong King at the head of affairs. Northumberland and Philip were strong enough, but the former lacked that " divinity which doth hedge a king," especially in English eyes, and the latter was a detested foreigner. Officials are incapable of ruling; they are not original; they can merely carry out instructions from above. Though Henry VIII. had great ministers, they never became like the Merovingian Mayors of the Palace. They rose from the lower ranks of life and were officials from first to last, wholly dependent upon the King's good will.

According to Herbert of Cherbury, the frame of Henry's Council at the beginning consisted of scholars and soldiers, their choice proceeding " rather from their sufficiency in the business they were to discharge and care of that authority they must support than from any private affection. . . Among them (though not many) there were divers able to execute and perform as well as counsel, so that without divulging any secret or descending from the dignity of their place to require advice from their inferiors, they moved in their own orb. This held up the majesty of the Council." (1) Herbert remarks that there was no Common lawyer in the Council. It certainly contained many noble names, but it was the organ neither of an official bureaucracy nor of a territorial aristocracy, but combined both elements in fair proportions. They were chosen largely for their high ability: Henry VIII. is said never to have rested until he had made the learned More one of his Council, (2) and Pace wrote to Colet and told him the reply he (Pace) had made to a gentleman who asserted, " By the body of God, I would sooner see my son hanged than a bookworm. It is a gentleman's calling to blow the horn, to hunt and to hawk. He should leave learning to clodhoppers." Pace's reply was to the effect that this prejudice excluded the sons of noblemen and gentlemen from employment in the state, and that learning was better than ignorance and noble blood. (3)

The Lady Margaret lived long enough to assist in the choice of her grandson's earliest counsellors, and the experienced band of diplomatists and soldiers who had served the father continued for a while to direct the counsels of the son. Warham, though still Chancellor, seems to have taken little or no share in the shaping of the national policy. Unambitious and perhaps a little weary of twenty years' official life, he was content to devote himself to his clerical duties and to dispense a generous patronage to impecunious scholars. With his effacement, the chief place in the direction of affairs belonged to Richard Fox, Lord Privy Seal—wary, alert, resourceful, quick to descry the currents of the age. He had been concerned in almost all the great transactions of the preceding reign, the Treaty of Etaples, the Magnus Intercursus, the Scottish and Spanish marriages and the alliance with the young Charles. In return for these services Henry VII. had named him one of his chief executors, and had specially commended the heir apparent to his charge. (4) Sir Thomas More told Erasmus that Fox was the real author of the famous dilemma later known as Morton's Fork. (5) He was, however, a devoted and able servant

(1) Henry VIII., p. 2.
(2) L. and P.: III. 881, 25th June, 1520.
(3 Ibid: II., 3765, October, 1517.
(4) If Nicholas Harpsfield may be believed: "A Treatise on the Pretended Divorce between Henry VIII. and Catherine of Arragon." (Ed. Pocock, Camden Society, 1878).
(5) Political History of England: Vol. VI., p. 162.

of the Crown and deservedly occupied the chief place in the King's counsels. In 1510 he is described by Badoer, the Venetian ambassador, as "alter rex." Thomas Howard Earl of Surrey appears his only serious rival, the Queen always excepted. He was now sixty-six, and had repaid Henry VII. for his release from prison and restoration to his earldom by signal military and diplomatic services; at Henry VIII.'s accession he was the first soldier in England, though apparently he had not yet earned his restoration to his dukedom.

The other members of the Council were less conspicuous. Ruthal, Bishop of Durham, was a hard working official; Poynings, Comptroller of the Household, had made a name both as a soldier and an administrator; while Sir Thomas Lovell had been Chancellor of the Exchequer since 1485. (1) George Talbot Earl of Shrewsbury had fought at Stoke and contributed an illustrious family reputation to the prestige of the government. Charles Somerset, Lord Herbert and afterwards Earl of Worcester, the Lord Chamberlain, had been brought up as a child in the court of Henry VII. He had seen something of war both by land and sea, but his rapid promotion was due rather to favour than to merit, and his weight in Henry's counsels inconsiderable.

The first document which gives a clear picture of Henry's Council is that containing the "Regulations for the Better Government of the Household," amongst which was the following for the "Establishment of a Council." (2) "And to the intent that as well matters of justice and complaints touching the greaves (i.e., grievances) of the King's subjects and disorder of his Realm and otherwise, which shall fortune to be made brought and presented unto his Highness by his said subjects in his demurre, or passing from place to place within the same; as also other great occurrences concerning his own particular affairs may be the better ordered, and with his Grace more ripely debated digested and resolved, from time to time as the case shall require; it is ordered and appointed by his Highness, that a good number of honourable, virtuous, sad, wise, expert and discreet persons of his Council, shall give their attendance upon his most royal person, whose names hereafter follow; that is to say, the Lord Cardinal, Chancellor of England; the Duke of Norfolk, Treasurer of England; the Bishop of London, Keeper of the King's Privy Seal; the Duke of Suffolk, Marshal of England; the Marquis of Dorset; Marquis of Exeter; the Earl of Shrewsbury, Steward of the King's Household; Sir Henry Guildford, Comptroller; the Secretary; Sir Thomas More, Chancellor of the Duchy; the Dean of the King's Chapel; Sir Henry Wyatt, Treasurer of the King's Chamber; the Vice-Chamberlain; the Captain of the Guard; Dr. Wolman. (3) And forasmuch as the said Lord Cardinal, Lord Treasurer of England, Lord Privy Seal, Lord Steward, and divers other Lords and Personages before mentioned, by reason of their attendance at the terms for the administration of justice and exercising of their offices, and other reasonable impediments shall many seasons fortune to be absent from the King's Court and specially in term times, to the intent the King's Highness shall not be at any season unfurnished of an honourable presence of Counsellors about his Grace, with whom his Highness may confer upon the premises at his pleasure: it is ordered that the persons hereafter mentioned shall give their continual attendance in the courses of his said Council, unto what place soever his Highness shall resort: that is to say, the Lord Chamberlain, the Bishop of Bath, the Treasurer and Comptroller of the King's Household, the Secretary, the Chancellor of the Duchy of Lancaster, the Dean of the King's Chapel, the Vice-

(1) D.N.B.: xxxiv., 175. Campbell: "Materials," I., 29th Sept., 1485.
(2) Dated January, 1526, and published by the Society of Antiquaries, 1790, pp. 159—160. Percy: "Privy Council under the Tudors," p. 14, erroneously gives the date as 1516.
(3) Note that the President of the Council is not mentioned.

Chamberlain, the Captain of the Guard; and for ordering of poor men's complaints and causes, Dr. Wolman." If any of these are absent on reasonable excuse, the Bishop of Bath, the Secretary, Sir Thomas More, and the Dean of the Chapel are always to be present, unless with leave of absence from the King. These, "appointed for continual attendance, are to apply themselves effectually, diligently, uprightly and justly in the premises; being every day in the forenoon by ten of the clock at the furthest, and at afternoon by two of the clock, in the King's dining chamber, there to be in readiness not only in case the King's pleasure shall be to commune or confer with them upon any cause or matter, but also for hearing and direction of poor men's complaints on matters of justice; which direction well observed the King's Highness shall always be furnished of an honourable presence of Counsellors about his Grace, as to his high honour doth appertain.'

The pre-dominance in this Council of bishops and nobles, and the fact that two-thirds of these latter classes of Councillors held other offices, is very noteworthy, and there was clearly no intention of making any separation between advisory and judicial functions. The administrative body was to consist of twenty persons, fourteen state and court officers, four peers and two bishops. For the smaller Council which was to remain continuously in close attendance upon the King ten members were designated, and for daily duty with the King the secretary and three others.

There was a marked tendency after Wolsey's fall and the inauguration of the new ecclesiastical policy to give clergymen less prominence in the council and to rely mainly upon laymen. In 1538 there was a significant suggestion to "withdraw the King's council more secret together, and to avoid spiritual men there hence for divers reasons." (1)

In 1536 there was a serious attack upon Henry VIII.'s Council—an attack which recalls the methods of the previous century but of which the outcome was very different. Incited by attacks on the Church, for which the Privy Council was known to be largely responsible, and from other motives more purely economic, the people of the northern shires made their noted pilgrimage and protest. Among the articles of complaint was one to the effect that the "King takes of his Council and has about him persons of low birth and small reputation who have procured these things for their own advantage, whom we suspect to be Lord Cromwell, and Sir Richard Rich, Chancellor of the Augmentations." (2) In Lincolnshire the insurgents asked the King to "take noblemen into his Council and remove Cromwell, the Chancellor of the Augmentations, and certain heretic bishops as the Bishops of Lincoln, Canterbury, St. Davids, etc." Others bound themselves by an oath "to expulse all villain blood from the Privy Council," and in a letter to the Queen of Hungary it was reported that they demanded "a shearer of cloths to be given up to them meaning Cromwell, and a tavern-keeper meaning the Archbishop of Canterbury, the Chancellor of the country, the Chancellor of the Augmentations, and certain other bishops and lords of the King's Council." (3) The King condescended to the following thoroughly Tudor reply in answer to the petitions of the Lincolnshire rebels: that he had never heard that princes' counsellors or prelates should be appointed by ignorant common people nor that they were meet persons to choose them. "How presumptious then are ye, the rude commons of one shire, and that one the most brute and beastly of the whole realm and of least experience, to find fault with your prince for the electing of his counsellors and prelates. Thus you take upon yourself to rule your prince." (4) To the Yorkshire rebels he deigned to be more explicit: "As to the

Vol. XIII

(1) L. and P.: Pt. 2, 974.   (2) Ibid: XI., 705.
(3) Ibid: XI., 828, 852, 714.   (4) Ibid: XI., 780.

beginning of our reign when ye say so many noblemen were counsellors: who were then counsellors I well remember, and yet of the temporalty, I note but two worth calling noble, the one, Treasurer of England, the other, High Steward of our House. Others, as the lords Marny and Darcy, were scant well-born gentlemen, and yet of no great lands till they were promoted by us. The rest were lawyers and priests, save two bishops, Canterbury and Winchester. Why then are you not better content with us now who have so many nobles indeed, both of birth and condition? For of the temporalty we have in our Privy Council, the Dukes of Norfolk and Suffolk, the Marquis of Exeter, the lord Steward when he may come, the Earls of Oxford and Sussex, lord Sandys our chamberlain, the lord Admiral, the treasurer of our house, Sir William Paulet comptroller of our house; and of the spiritualty the Bishops of Hereford, Chichester, and Winchester. How came you to think that there were more noble men in our Privy Council then than now? But it does not belong any of our subjects to appoint us our Council." (1)

The list of Privy Councillors in 1526 agrees very nearly, as regards the great offices of State, with the one given in August, 1540, in the Council Register, when it is said to have consisted of the Archbishop of Canterbury, the Lord Chancellor, the Lord Treasurer, the Great Master or Steward of the Household (then also President of the Council), the Lord Privy Seal, the Great Chamberlain of England, the Great Admiral of England, the King's Chamberlain, the Treasurer and Comptroller of the King's Household, the Master of the King's Horse, the King's Vice-Chamberlain, the King's Principal Secretary, the Chancellor of the Augmentations of the Revenues of the Crown, and the Chancellor of the Tenths and First Fruits, (2) many of whom were members virtute officii, and the remainder were probably appointed because their offices render their presence in the Council desirable. The only persons chosen on account of their rank or abilities, without reference to their official stations, were the King's brother-in-law, Edward Seymour, Earl of Hertford, and the Bishops of Durham and Winchester, two prelates eminent for their knowledge of civil and canon law. There were nineteen in all, an increase of eight since the beginning of the reign. (3)

Long before August, 1529, Henry had become conscious of his own powers of management, and Wolsey fell. The nobility and landed gentry hated him; he had no hold over the nation, but Henry seemed to have given over his royal authority into Wolsey's hands with a blind and unreasoning confidence, although in reality Wolsey never carried out any policy but that of his royal master's. Before another decade had passed, however, Henry was King and Government in one, and nobody in the kingdom counted for much except the Sovereign. Before Wolsey's ruin his enemies obtained prominent places in the Council chamber. Norfolk was made President and Suffolk Vice-President; the Great Seal was given to the most eminent layman in England, Sir Thomas More, while Stephen Gardiner succeeded to the see of Winchester. There had always been parties in Henry VIII.'s Council. According to Herbert (4) the Councillors agreed during the lifetime of the Countess of Richmond, but after she died " some smothered jealousies broke out into open faction. Inasmuch that Thomas Howard, Earl of Surrey, and Richard Fox, Bishop of Winchester, out of a competition for being most eminent in the King's favour, became at last not sufficiently united between themselves. . . Now these two (as Polydore relates) had brought all business within their verge. . . I doubt not yet but their fellow counsellors were often admitted; though perhaps not being acquainted with all the

(1) Ibid: XI., 957.　　　　　　　　(2) See Appendix.
(3) Nicholas: " Proceedings and Ordinances " vii., p. 1.
(4) Henry VIII.: II., 4.

premises they were hardly able to ground a solid advice. The Bishop [Fox] was an old and intimate counsellor to King Henry VII., and knew all the mysteries of State. The Earl of Surrey . . . Lord Treasurer . . . ever since 16 Henry VII." was much in request " as one who both kept and dispensed that mass of wealth left by Henry VII." This denotes, perhaps, an early trace of departmentalism though there was little enough under Henry VIII., for after the fall of Cromwell the King issued his commands to any of his Ministers without regard to their peculiar duties, and their attention was by no means confined to their particular departments. The Duke of Suffolk after his marriage with Mary in France is said to have been hated by all the Council except Wolsey, and the latter wrote to Suffolk that in order to appease Henry and enable him to satisfy his Council he must induce Francis to intervent in his favour and pay the King 200,000 crowns. (1) The party against Wolsey in 1528 was united by a bond of common hatred to the Cardinal. After his fall, the new Government was eminently aristocratic with strong leanings to France. Norfolk, Suffolk, Boleyn, Fitzwilliam, and More were all in receipt of pensions from Francis (2)

Henry had one more great Minister who dwarfed all the other Privy Councillors before he decided to cease issuing his commands to any one individual. This last of Henry's predominating Ministers was Thomas Cromwell. As Vicegerent he held first place among the Privy Councillors, but after the King's disappointment concerning Anne of Cleves, Cromwell's star waned while that of Gardiner, the head of the Catholic party, seemed in the ascendant. Few men who have served England knew more of the details of English life; for ten years he managed Parliament, and his force of will is shown in the fact that no one seriously challenged his pre-eminence. Audley, the Chancellor, admitted that Cromwell had seriously reduced the significance of his office; Norfolk cringed to him; the Lord Admiral was his humble servant; and beneath these was a crowd of henchmen, pliable, adroit, hard and exact in business, as unscrupulous, overbearing, and unpopular as their master. At last the storm burst. On 10th June, 1540, Cromwell was arrested, and shortly afterwards, protesting that he died in the Catholic faith, was executed.

Though Cromwell had fallen there was still a Reforming party in the Council led by the Primate Cranmer, and by Audley, the Lord Chancellor. By 1545 a spirit of religious debate had fastened upon the nation—in the Council the struggle was carried on with covert but internecine ferocity. Cranmer, however, had very great theological influence with the King, and one by one the Catholic plots failed. In 1544, however, Audley died and was succeeded as Lord Chancellor by Wriothesley, who had been made Lord Keeper a fortnight before Audley's death, and who was understood to be a Catholic. Sir Edward Poynings had died in 1521, the Duke of Suffolk in 1545, and this had left the Reforming party the poorer, but Lisle and Hertford returned from France, and the position of the Reformers became stronger at Court. The Reforming party was rapidly growing in the Privy Council itself. Henry's marriage with Catherine Howard might have been the outcome of strong Howard influence over the King and his Council, but after her disgrace the Catholics certainly suffered a reverse. In 1546 Cranmer still retained his curious hold over the King's mind; Hertford was steadily rising into favour, and the majority of the Council was prepared to accept the authorised form of religion, whatever it might happen to be. Besides the Howards, Gardiner was the only convinced and determined champion of the Catholic faith (3) and he was strongly anti-Papal.

(1) L. and P.: II., 367.
(2) Friedmann: "Anne Boleyn" I., p. 99.
(3) Pollard: Henry VIII. p. 416.

The Privy Council Register affords practically no information concerning parties the Council of Henry VIII. What there is of it for Henry VIII.'s reign resembles the " Book of the Council " of the time of Henry V. and Henry VI., in which the decrees rather than the deliberations of the Privy Council are entered. These differed materially from the original minutes for the same period, which often contained the individual opinions of members upon the business which happened to be under discussion. (1)

As the King's grasp upon the situation weakened, the struggle for the helm of state became more severe. Early in November, 1546, in full Council, Lisle struck Gardiner. Rumours of plot and counterplot filled the town, and then in December, 546, Norfolk and Surrey were thrown into the Tower. Later in the same month it was observed that Hertford and Lisle had taken up their residence at Court, and the Councillors swung over in their direction. They seemed to have complete control of the Council, which met for the most part at Hertford's house, and it was asserted " that the custody of the Prince and government of the Realm will be entrusted to them; and this misfortune to the House of Norfolk may have come from that quarter." On the 29th January, 1547, Chapuys wrote that the Earl and Admiral had plans to obtain the government of the Prince, and that " to gain a party they drag the whole country into error, to which is no counteracting influence among the secular nobility except Norfolk, who has great favour with the people of the North. This is the cause of his and his son's detention. The only obstacle is the authority of the Bishops; therefore it is to be feared that in the coming Parliament they will be divested of property and given pensions from the King's coffers." (2)

At Henry's death, his Privy Council numbered twenty-nine. There had been several changes and additions since August, 1540, and in 1547 the most influential of the Councillors were Hertford and Lisle. No member of Henry's Council in 1547 held a peerage more than twelve years old. Henry VIII. had filled his Council with middleclass men, and after Cromwell's fall gave his confidence to no one individual.

The effect of his death was clearly visible. The active control of the work of government by the sovereign was an essential feature in the English constitution, and the Privy Council without the King was as unfinished an administrative machine as a modern Cabinet without a Premier. Henry appointed sixteen executors in his will to carry on the work of government..

His Privy Council was dissolved at his death and a new one should have been elected by the new King. He was a minor, however, so that his Council consisted merely of a number of executors acting in virtue of their appointment by Henry VIII.'s will, which limited their powers and controlled their action. The executors were elected from both parties, the Reformers being represented by Cranmer, Hertford, Russell, Lisle, Denny, and Herbert; the Catholics by Wriothesley, Tunstal, Browne, and perhaps the two Wottons. There was a third party of no pronounced views, St. John, Paget, and North, while Montague, Chief Justice of the Common Pleas, and Bromley, Chief Justice of the King's Bench, were expected to take small share in the party conflict, and, indeed, rarely attended the Council. No sharply defined lines can, however, be drawn between Reforming and Catholic parties as yet even for Churchmen, and in Edward's Council men of the New Learning were dominant. (3)

Before Henry died, Hertford had formed an alliance with the King's principal secretary, Sir William Paget, who knew all the secrets of the Court (and invented many more), and together they had been predominant in Henry's Council. Thus, when Henry died, Hertford, with the aid of Paget and Sir Antony Browne, Master of the Horse and a staunch Catholic, made himself supreme. The rest of the executors and the King acquiesced,

(1) Nicholas: P. and O. VII., p. xiv.   (2) L. and P.: XXI., 605, 756.
(3) Pollard: " Protector Somerset," pp. 21—22.

and the Patent conferring the office of Protector upon him was entered in the Council Book 13th March, 1547. (1) These same Letters Patent also created a new Privy Council of twenty-five members, of which Lord St. John was made President. Somerset was also given authority to appoint other Privy Councillors if he wished. This authorisation afforded him the opportunity of surrounding himself with his personal adherents and excluding all who showed any hesitation in obeying his will; but as a matter of fact Somerset made practically no change in the composition of the Council. After the grant of the Letters Patent, the Privy Council was identical with that of Henry VIII. with the three exceptions of Gardiner, Thirlby, and Wriothesley, and the three additions of Baron Seymour of Sudeley, (2) Sir Richard Southwell, and Sir Edmund Peckham. It was composed of the executors and assistant-executors appointed by Henry's will, acting now as one body, but neither deriving their authority from nor being bound by the limitations of that document. At Somerset's fall there were only three additions— Southampton, Shrewsbury, and Sir Thomas Smith, who were no doubt designed to supply the places of those who had meanwhile died: Lord Seymour, Sir Anthony Browne, and Sir Anthony Denny. Thus the government under Somerset was practically the same in composition as under Henry VIII. The exclusion of Gardiner and Thirlby had given it a more distinctly secular tinge than had been the case perhaps since the Privy Council came into existence, and it was the result of the anti-sacerdotal and Erastian character of Edward's legislation. Two bishops only, Cranmer and Tunstall, remained in the Council, and Tunstall soon withdrew to his northern diocese.

After Somerset's fall and under Warwick the process went still further, for Cranmer took little part in civil affairs after Somerset's exclusion from the Council, and though Goodrich, Bishop of Ely, held for a time the Great Seal, he had little weight in the deliberations of the King's advisers. The separation from Rome was followed by a gradual banishment of ecclesiastical influence from the sphere of civil government and an increasing subjection of Church to State.

The composition of Edward's Council admirably illustrates the Tudor policy of neglecting the old nobility and depending for support on new men who owed their rise to Tudor rule. There were seventeen commoners, two prelates and only seven temporal peers. Of these one only, Henry Fitzalan, twelfth Earl of Arundel, could claim a noble ancestry. The senior peer, after Arundel, was Somerset, who had been created Viscount Beauchamp in 1536. The peerages of Russell, St. John, and Northampton dated from March, 1539, and that of Warwick from 1542, while Rich and Thomas Seymour were created peers in the first year of Edward VI. Never before or after was England governed by such an assembly of parvenus.

The quarrels of parties in the Council reached their height during the short-lived elevation of Lady Jane Grey. The reign of the nine days' Queen came to an end with the proclamation of Mary in London on 19th July by Lords Arundel, Pembroke, Shrewsbury, and others of the Council. On 3rd August Mary rode into town, and no sooner had the prison gates closed behind Northumberland than they opened to liberate his victims. The composition of the Privy Council underwent a revolution. (3) Hitherto since its gradual evolution it had been a comparatively small and select body. Under Henry VIII. its numbers had fluctuated between eleven and twenty-five: sixteen executors with twelve assistants had been nominated in his will. Somerset had somewhat reduced the

(1) A.P.C., II.
(2) Who had been sworn before Henry's death, 23rd January, 1547, but had not attended.—A.P.C. I.
(3) A.P.C., vol. 4 (passim).

number, but in 1551 under Warwick it rose to thirty-three. Mary necessarily began with a ring of personal advisers having no connection with those of the late King's Council in London, and to these she added members of the old Council as they gave in their adherence. Not unnaturally her first act on reaching London was to reward her faithful servants by appointing them to discharge those honorable offices at Court which brought their holders into daily communication with the Sovereign. The result of this was nearly to double the size of the Council; before March, 1554, it numbered forty-four members. Of these nearly three-fifths had never sat at the Council Board before. One or two were men of good abilities; half-a-dozen or so, such as Rochester, Waldegrave, and Englefield, had been Mary's faithful household servants in her time of trouble, but the majority had no claim to their position beyond religious sympathy and the promptitude with which they had espoused her cause. In their counsel there was little wisdom and in their multitude no safety.

Of the Privy Council as it was in June, 1553, a score lost their seats, including Cranmer, Cecil, Cheke, Clinton, Goodrich, Sadler, and Huntingdon, as well as the chief of Northumberland's faction Suffolk, Northampton, and Gates, while seven who had been councillors of old, but had been deprived of liberty or influence, were restored. These were all men of mark: Norfolk, Gardiner, Thirlby, Tunstall, Southwell, Rich, and Paget, and they guided Mary's government during the first part of her reign. Twelve who had been active to the last under Northumberland retained place and power, for some of these Mary could not afford to displease. The Marquis of Winchester continued to hold office as Lord High Treasurer, and the Earl of Bedford as Lord Privy Seal, while the Earl of Arundel succeeded Northumberland as Lord Great Master. Together with these, the Earls of Shrewsbury and Westmorland, with Petre, Mason, Gage, Cheyne, Baker, and Peckham, were re-admitted to the Council. Winchester seemed to regard himself as the permanent head of the civil service, and retained the Lord High Treasurership in spite of Norfolk's claim to his old office. Lord Arundel had done much for Mary at the crisis. The other peers were perhaps retained partly for their compliance and partly for their local influence: Bedford for the South-West, Pembroke for Wales and the Welsh Marches of the Council of which he was President, Shrewsbury held like office in the North, and Westmorland's influence counted for something on the Scottish borders. Cheyne had been Warden of the Cinque Ports, Petre secretary for ten years, Baker Speaker of the House of Commons and Chancellor of the Exchequer in Henry VIII.'s reign, and nearly all were tried officials of reactionary tendencies. Gardiner became Lord Chancellor instead of Goodrich Bishop of Ely; Lord William Howard, later renowned as Effingham, became Lord High Admiral in Clinton's place. The Lord Great Chamberlainship of England, which, though by right hereditary in the Earls of Oxford, had been held by Somerset, Northumberland and Northampton, lost its political importance and relapsed into hereditary insignificance. Sir John Gage succeeded Lord Darcy as Chamberlain of the Household and Lord Clinton as Constable of the Tower, while Sir Henry Jerningham succeeded Gates as Vice-Chamberlain and Captain of the Guard. All other household officials were changed, and Sir John Bourne took Cecil's place as Secretary.

The new Government had the goodwill of the nation, however. Men were ready to support a settled Government, for during Jane's brief reign it was said " the State of this Realm might well seem most miserable, wherein the nobility and counsell on the one part, and the gentlemen and commons of the other appeared to be fully bent to maintain two contrary titles." So numerous a body as Mary's Privy Council, however, must have been far too unwieldly for deliberative purposes. It approximates most nearly of all the Privy Councils of the Tudors to the Privy Councils of to-day, so far as its size is concerned. Very soon it was found convenient for administrative purposes to form what were called committees of the Council, the amount of ordinary routine business which came before the Council daily rendering necessary some such sub-division of labour. (1)

Soon after Philip's marriage with the Queen, he appears to have reduced the real working Council to six or eight. On 3rd April, 1557, the Venetian ambassador wrote to the Doge and Senate: "The Count de Feria . . . told me as a great secret that the King having found that the Queen has twenty-six councillors, the grade being an honorary one conferred on all those from whom she had anything to hope or fear, in order to keep them under obligation to her, has reduced them to only six of his most trusty adherents, without, however, displacing the others, so as not to provoke them, but has so arranged with the Queen and those six that matters of importance are to be treated by them alone, less momentous business being discussed by all together." (2) On 13th May of the same year, "On the King's departure, he and the Queen had ordained a new form of Council, almost in the fashion of a Council of State, to exclude from it any sort of members who had seats in the old and customary one, persons who, although of noble birth and true to the Queen, were, however, not considered either adapted to State affairs or capable of treating them. These new councillors were nine in number, all chief personages, some temporal and others spiritual, over all of whom, by reason of his grade and nobility, the Cardinal was appointed superior." (3) Cardinal Pole seems never actually to have been sworn of Mary's Privy Council, though he is twice recorded as present. (4) There is a curious entry in the Council Register (5) under date 14th June, 1556. The Council was at St. James', and fourteen appearances are recorded; then, "This day my Lord Cardinal's Grace, my Lord Chancellor, my Lord Treasurer, my Lord Privy Seal, my Lord of Ely, Master Comptroller and Master Secretary Petre being with the Queen's Majesty, Her Highness declared unto them her pleasure was " that five Privy Councillors whose names are given, should take charge of the affairs of the Mint. On 7th October of the same year he appears to be acting as the Queen's mouthpiece to declare, in the presence of certain members of the Council, to the wife of Sir Nicholas Throgmorton that she was "for that once" permitted to send "some present relief" to her husband, a fugitive in France.

The Cardinal undoubtedly had great influence over both Mary and Philip. Michiel, the Venetian envoy, records, 9th September, 1555, (6) that a sort of Privy Council was to be established for matters of State and importance, ordinary affairs and "such as relate to justice being referred to the one which already exists, wherein many persons who are considered sage have seats, but they apparently do not enjoy such esteem and repute as to qualify them for this other," for which, as Michiel understands, the only persons already destined were the Cardinal, the Chancellor, the Earls of Arundel and Pembroke, the Treasurer, the Bishop of Ely, Lord Paget, and Secretary Petre. But until the King returned, nothing was known for certainty, and matters were treated as before, except that when necessary "those of weight are communicated to Cardinal Pole." Pole himself wrote on 10th October, 1555, to Cardinal Caraffa telling him that Philip, on his departure, had left eight of the principal members of his Council to consult about the most important affairs, and had earnestly begged Pole, in the presence of the

(1) A.P.C. 4, 5, 6 (passim).
(2) Venetian Calendar: VI. 852. (3) Ibid: 884.
(4) Stype twice records Pole as a Privy Councillor.
(5) A.P.C., 5, 6. (6) Venetian Calendar: VI. 209.

Lords of the Council, to attend their consultations. This Pole had agreed to do, and had attended assiduously, together with the Queen and the other deputies, but had not signed any of the decrees made until he knew the wishes of His Holiness, the Pope. (1) It is impossible to judge from the evidence we have whether this was a permanent inner ring of the Privy Council or only a kind of Council of Regency to aid the Queen during Philip's absence abroad.

Mary's huge Council was by no means a passive one, nor was it ready to consent without a struggle to the measures taken by Mary against its advice, although in a letter to Pole the Queen speaks of the unanimous consent of the Council when the return of England to the fold of the Church was proposed, so much so that they "seemed really to have been moved by the Holy Spirit." (2) Renard wrote to the Emperor, however, in April, 1554, that " the party squabbles, jealousies, and ill-feeling of the Councillors have so increased and become public, that, at this moment, some from animosity against others will not attend the Council; what one does, another undoes; what one counsels, another contradicts; one advises to save Courtenay, another Elizabeth; and all at last has got into such confusion that we only wait to see the the quarrel end in arms and tumult. Thus is the Queen of England treated by those who ought to be her most intimate and devoted servants. The Chancellor (Gardiner), the Comptroller (Sir Robert Rochester), Walgrave, Inglefield, Southwell, the Chamberlain, Vice-Chamberlain, and Secretary Bourne form one party; the Earls of Arundel, Pembroke, Sussex, the Master of the Horse, Paget, Petre, Cornwallis, and the Admiral make another; and whereas it was thought that the last reduction and reform in the Council of State to six, ought to be continued and become permanent, the Comptroller and his friends have murmured against it; they assert that they were the agents in maintaining the Queen in her royal right, and merited as well to belong to the Council of State as the others; that they were Catholics, and the others for the most part heretics, and they have so overwhelmed her Majesty that she is disgusted with Paget and Petre." (3) Gardiner, whom Soranzo the Venetian Ambassador described as Mary's Prime Minister, was averse to her marriage with the Spanish King; he held the restoration of Papal authority tolerable, but he dreaded the return of Pole as likely to supersede himself. At least a third of the Council agreed with him in disliking the Cardinal and the marriage, but disagreed with him about the Pope. Paget on the other hand was in favour of the marriage, but inclining with Arundel and Pembroke to the Reformers as the Catholic views of the Queen became more obvious. (4) No wonder, therefore, the Council was in confusion and at cross purposes, or that Philip wished to reduce it when he came to England. The unwieldly bulk of Mary's Council fostered faction and cabal, and personal feeling embittered political differences. Paget, Gardiner's rival for Mary's confidence, led the *politiques*, Arundel, Pembroke, Sussex, Petre, Hastings, and Lord William Howard; all with the excepton of the two last had served on Northumberland's Pirvy Council. Gardiner's partisans were Rochester, Englefield, Jerningham, Bourne, and Waldegrave, jealous Catholics, who, having had no connection with Edward VI.'s Government, had been the first to raise Mary's standard. Philip on his departure from England in 1555 had selected a small council, as we have already seen, from all parties.

(1) Ibid: VI., 244.   (2) Ibid: V., 11th November, 1554.
(3) Tytler: " England under the reigns of Edward VI. and Mary," II.,
       pp. 371—372.
(4) Froude: V., 267.

Mary's Privy Council came to an end with her death in 1553. It consisted then of thirty-eight. Elizabeth could summon whom she pleased to the board. Only three of Mary's Council, Pembroke, Clinton, and Howard had attended the small meetings held at Hatfield before Elizabeth removed to London, but besides these Elizabeth admitted eight more of the old members, Cheney, Heath, Arundel, Winchester, Shrewsbury, Derby, Petre, and Sir John Mason, and nine new ones, Sir Thomas Parry, Sir Edward Rogers, Sir William Cecil, Lord Northampton, Nicholas Bacon, Sir Richard Sackville, Sir Ambrose Cave, Sir Ralph Sadler, and the new Earl of Bedford. Elizabeth's new additions were indicative of the composition of the Council throughout her reign. It numbered as a rule about seventeen or eighteen persons, most of whom were high officers of State. Under Elizabeth, moreover, the Councillors were, with rare exceptions, laymen; the Church had now resigned all claim upon the great temporal offices, and no Churchmen held such offices under the last of the Tudors. Heath, the only ecclesiastic in the Council at her accession, and who ceased altogether to attend in January, 1559, was succeeded in his office of Chancellor by Sir Nicholas Bacon, who was styled Lord Keeper; Winchester as Treasurer, Clinton as Admiral, Arundel as Lord Steward, Howard as Lord Chamberlain, and Cheyne as Treasurer of the Household, retained their places. Paget lost his seat and Cecil more than filled the two places he held, while the secretaries Bourne and Boxall.

"The choice of her Council bespake also her wariness and great discretion, and contributed much to her first successes. For such she picked out to save her . . . as were neither of common wit nor common experience, of whom some by travel in strange countries, some by learning, some by practice and like authority in other rulers' days, some by affliction, either one way or other, for their great gifts and graces which they had received at God's hand, were men meet to be called to such rooms." (1) Elizabeth meant to imitate her father and constitute her Council so as to retain for herself the greatest weight in determining the issue of its deliberations. As Camden says, on all whom she admitted "she bestowed her favours with so much caution and so little distinction as to prevent either party from gaining the ascendant over her, whereby she remained mistress of her own self and preserved both their affections and her own power and authority entire." (2) Feria wrote within a few months of her accession: "She gives her orders and has her way as absolutely as her father did." (3) She was not bound to act on the decisions of her Council, even though they might be unanimous, for the function of the Privy Council was merely to advise—and on many occasions the Council failed to persuade Elizabeth to adopt the causes it recommended or to abandon those of which it disapproved.

As Elizabeth's reign drew on, her Council became gradually smaller and limited almost entirely to office holders. In July, 1577, it consisted of fifteen, all except two having office; in July, 1588, it had increased slightly to seventeen; in March, 1591, it numbered eleven; in July, 1596, twelve; in December, 1600, eleven; and thirteen in December, 1601. (4)

In spite of the continuity between Mary's and Elizabeth's Councils, Feria asserted that England was "entirely in the hands of young folks, heretics, and traitors," and that

(1) Strype: "Annals of the Reformation," p. 3.
(2) Camden, "Queen Elizabeth."
(3) Spanish Calendar: I., 7.
(4) A.P.C., 9, 16, 20, 26, 30, 32 (passim).

izabeth did not favour a single man whom Mary would have received. Nevertheless, the iciency of the Government could not have been maintained with a Council in general agreement with the Crown. Elizabeth was not, as a rule, impervious to remonstrance, d her selection of Privy Councillors conveyed a fairly accurate indication of the prin-)les on which she meant to rule. The composition of her Council in 1589 is typical for r reign; Lord Buckhurst, who in 1591 received the title of Lord High Butler, Burgh- r Treasurer, Whitgift, Cobham Lord Warden of the Cinque Ports, Sir James Crofts mptroller of the Household, John Fortescue Master of the Great Wardrobe and Vice- easurer of the Exchequer, Hatton as Chancellor, Sir Thomas Heneage Vice-Chamberlain,)ward of Effingham Admiral, Lord Hunsdon Lord Chamberlain, Sir Francis Knollys easurer of the Household, Sir John Perrott, Sir Francis Walsingham Principal Secre- ry, Earl of Warwick Master of the Ordnance, John Wolley Latin Secretary to the ieen. The Sovereign nominated the Council and personally superintended all the higher partments of State, but no matter how watchful or labourious, he was forced to leave ich to his subordinates. Men of the type of Burghley and Walsingham, Mildmay and inry Sidney, Knollys and Robert Cecil were no servile instruments, and apart from the ce of routine and the say wait parable from the management of details, the counsel d experience of such and treated by largely modified the policy of the State. (1) "The blic policy of the councillor (Gardiner), as far as Elizabeth would permit, by Burghley d Walsingham, who with Sadler, Mildmay, Knolles, Bedford, and Bromley, were the althy elements of the Council. But by the side of these was the circle of favourites, teful as the 'minions' of Henry of France." . . (2) Elizabeth, though she had her vourites, never trusted them with supreme control: Leicester, Hatton, "the Captain of e Guard whom the Queen is said to have loved after Leicester," (3) and Essex were ided with gifts and had ready access to the Sovereign's ear, but it was Burghley who verned for the Queen.

The Council was composed largely of staunch Protestant laymen such as Cecil d his son Robert and the Earl of Bedford. The substitution of a layman as Chan- llor for Archbishop Heath was as significant of the change in the relations between iurch and State as was Henry VIII.'s consistent appointment of laymen to the office ter Wolsey's downfall. Not until 1586, and then largely owing to the influence of Sir iristopher Hatton, the "enemy of the gospel" according to the Puritans, was Whitgift th his two allies, Lords Cobham and Buckhurst sworn of the Privy Council, a privilege iich none of Elizabeth's archbishops had then as yet enjoyed. In 1587 Hatton became iancellor, and, with the Archbishop and Cobham, the principal advocate of ecclesiastical gour.

There were always parties in Elizabeth's Council. From the beginning the Spanish id French Ambassadors had begun to bribe the Councillors and had formed their parties iongst those who surrounded the Queen. (4) Philip's paid agents in the Council were er whispering against Cecil and his religious reforms: the Howards, Arundel, and Mason ere all "Philippians." Cecil's friends, Suffolk, Bedford, and Clinton often grew im- itient at his (Cecil's) moderation, but, with him they opposed Leicester as being danger- is to the national welfare since he was ready to swear allegiance to any cause in order

(1) Prothero: "Statutes and Constitutional Documents," p. xcix.
(2) Froude, xi., p. 470.
(3) "Journey through England and Scotland, 1584 and 1585"; Trans- actions of the Royal Historical Society; N.S. ix., p. 263.
(4) Hume: "Burghley," 95.

to serve his purpose of dominating the Queen. He had much influence with the Queen, and in 1565 managed to obtain the office of Comptroller of the Household and a seat in the Privy Council for one of his servants, Sir James Crofts by name, who had been implicated in Army Robsart's death, and dismissed for incapacity if not for treachery and cowardice in one of the Scottish expeditions. He was one of Philip's paid agents all the time he was in the Council. (1)

It was Burghley who first introduced Walsingham into the public service, and obtained for him his appointment as ambassador in France in 1570, but Burghley was soon deserted in favour of Leicester. Walsingham was radically Protestant in religion, and his religious views ordered his foreign policy. He was quite prepared to sacrifice English interests for the sake of what he considered the greater cause, and here he clashed with Burghley, who was an opportunist in religious matters. In this difference on the fundamental question of the times lay the seeds of a division which developed into open opposition on matters of public policy as Walsingham's influence in the Privy Council increased. Bernardino de Mendoza, Spanish ambassador at London, wrote 31st March, 1578, "Although these are seventeen councillors with two secretaries, Hatton and the new ones, the bulk of the business really depen___ __n the Queen, Leicester, Walsingham, and Cecil, the latter of whom, though h___ ___part in the resolutions of them by virtue of his office, absents himself on many ___ions, as he is opposed to the Queen's helping the [Dutch] rebels and thus weakening her own position. He does not wish to break with Leicester and Walsingham on the matter, they being very much wedded to the States [of the Low Countries]. . . . They urge the business under the cloak of religion, which Cecil cannot well oppose. Nor can he afford to make enemies of them, as they are well supported. Some of the Councillors are well disposed towards your Majesty, but Leicester, whose spirit is Walsingham, is so highly favoured by the Queen, notwithstanding his bad character, that he centres in his hands and those of his friends most of the busines sof the country." (2) Leicester had joined with Norfolk's party in 1569, impelled by his old desire to turn Burghley out of office. Norfolk's plans failed, and Leicester allied with Walsingham, the strong man in the Protestant party. From 1578 two groups are discernible among the Councillors, one supporting Burghley's views, the others Leicester and Walsingham combined. There was nothing like party organisation in the modern sense of the term, but each group had its leader and its programme, to which each lent a fairly consistent support. Burghley's views, and to a considerable extent his antagonism to Leicester, were shared by the older members of the Privy Council, such as Sussex, the Lord Chamberlain, and after his death in 1583 Lord Hunsdon, Lincoln the Lord Admiral, Bacon, Whitgift, Cobham, and Buckhurst were made Councillors in 1586 for the express purpose of counter-balancing the influence of Leicester's friends. On the other side, Walsingham, Leicester, Bedford, Warwick, and Knollys formed the nucleus of an aggressive Protestant party in the Council. Generally speaking, on disputed questions of public policy the Council split along this line of cleavage. For some time Leicester and his partisans commanded a numerical preponderance in the Council, and after the death of Secretary Smith in 1577 both the principal secretaries belonged to his party. The Council was divided on foreign policy, on religious affairs at home, on the Anjou marriage question, and on the problem of the treatment of Mary Queen of Scots. The final issue of the struggle between the conservative and aggressive Protestants, between the peace party and war party in Elizabeth's Privy Council, did not result in a complete victory for either side. In foreign affairs the war

(1) Spanish Calendar: II., 571.   (2) Spanish Calendar: II., 486.

These phrases come from ____'s article on ____ — but no credit is given!

party ultimately prevailed, and in the settlement of religion the conservatives on the whole won the day. (1)

After Burghley's death and his son's rise to power, the parties in the Council centred round Essex and Robert Cecil. After the former's fall, Cecil's elder brother, Lord Burghley, wrote to him 21st July, 1601, "Now your voice is freer" and "the world is informed you carry most sway in these matters of highest nature." Before Essex's death, there had been divided worship on the part of many men, though of so jealous a humour was Essex and so apparent was the opposition between them that there was no possibility of combining any sort of active allegiance to both. Sir Ferdinando Gorges wrote to Robert Cecil 27th April, 1601, "I vow to God that I did endeavour by what means I was able, the reconciliation of your Honour and him: but he answered me that he would receive no good from you or by your means." (2) With Essex gone, however, there was little hesitation on the part of men in general to acclaim his former rival.

The extinction of the last surviving dukedom on the execution of the Duke of Norfolk in 1572 marked an epoch in English history; it sealed the ruin of the old nobility which was incompatible with the new monarchy. By 1571 the old influences had almost disappeared from Elizabeth's Privy Council. She told La Mothe in April, 1572, that of the principal lords who used to frequent her Court, all were dead, fugitives or prisoners. Pembroke had died in 1570, Northampton in 1571, Winchester early in 1572, and Norfolk and Arundel were in prison. The nobles in the Council were now all of Tudor creation, and the control of English affairs had passed into the hands of new men prepared to give full play to the new forces which were making for the expansion of England and for a revolution in diplomatic relations. Few of the men who wrought the greatness of Elizabethan England were born of noble parentage.

No chapter upon the composition of the Tudor Privy Council should close without some mention of the office of Secretary, which is deserving of more than passing notice. These officers were characteristic instruments of the Tudor system. Their origin, indeed, lies much further back, but their political importance dates from the establishment of the autocracy and is indicative of the beginning of government in the modern sense. The King's Secretary is first heard of in the reign of Henry III. His duties had doubtless in earlier times been discharged by the Chancellor and his staff. Administrative business, however, increased—the severance of Chancery from the Exchequer at the end of the twelfth century indicates the increasing importance of both departments—and the King's Clerk or Secretary became an officer distinct from the clerks and chaplains who acted under the Chancellor. The standing and character of the men holding the post undergo a gradual and profound change; the general tendency is towards greater dignity in the office. During the next two reigns the only apparent change is that the Secretaries begin to be associated with the Privy Council. A Secretary under Henry IV. was a Privy Councillor at the time of his appointment (John Prophete), and in Henry VI's time William Alnewick was present in the Privy Council, apparently by virtue of his office, for he was not previously a member. In the reign of Henry VI. two Secretaries were appointed for the first time, one by delivery of the King's Signet, the other by patent: the second Secretary had become necessary for the transaction of the King's business in France, and is

(1) E.H.R., January, 1913, "Walsingham and Burghley in Queen Elizabeth's Privy Council."

(2) Hatfield Papers, xi. Also Dom. Cal., Elizabeth (passim), for the struggle between Essex and Robert Cecil.

first mentioned in 1433. Moreover, during this reign there is the first clear instance of political importance being attached to the Secretaryship. (1) Under Edward IV. the Secretary ranked next to the Knights of the Household and before the Chaplains, and he had four clerks and " sufficient writers of the King's Signet." He did his work in the Court premises, and had, like other officers of State, his appointed Diet at Court. Edward Hatclyffe was Secretary in 1464, " our Secretary and Councillor," and Oliver King was " the King's first and principal Secretary in the French language." (2) The Secretaryship was carried over from one reign to another ; though as a matter of course new Letters Patent had to be taken out. Oliver King was Secretary again under Henry VII. Stephen Frion is also mentioned as " the royal secretary " in 1489, and Robert Sherbourne in 1496. (3) Ruthal Bishop of Durham, a later Secretary of the same King, continued his duties under Henry VIII.: evidently the office was important for itself alone.

The reign of Henry VIII. was a striking epoch in the history of Government departments. In every direction the administrative official became more firmly established, his work more highly organised. Since the officials of Government were the King's officials, it is a natural consequence of their higher development that the mainsprings of the machine should be the King's Treasurer and the King's Secretary. The immense difference in the position of the Secretary can be gauged by the fact that Thomas Cromwell rose to power by means of the secretaryship (1534—1536). In a lesser degree it can be seen in the security with which a Secretary could remonstrate with no less a person than Cardinal Wolsey. Dr. Pace, one of the Secretaries with Cromwell, wrote to Wolsey to complain of an irregularity by which a document had been sent by the Lord Mayor of London direct to Wolsey, instead of to the Secretary, who would then communicate it, together with the King's pleasure, to Wolsey.

Responsibility for the use of the Signet, indicated by the ordinance of 1443, was confirmed by the Statute 27 H. VIII., c. 11. The Secretaries were still members of the King's Household, but they ranked next to the greater household officers, (4) and in Parliament and Council they have their places assigned by Statute. 31 H. VIII., c. 10, s. 6, provided that King's Chief Secretary, if a baron of Parliament, should sit before and above all other barons, and if a bishop, before and above all other bishops. Further, " if any person or persons which at any time hereafter shall happen to have any of the said offices of Lord Chancellor, Lord Treasurer, Lord President of the King's Council, Lord Privy Seal, or Chief Secretary shall be under the degree of a Baron of Parliament . . . shall sit and be placed at the uppermost part of the sacks in the midst of the great Parliament Chamber." Evidently the Secretary had risen to be ranked with the four great officers of State: his work " to answer of such letters or things passed in counsell whereof they have the custody and knowledge " (5) was now of such importance that he was to sit in the Lords even if not a member of that House. A few years later it was ordained that when the King or Speaker was present in the House of Lords, both Secretaries were to be on the woolsacks; on other days they were to sit alternately week by week—one in the Lords, the other in the Commons, but if important matters were before the Commons they were both to be there. (6) The names of Cromwell, Wriothesley, Sadler, Paget, Petre, Walsingham, Davison, Cecil, and Herbert, some of the Secretaries during the Tudor period, serve to show what kind of an office the secretaryship had become. Yet they lived in extreme discomfort. In 1545, Paget, one

(1) Nicholas: " Proceedings and Ordinances," VI. clxxxviii.
(2) Gretton: " King's Government," p. 31.
(3) Venetian Calendar: I., 556, 691.
(4) " Ordinances for the Royal Household," p. 162.
(5) Smith: " De Republica Anglorum," 51.
(6) Gretton: " King's Government," 33.

of the Secretaries, and at that time ambassador in France, wrote to the other Secretary, Petre, to beg his lodging might be changed for the better. "You know that the chamber over the gate will scant receive my bed and a table to write at for myself. The study you know is not mete to be trampled in for diseasing his Majesty. I must needs have a place to keep my table in." (1) In 1547 Paget was made Comptroller of his Majesty's Household and was given £75 in lieu of "three quarters of a year's exercise of the room of one of His Majesty's Principal Secretaries." (2) Sir Francis Walsingham, though he held the offices of Chancellor of the Duchy of Lancaster, and of the Order of the Garter, together with that of Secretary, was not thereby prevented from dying in very necessitous circumstances in April, 1590, with the reputation of having carried on the public service at the expense of his fortune. (3) His diary gives a vivid picture of the work of a Secretary. (4)

In 1539 a warrant issued to Thomas Wriothesley and Ralph Sadler gave them "the name and office of the King's Majesty's Principal Secretaries during His Highness' pleasure," requiring them to keep two Signets and a book of all warrants which passed under their hands, and placed them in Council next after the Great Chamberlain.(5) Hitherto there had been only one Signet, and the second Secretary had not been on quite the same level as his fellow. Now they were both of equal rank and title.

After the reign of Henry VIII. it would seem that the Secretary ceased to be an officer of the Household; he does not appear as an item in the household expenditure of Elizabeth. During the greater part of Elizabeth's reign only one Secretary appears, but at the close of it Sir Robert Cecil shared the duties with another, he being called "Our Principal Secretary of Estate" and the other "one of our Secretaries of Estate." From this date the new style of nomenclature was always used, and would seem to imply that the office of Secretary was a constitutional rather than a personal service.

From the reign of Henry VIII. the Secretary was the channel through which alone the Crown could be approached in home and foreign affairs, and the medium through which the pleasure of the Crown was expressed. The rules made by Edward VI. for the conduct of business in Council made the Secretary the medium of communication between the King and his Council or its committees. (6) Cecil, or whoever did write that short treatise attributed to him, on "The State and Dignity of a Secretary of State's Place, with the Care and Peril thereof," speaks of the Secretary's liberty of negotiation at discretion, at home and abroad without "authority or warrant (like other servants of princes) in disbursement, conference or commission, but virtue and word of his Sovereign." He seems to complain somewhat of the unconstitutional indefiniteness of his office, "the place of Secretary is dreadful if he serve not a constant prince, for he that liveth by trust, ought to serve truly." (7)

The duties of a Secretary were clearly set out in a memoranda probably by Dr. John Herbert, second Secretary, in 1600. It is a formidable list. The Secretary was expected to possess general knowledge of the relations between this country and others, the affairs of Wales, and the state of Ireland, while he also had charge of all the Queen's

(1) Thomas: "History of Public Departments," p. 26.
(2) A.P.C. II., 29th June, 1547.
(3) T. Birch: "Memories of the Reign of Queen Elizabeth," 7.
(4) Camden Society: "Camden Miscellany," 1870.
(5) Gretton, p. 40.
(6) Grenville Correspondence, III., 16 note.
(7) Harleian Miscellany, II. 281.

correspondence with foreign princes, and, as it would seem, of the preparation of business for the Council, including the assignment to the Council, Star Chamber, and Court of Requests of matters within their respective provinces. (1) The growing importance of the Secretary in Henry VIII.'s time is admirably illustrated in Cécil's correspondence. (2) Throughout the Tudor period he is the King's mouthpiece. He obtains the Sovereign's dispensation for a member to be absent from Parliament (3): he gives permission for petitions to be addressed to the Council. (4) From the first they had been peculiarly connected with the King's business abroad, and were often sent on embassies and missions. (5) 22nd April, 1587, Secretary Walsingham released a man from his bond to appear before the Council, and gave him licence to depart. (6) 20th April, 1589, he is asked to hear a case and order some " good and friendly agreement." between the litigants." (7) The Secretary was responsible, too, for the minutes of the Council, and through him the Sovereign conveyed his wishes to the heads of departments, to the Lords-Lieutenant, to the Councils of the North and of Wales, to the Lord Deputy in Ireland, and to the ambassadors abroad.

The reign of Elizabeth was as striking an epoch in the history of the Secretary-ship as was that of Henry VIII., though for a very different reason. Henry VIII. gave to the office statutory powers and so prepared one line of subsequent development of Ministries. Under Elizabeth the change was more profound and subtle. The office changed little in theory, but during her reign it was made clear how much the quality of the Secretary's power depended upon the character of the holder of the office. The Secretaries were members of the Privy Council, but not until the Privy Council ceased to combine deliberative and executive functions did the office of Secretary of State assume its present importance. Before that change took place, the Secretary assisted at private discussions of business to be brought before the Council, was the necessary instrument for carrying out the pleasure of the King, and might even be a personage whose opinions carried great weight (as were Burghley and Robert Cecil), yet he exercised little independent discretion in the executive government. He was responsible directly to King and Council—remotely to Parliament. The rise of the Secretary meant diminished independence for the Council. " The Tudors from their own force of character gave importance to the office: it was something to be the exponent of the will of one who always had a will of his own." (8)

(1) Prothero: "Statutes and Documents," p. 166. Also A.P.C. XVIII.,
    8th October, 1589.

(2) H.M.C.: Hatfield MSS. I.—V. (passim).

(3) Ibid: VII., 28th September, 1597.

(4) Ibid: IX., 30th July, 1599; X., 22nd March, 1600.

(5) A.P.C. and Calendar Domestic (passim).

(6) A.P.C.: XV.

(7) Ibid: XVII.   (8) Anson: II. pt. I., 162.

IV. OFFICIALS OF THE COUNCIL.

————:o:————

THE Register of the Privy Council for the years 1460—1540, if one was ever kept, does not now seem to exist. Consequently for this period little can be gathered about the officials of the Council. That there were clerks we know (1), and from this it may be argued, though not conclusively, that records were kept which have now disappeared.

The Clerks of the Council were under the control of the Secretary, and in Henry VII.'s reign the most notable seem to have been Robert Rydon and John Bladiswell. Very little else is known concerning them, but even in Henry's reign they occupied no insignificant position. (2)

The next reference to a Clerk of the Council is in the reign of Henry VIII. On 19th October, 1509, a warrant is recorded for John Meautys, the King's French Secretary, to be Clerk of the Council in place of Robert Rydon, deceased. His salary was to be forty marks a year. (3) He would seem later to have given up his office of clerk, for on 21st October, 1512, there was a warrant passed for Richard Eden to be Clerk of the King's Council with forty marks a year, in the place of John Meautys, the King's Secretary for the French tongue, appointed during pleasure by patent 19th October, 1 H 8; to enjoy the office in the same manner as Meautys or Robert Rydon. (4) In 1516, amongst the fees and annuities paid by the King, Meautys receives £40 for life, while Richard Eden, "Clerk of the Council in place of Robert Rydon," gets for life £26 13s. 4d. (5) Eden appears to have held the office for some time alone, but on 5th May, 1516, Richard Lee is mentioned with him as being Clerk of the Council. (6) In 1519 they still held office, and Eden is recorded as drawing on Lady Day half a year's wages due to him, being the sum of ten shillings. (7)

In August, 1527, however, Richard Lee is mentioned as Clerk of the Star Chamber (8), and to take up this post he seems to have given up his appointment of Clerk of the Council, the former probably being the more lucrative of the two, as it certainly was later. Adrian Dyer evidently took his place, but did not hold office for long, for amongst the grants in December, 1527, is one to Thomas Derby, clerk of the Signet, and John Almain. They were awarded the grant in survivorship of the office of clerk of the Council vacant by the decease of Adrian Dyer. (9) It appears customary throughout Henry's reign to have had at least two clerks of the Council, if not more, holding office jointly. Thomas Derby held the clerkship of the Signet together with that of the Council for many years, and in December 1539 he was given an advance " of his whole year's fee of clerkship of the Privy Council beforehand, the same year to begin 1st January, anno 30 (sic), £20," a marked increase upon Richard Eden's half-year's wages in 1519. (10) Four months after Thomas Derby and John Almain had obtained their grant in

---

(1) Baldwin: 435. Scofield: 5. (2) See above, p. 10.

(3) L. and P., I. 588. His name is spelt in various ways. The method adopted above seems the most used.

(4) Ibid: I. 3478.

(5) Ibid: II. 2736. (6) Ibid: II. 1857.

(7) Ibid: III. King's Book of Payments. This is difficult to explain; it may have been that Lee had bought him out as regards wages.

(8) Ibid: IV. 3380. (9) Ibid: IV. 3747 (16).

(10) Ibid: XIV. Part II. 781 (64b).

survivorship, Thomas Elyott, on conditional surrender by Richard Eden of the patent 21st October, 4 H. 8, which granted the office to him, was made clerk with a salary of 40 marks a year, April, 1528. (1) He was a man of some standing, an author and diplomatist, and, on giving up his clerkship in 1530, obtained a knighthood. If the conjectural date of his birth, 1499, in the Dictionary of National Biography, is correct, he was young to fill the responsible position of clerk to the Privy Council. Richard Eden came back into office again when Elyott resigned, and in April, 1530, he and Thomas Eden obtained a grant in survivorship of the office of clerk of the King's Council with the usual salary of forty marks a year. (2) Thomas Derby also was still clerk of the Council. In January, 1534, a Master Eden is mentioned as the Clerk of the Star Chamber. Whether this was Richard or Thomas we do not know, but in all probability it was Richard, for a new clerk of the Council, Thomas Bedyll, is mentioned about that time. (3) The clerkship of the Council and that of the Star Chamber seem to have been offices quite distinct from each other. There is, however, no record of Eden's second surrender of his patent of Clerkship of the Council, and both he and Richard Lee after him may have held both offices. Might it not even be conjectured, if the Court of Star Chamber was still very closely connected with the Privy Council, as it was in Henry VII.'s time, that the office of clerk to the Council implied also that of clerk of the Star Chamber, at any rate previous to about 1536?

The new clerk, Thomas Bedyll, was a divine, and secretary 1520—1532 to Archbishop Warham. He then became a royal chaplain and clerk to the Council, (4) and was employed by Henry VIII. in business relating to his divorce and the royal supremacy. In 1535 he is mentioned together with Cromwell and John Tregonwell as a "King's Councillor," (5) and in June of the same year, both he and Richard Layton are spoken of as clerks of the Council. (6) Layton was one of Cromwell's henchmen and his chief agent in the suppression of the monasteries. He began visiting them in 1535, was made Dean of York in 1539, and English ambassador at Brussels in 1543, dying there in 1544. Already the clerks of the Council were men of sufficient standing and importance to be sent as envoys abroad. In Elizabeth's reign one of the clerks of the Council was generally at some foreign court engaged in diplomatic business. (7) On 7th April, 1538, "Master Needham" is mentioned as clerk of the Council (8), and very little else is known about him. There was a James Needham or Nedeham in Henry VIII.' reign, an architect and master carpenter, who was appointed clerk of the King's works in 1530, and overseer in 1533. He may have become clerk of the Council later, but it is very unlikely. (9)

From 10th August, 1540, we have again the Register of the Council until 1601, although there are considerable gaps at times. The first entry in the Register recorded that "there should be a clerk attendant upon the said Council to write, enter, and register all such decrees, determinations, letters, and other such things as he should be appointed to enter, in a book, to remain always as a register, as well for the discharge of the said Councillors touching such things as they should pass from time to time, as also for a memorial unto them of their own proceeding." (10) William Paget, of late secretary to the Queen, was appointed by the King to this office and sworn in. In September, 1541, Paget was sent ambassador to France, the King's French Secretary, John Mason, being sworn and admitted clerk during his absence. On his return from France, Paget was made one of the two principal secretaries and a Privy Councillor, while John Mason and William Honnings were sworn as clerks. In 1549 Wriothesley speaks of Mason as still " the chief clerk of the Council." (11). He had a remarkably interesting career, being

(1) Ibid: IV. 4231. D.N.B. asserts he was clerk of the Privy Council 1523—30, and it also records him as being clerk of assize on the western circuit 1511—1528. (2) Ibid: IV. 6490 (1).
(3) Ibid: VII. 47. Scofield, p. 67, speaks of Richard Eden as clerk of the Star Chamber.
(4) D.N.B. gives the date 1532, but 1534 would seem the more correct.
(5) L. and P.: VIII. 974. (6) Ibid: VIII. 858.
(7) A.P.C., IX. passim. (8) Ibid: XIII. 696.
(9) D.N.B.: XL.
(10) Nicholas: Proceedings and Ordinances VII., 10th August, 1540.
(11) Wriothesley's Chronicle: Vol. II. p. 31. Camden Society, 1877.

38

employed very largely as an envoy abroad. In 1551 he was clerk of the Parliament, and though he gave up his ecclesiastical benefices under Mary, he was favoured by her and lived to influence Elizabeth's foreign policy in her Privy Council. He retained his office as French Secretary while he held the Clerkship of the Council. William Honnings, his colleague, received an increase in salary in 1545: £20 a year was granted to him as clerk of the Privy Council on the surrender of his patent 10th May, 35 H 8, appointing him one of the said clerks with £10 a year. (1) In Edward VI.'s first Parliament he sat in the Commons for the city of Winchester, (2) and 17th April, 1548, the Council Register records an increase in the salaries of the three clerks of the Council, William Honnings, Sir Thomas Chaloner, and Armigill Wade, Waad, or Ward. (3) The last mentioned also sat in the same Parliament for the borough of Chipping Wycombe, Bucks. Honnings seems to have been involved in the Protector's disgrace, and on 19th April, 1550, William Thomas became clerk of the Council (4): he seems to have acted as political mentor to the young King. (5)

Thus, in Edward VI.'s reign for the first time there is a distinct record of three clerks of the Council. Sir John Mason was taken into the Privy Council on the same date that William Thomas was sworn clerk. (6) Thus two former clerks, Mason and Paget, became later Privy Councillors. Thomas was a Welshman and an author of some repute. Herbert of Cherbury records that " Though William Thomas, a clerk of the Council to Edward VI., and living about the latter times of Henry VIII.'s reign, did in great part defend him [Henry VIII.] in an Italian book, printed anno 1552, it hath not availed." (7) He was given a prebend at St. Paul's and other rewards, but he lost all his preferments at the accession of Mary. After taking an active part in Wyatt's conspiracy, he was, according to Machyn, " beheaded and quartered " 18th May, 1552. (8) When Thomas was appointed to the Clerkship, there were then three holders of the office, Honnings, Chaloner, and Wade, whose salaries at that date were respectively £50, £40, and fifty marks a year. Obviously there was not one clerk but several, for one salary was not divided between those holding office. Honnings, however, did not remain long in office after Thomas' appointment. Sir Thomas Chaloner had been made Clerk in 1547. He managed to enrich himself while in office, acquiring the grant of Guisborough Priory and its lands in 1550, and though he no longer held office after 1551, he was given many other lands, and continually employed as envoy abroad, in Edward's, Mary's, and Elizabeth's reigns, to Scotland, France, the Emperor, the Spanish Netherlands, and Spain. (9) The Clerkship of the Council seems often to have led to higher and more lucrative office. Armigill Wade, Chaloner's colleague in office, was equally fortunate, and, though he, too, lost office on Mary's accession, he was sent abroad by Elizabeth, and employed by her generally in the public service. (10) On 24 Sept., 1551, Bernard Hampton was sworn and admitted a Clerk of the Council (11); Chaloner appears to have given up office soon after, and Hampton and Wade filled the position until the end of Edward's reign. (12)

At Mary's accession she appointed Francis Aleyn and William Smith in succession to her brother's clerks, 30th July, 1553 (13), but in the next year Hampton was back in office in place of Aleyn. Mary employed these two men throughout her reign as clerks.

(1) L. and P. XX., Part ii., 910 (41).
(2) Returns of Members of Parliament.
(3) A.P.C., II.   (4) Ibid., III.
(5) D.N.B.
(6) King Edward's Journal, p. 15. Clarendon Hist. Soc., Reprints.
(7) Herbert: Henry VIII., p. 268.
(8) Machyn's Diary, p. 60. Camden Soc., 1848.
(9) D.N.B.   (10) D.N.B.
(11) A.P.C., III.
(12) D.N.B., X. 178, gives Sir John Cheke as clerk of the Council in Edward VI.'s reign; there is no record in the Council Register of his holding that office, though he may have the office of a clerk as a sinecure.
(13) A.P.C. IV.

Elizabeth, following out her policy of dislocating the public service as little as possible, continued William Smith in the office (1) For some years he apparently held office alone (2), but in May, 1571, a colleague was appointed in the person of Edward Tremaine. Smith must have given up his position about this time, for in the volume of the Council Register dealing with the years 1571—5, two clerks only are mentioned, Edmund Tremaine and Robert Beale, the latter being appointed in July, 1572 (3) Tremaine had done secret service work for Cecil in Ireland in 1569, and the clerkship was evidently conferred as some reward for the same. In 1572 he sat in the Commons for Plymouth. (4) Robert Beale, on the other hand, was one of Walsingham's party, being the latter's brother-in-law. He had been compelled to leave England under Mary owing to his religious opinions, and in 1570 became secretary to Walsingham while the latter was Ambassador in Paris. He sat for Totnes in the Parliament which met in 1572, and in 1578, 1581, and 1583 acted as Secretary of State during Walsingham's absence. (5) He sat in Parliament again in 1585, 1586, and 1588, and again in 1592, in that year being banished both from Court and Parliament for his attitude in debate upon supply and towards the inquisitorial practices of bishops. (6).

The increase in the business transacted by the Council necessitated the appointment of two additional clerks in 1579, Henry Cheke and Thomas Wilkes. The former was the son of Sir John Cheke, Cecil's college friend, and in 1581 was appointed secretary of the Council of the North for life. (7) William Wade, son of Armigall Wade, took his place in 1583, and held office until 1613. He, like his father, was a member of Parliament while being employed by the Crown, both in 1588 and 1601. He was instrumental in tracking down Roderigo Lopez's plot in 1574, and three other Catholic schemes. During Elizabeth's reign the clerkships of the Council seem largely to have been conferred as rewards upon the secret service agents of the Government who could hold their tongues and were thus suitable for these posts. On 19th March, 1587, Anthony Ashley was sworn into the office (8), probably in succession to Edmund Tremaine, who disappeared from public life about this time.

In 1587 the number of clerks was raised to five, Daniel Rogers being sworn 7th May, 1587. He died, however, in 1591, and apparently no successor to him was appointed. The numbers were further reduced to three when in 1596 Anthony Ashley was attached in a civil capacity to the "honourable voyage to Cadiz." Thomas Smith took his place, however, in 1597 (9), and although appointed 30th September, 1597, to the office of clerk of the Parliament for life with a fee of £40 per annum, he retained that of clerk of the Council. In 1598 Wilkes died, and Thomas Edmondes, French secretary to Elizabeth, was rewarded for his careful negotiations with the Archduke Albert at Boulogne with a clerkship. He owed his advancement to Sir Robert Cecil (10), and a clerkship to the

(1) He had been made, with William Pope, clerk of the Star Chamber, December, 1534. L. and P., VII. 1601.
(2) Hatfield Papers, I. One Harris is mentioned as being clerk of the Council in a letter dated 28th March, 1560. The Council Register is missing 12th May, 1559—28th May, 1562.
(3) A.P.C., VIII.   (4) D.N.B.
(5) Hatfield Papers, VII., 28th September, 1597.
(6) D.N.B.
(7) D.N.B. does not mention his being made clerk of the Council in 1579.
(8) A.P.C., XIV.
(9) Hatfield Papers V. mentions him as clerk of the Council in 1595, December 5th. A.P.C. XXVIII., September, 1597—July, 1598, does not mention him as being clerk as yet.
(10) D.N.B.

Council was often the reward for service done to one or other of the parties at Court and in the Council. In 1601, when the Council Register ceases, Ashley, Edmunds, Smith, and Wade are still acting as clerks. The extracts only of the Register which remain to us for the rest of Elizabeth's reign shed, unfortunately, no light upon the office of clerk of the Council.

In 1601 Elizabeth wrote to the Archbishop of Canterbury concerning "our servant William Mill, clerk of our Council for three years past." (1) He is also referred to in the Hatfield Papers as Clerk of the Council. (2) He was, however, clerk of the Star Chamber, (3) and the distinction between the two offices of clerk of the Privy Council and clerk of the Star Chamber is explained in the following speech of Lord Burghley in the Star Chamber, in which he " declared before all the presence that the same Court [of Star Chamber] was the Council of State of this Realm and the Clerk thereof the only Clerk of the Council of State and the Clerk of the Council of England, and that there was no other Clerk of the Queen's Council of State but only the Clerk of this Court, and that the others were Clerks of the Privy Council attendant upon her Majesty's royal person, and those other Clerks were to attend the Council table." (4) The Clerkship of the Star Chamber was less important than that of the Privy Council, but it was highly lucrative. It was in the gift of the Crown and the yearly wages were £26 13s. 4d., but numerous fees also pertained to the office, which was usually delegated, men of high station being glad to secure so profitable a post and to get the work done by a deputy. In 1589 Lord Bacon secured the reversion of it from Burghley: it was not vacant, however, till the death of William Mill, July, 1608, who had held it since 15 Eliz.

The Clerks of the Council took an oath before entering upon their duties. It was as follows: " You shall swear to be a true and faithful servant unto the Queen's Majesty as one of the Clerks of her Highness' Privy Council. You shall not know or understand of any manner thing to be attempted, done, or spoken against Her Majesty's person, honour, crown, or dignity royal, but you shall let or withstand the same to the uttermost of your power, and either do or cause it to be revealed either to her Majesty's self or to her Privy Council. You shall keep secret all matters committed or revealed unto you or that shall be treated of secretly in Council, or if any of the same treaties or counsels shall touch any of the same Councillors, you shall not reveal the same unto him, but shall keep the same until such time as, by consent of her Majesty or of the Council, publication shall be made thereof. You shall to your uttermost bear faith and true allegiance to the Queen's Majesty, her heirs and lawful successors, and shall assist and defend all jurisdictions, pre-eminences, and authorities granted to Her Majesty and annexed to her Crown by Act of Parliament or otherwise against all foreign princes, persons, prelates, or potentates, etc., and generally in all things you shall do as a faithful and true servant and subject ought to do to her Majesty. So help you God and the holy contents of this Book." (5)

The duties of the clerks in attendance upon the Council will be dealt with more fully later in connection with the Council Register. It is impossible to say with any degree of certainty whether the clerks were present at the metings of the Council, for though it was their duty to write up the Council minutes, they entered only what they were told to enter. (6) They themselves, moreover, did not always write the entries, but

(1) Dom. Calendar, Feb. 1st, 1601.   (2) Hatfield Papers X., p. 435.
(3) Egerton Papers, p. 316, Camden Society, 1840; and A.P.C. XXX., p. 31.
(4) Hargreaves MS. 216—printed in Scofield, p. 62.
(5) A.P.C. VIII., 8th and 9th July, 1572.
(6) P. and O. VII., p. 1., 10th August, 1540.

employed deputy clerks, and this work in connection with the Register seems to have been one of the most insignificant of their duties. Apparently, however, they attended most of the Council meetings, for in June, 1552, the Register records the answer to a petition of theirs concerning this same matter. The petition was granted: two clerks were always to be present at the Council Board, and a third absent, for a fortnight at a time. (1) In 1579 an order was taken at the beginning of the year for the attendance of the four clerks throughout that period: two were always to be in attendance, each clerk being present for two months at a time, changing every month. (2) Apparently, however, the clerks were sent away when important business was being discussed: on 7th October, 1579, the Council were in session, concerning the Queen's marriage, from eight in the morning till seven at night, "without stirring from the room, having sent the clerks away, which, as I have told your Majesty, is very rarely done, and only when something very secret and important is being discussed. (3)

The more important part of the duties of the Clerks consisted of confidential negotiations, and the transaction of important business in connection with the interests of the Crown and its relations with foreign princes. There is continual reference to one or other of the Clerks being sent abroad. (4) It was also their duty to summon foreign ambassadors to the Court or Council when their presence was requested. (5) They were also used as messengers on important business; (6) were allowed to take action in pressing matters arising on days when the Council was not sitting, and formal attendances before them of prisoners on bail are recorded. (7) In 1516 they are seen engaged upon an inspeximus of a writ of certiorari in a suit (8); they examined prisoners, took charge of seditious books, and of the inventories of prisoners' goods. (9) They could commit to prison. (10) On 8th October, 1589, it was ordered by the Council that all private suits were to go first for examination before the Secretary or the Clerks of the Council. (11) They sometimes tried cases, and their decisions were confirmed by the Council. (12) Evidently they acted herein much as the later Masters in Chancery. They wrote letters for Elizabeth (13), and petitions to the Lords of the Privy Council apparently went first to them." (14) Late in Elizabeth's reign the Council abolished the office of Muster Master, and decided that the duties of the office should be performed by one of the clerks of the Council, paid at the rate of six shillings and eightpence per day. (15) At Council meetings the clerks read the dispatches to the assembled Councillors, (16) and as early as

(1) A.P.C.: IV., 18th June, 1552.   (2) Ibid: XI., 3rd January, 1579.
(3) Spanish Calendar: II., 606.
(4) A.P.C.: III., 11th February, 1552, and passim.   Hatfield Papers,
     VIII.; X., 13th May, 1600.
(5) L. and P.: xvi. 1482.
(6) A.P.C.: XIV., 26th August, 1586.   Birch "Memoirs of Queen Elizabeth," p. 434.
(7) A.P.C. VIII., 13th May, 1574, and passim.
(8) L. and P.: II. 1857.
(9) P. and O. VII., 28th February; 16th January; 4th February, 1542.
(10) Dom. Cal., 21st May, 1599.
(11) A.P.C., XVIII.   (12) Ibid: XIX., 30th April, 1590.
(13) Hatfield Papers V., 5th December, 1595.
(14) Ibid: VIII. May, 1598.
(15) A.P.C. XXVIII., 23rd July, 1598.
(16) Sprinia Ceciliana, 1st October, 1568.

Edward VI.'s reign in, was ordered that no Treasurers were to pay any warrants unless the same were signed by one of the clerks to whom that duty had been specifically assigned.

Under both Edward and Mary, the clerks of the Council, as we have seen, managed to acquire riches: on 26th May, 1552, a grant of Trinity Church, York, was made to Armigill Wade and Barnard Hampton. (1) Under Elizabeth, however, although prospects of advancement seem to have been as good as under previous Sovereigns, one clerk at least was not wealthy when he died. This was David Rogers, whose widow was said to have been left with "but small ability to maintain her [self] and her children." (2) In 1587 Robert Beale solicited the Queen for a grant of £60 a year for thirty or forty years in consideration of his poverty and services, or leave to resign and serve in some other place, for being in debt he was not able to continue in office any longer. (3) Elizabeth's poverty was felt even by her clerks of the Council. Ten years later, in 1597, Beale wrote in despair to Sir Robert Cecil: "For twenty-five years and more I have been a clerk of the Privy Council. I am a Master in Chancery, have served as a counsellor for the Queen with the Estates of the United Provinces, and am one of the Council established in the North parts." Two years later: "I have been a long time a suitor unto Her Majesty for the means to relieve my necessities, and to be better able to serve her . . . I receive not any benefits by my fee of clerk of the Council, which is spent in subsidies and many other charges of my extraordinary employment . . . And for that I am loth in these chargeable times to demand too much, I would humbly beseech your Lordship to be a means to Her Majesty that I may surrender up my fee of £50 yearly for the clerkship of the Council and have a lease of some 100 marks by the year for forty or fifty years." (4)

The clerks of the Council occasionally obtained monopolies, and these letters patent were enforced by the Council itself. (5) A certain amount of dignity was attached to the office from the beginning of the Tudor period. In Henry VII.'s reign an act was passed concerning "the forfeiture of him who goeth not in person with the King in his wars when he is in person." (6) It enacted that every subject by the duty of his allegiance was bound to serve the King when required, especially those who had received at his hands promotion or advancement, such as grants and gifts of offices, fees and annuities; the clerk of the King's Council, however, was excused such attendance. The credit of the Council office was maintained under Elizabeth by Anthony Ashley, who extorted from one Thomas Kelloway an apology for defamation of character. Kelloway was committed by the Lords of the Council (a familiar phrase in Tudor times), to the Fleet, "for divers matters of great misdemeanour as well towards their Lordships as against Anthony Ashley Esquire, one of the clerks of the Council," and order was taken that he was not to be liberated till he had apologised to Ashley. (7).

The Council had other functionaries attendant upon it besides the clerks. In connection with the Marprelate controversy, nine Privy Councillors, together with the Lord Bishop of Rochester, were appointed by the Queen and Council to examine certain

(1) A.P.C.: IV.
(2) A.P.C., XXII., 16th April, 1592.
(3) Dom. Cal., April (?), 1587.
(4) Hatfield Papers: VII., 28th September, 1597; IX., 5th May, 1599.
(5) A.P.C.: XIV., 22nd March, 1587; XIX., 5th June, 1590.
(6) 11 H. 7, c. 18.
(7) A.P.C.: XXII., Sunday, 2nd April, 1592.

suspected persons; they were to report proceedings to the Council and to appoint certain times for their meetings, "calling Bedell the Register (i.e. Registrar) to set down the examinations taken, and to keep an account of their doings in this service." This officer was probably appointed solely for the judicial work of the Council, which was extremely heavy throughout the whole Tudor period, judging from the Council Register.

The Council Chamber was kept in order by a keeper, of whose name and duties we know nothing until Elizabeth's reign. Robert Jones held the office in 1565. He was succeeded by Robert Langham, who occupied the post for many years, but about 1581 Humphrey Rogers took his place. On 1st April, 1582, he was allowed £10 a year for "the provision of boughs and other necessaries," for the Council Chamber. (1) It was his duty also to look after the Council stationery, though the money for the same was given sometimes to the clerks, sometimes the keeper. On 27th July, 1576, "standishes" (i.e., inkstands). pens, ink and paper for the Council table cost £13 6s. 8d., and a new Register Book 8s. In 1577 there was a warrant recorded to the Treasurer of the Chamber for £13 6s. 8d. to the Clerks of the Council for paper, pens, ink, wax, and other necessaries for the Council chest for the year ending at the Feast of John Baptist last, and for four new "standishes" 15s.; for a fire shovel, pair of tongs, bellows, and fork 13s. 4d. (2) The Council chest must have been of considerable capacity judging from the documents it was said to contain; in 1576 the sum of 40s. was paid for a new one.

From the Register it appears that the usual wage of the keeper was £10 (3) for the provision of boughs and flowers with which to beautify the Chamber, and for his diligence and pains. In June, 1578, the stationery cost 20 marks, a chest in which to keep the Muster Books 20s., and a book of penal statutes 6s. (4) A dozen cushions were provided in the following year at a cost of £4 16s. (5) Ten years later the cost of stationery was £15, two standishes 8s., and a paper book 4s., while a dozen and a half of "cooshins" came to the sum of £12. (6)

In 1593 the clerks of the Council appear to be sharing a servant between them to assist them in the Council Chamber. On 26th August of that year there was a warrant to the Treasurer of the Chamber "to pay unto the Clerks of the Council or else unto Randolph Bellin their common servant attending on the Council Chest, for four standishes at 6s. a piece, for a paper book and two canvas bags, for a hinge and mending the Council Chest, the sum of 37s. 10d." (7) It might be that the "common servant" of the clerks was the keeper of the Council Chamber. It would seem that he followed the Councillors, in order to prepare the Chamber where they sat in Council, when they went on progress with the Queen: he was granted £24 in 1598 "for his attendance and pains taken, and for provision of boughs, flowers, and other necessaries for the said Chamber, and for his charges in the Progress time for his stuff and lodging for one whole year." (8)

(1) A.P.C.: XIII.
(2) A.P.C. IX., 6th July, 1577; 15th April, 1576.
(3) A.P.C.: VII., 11th April, 1565; VIII., 31st March, 1572; IX., 22nd April, 1577.
(4) A.P.C. X.   (5) Ibid: XI., 9th December, 1579.
(6) Ibid: XVII., 29th June; 26th May, 1589.
(7) A.P.C.: XXIV., p. 486.
(8) Ibid: XXVIII., 5th April, 1598.

V. THE MEETINGS OF THE COUNCIL.

———— :o:— ————

EACH Privy Councillor, after having been appointed by the King, was supposed to be
in continual attendance upon the Sovereign. He took a prescribed oath, (1) and
thus became a member of that body which the Venetian ambassador described as
assembling, following the King's person, (and for this purpose having board and lodging
at the Court being served with great pomp and respect,) and thus saving the King the
fatigue and inconvenience of governing: being, in short, the "ears, person, and voice
itself of the King." (2)

Since it was the primary duty of the Council to follow the King in order to be
always at hand to give advice when asked to do so, it held its meetings wherever the King
happened to be. This was often at one of the royal manors round London, such as
Richmond, Greenwich, Oatlands, Woking. When in town the Council assembled in the
Star Chamber, or in the palace at Whitehall or Westminster; or, sometimes, in St.
James' Palace. Owing to the disappearance of the Council Register for 1460-1540, there
is no record of the places at which the Council sat during that period. In the reign of
Henry VII., however, the Star Chamber was the favourite place of assembly, for though
the Council never did any but Star Chamber business when it sat in the Court of Star
Chamber, yet it often used the Star Chamber for its work when sitting as the King's
Privy Council proper. Whenever the King moved out of town the Council went with
him. Between 10th August, 1540, and 8th April, 1542, the advisers of the King sat in
Council at forty-two different places: Ampthill, Bishop's Norton, Buckingham, Canter-
bury, Cawood, Chenies, Collyweston, Dartford, Dunstable, Enfield, Eweleme, Fothering-
hay, Gainsborough, Grafton, Greenwich, Grimesthorpe, Hampton Court, Hatfield, Higham
Ferrers, Hull, Kettleby, Leconfield, Lincoln, Loddington, "More Park" (3), Norton,
Notley, Northampton, Pipewell, Pomfret, Reading, Rochester, Rycot, St. Albans, Scrooby,
Sittingbourne, Sleaford, Thornton, Waltham, Westminster, Windsor, Wressel, York, "Mr.
Gostwick's House," and "Lord Russell's House." (4) After 1542 the northernmost point
at which a Council is recorded is Tichfield (Yorks.); Portsmouth was the most distant in
a south-westerly direction. The most common meeting-places were Westminster,
Greenwich, Hampton Court, and Windsor. (5)

Edward's Councils were never held very far from London, and were nearly all at
circumjacent royal manors. Westminster was by far the most favoured spot; after it,
Greenwich and Hampton Court, Oatlands, Windsor, Richmond, Nonsuch, and Guildford.
The Council in his reign sat nearly a dozen times in the Star Chamber; it also met at the
Tower; at the Lord Admiral's House by Temple Bar on one occasion; at Somerset

(1) Prothero, p. 165.
(2) Ven. Cal., 13th May, 1557.
(3) Probably Moor Park, Richmansworth, Herts.
(4) P. and O., VII., passim.
(5) A.P.C., I.

Place, Strand (1), eleven times; at the Guildhall once; at Mercers' Hall once; and at the house of Master Sheriff York three times. The young King seems to have made few royal progresses, and the bitter partisan hostility between his Councillors may account partly for his residence close to London (2).

Mary, too, travelled about very little. The Council sat most frequently at Westminster, St. James', and Greenwich in her first year, constantly moving between the royal manors around London, but from March 1554 to September 1556 the Council met at only seventeen different places, Bishop's Waltham, the Clink, Eltham, Farnham, Greenwich, Guildford, Hampton Court, London, Oatlands, Richmond, at "the Star Chamber," the Tower, Winchester, Windsor, at Westminster and St. James'. After 1556 Mary rarely left London; her Council sat in the Treasury Chamber, at Westminster, at St. James', at the Lord Chancellor's House, at the Star Chamber, at "London"; beyond the precincts of the city only at Eltham, Greenwich, Otford (Kent), and Richmond (3).

Elizabeth, on the other hand, was extremely fond of royal progresses; she was her father's daughter in her love of pomp and show and admiration. There are such gaps, however, in the Council Register between her accession and the end of 1570 that we have very imperfect records of the Council meetings for that time. The most westerly point to which Elizabeth is recorded as penetrating was Tuddington in Gloucestershire, where one Council was held. Westminster was still the most frequent place of meeting, Greenwich and Windsor coming second and third. Three meetings are recorded at Hatfield, seventeen at St. James', and fifteen at Strand House. Others were held at Cambridge, the Charterhouse, Chenies, Hampton Court, Nonsuch, Oatlands, Penleys (Wilts.), Reading, the Tower, Richmond; and Rycote in Oxfordshire (4).

From 1571 to 1575 most of the Council meetings were held at Greenwich, Hampton Court, and Westminster. Elizabeth was constantly moving, however, and the Council assembled three times at Cecil's mansion, Theobalds, twice at the Lord Keeper's House once at Salisbury, and once at "Mr. Fisher's House outside Bishopsgate." Other places mentioned are the Star Chamber, Bath, Canterbury, Croydon, Farnham, Grafton, Reading, St. James', Exchequer Chamber, Westminster, Knole (Kent), Lees (Essex), and Woburn (5). Later in Elizabeth's reign the places at which the Council met are very often not recorded in the Register (6).

Between 1575 and 1577 twenty-six different places are mentioned, few Council meetings being held at each, the greatest number, fifty-six, at Greenwich. Elizabeth's Council seems generally to have sat at each place the Queen visited, even when she was bent entirely on pleasure. It met at "Havering atte Bower," Hallingbury, Morley, Kenilworth, Hertford Castle, Stafford Castle, Sudely Castle, St. Albans, and Deptford (7). Ofter assemblies were held at the houses of private persons; Mr. Altam's house, Mr. Rivett's house, Mr. Stoner's house, Sir William Cordell's (8) house, and Sir John Cutts' house (9).

(1) Somerset House.

(2) A.P.C., II., III., IV., passim.

(3) A.P.C., V.

(4) A.P.C., VII.

(5) A.P.C., VIII.

(6) A.P.C., X., records ninety-four meetings the place of which is not stated; XI., a hundred and four; XII., sixty-one; XIII., sixty-three; XV., eighty-five; XVII., a hundred and seventy-one.

(7) A.P.C., IX.

(8) The Master of the Rolls.

(9) A.P.C., X.

For the next two years Elizabeth's favourite residences seem to have been the royal manors at Greenwich, Richmond, Oatlands and Nonsuch, and Councils were held there very frequently. Occasionally the Councillors met in the Star Chamber, at the Lord Treasurer's house, at Leicester House, Somerset House, and Theobalds, but they were never more than a few miles from London (1) and, indeed, this is the case until the end of the reign. From 1590 until Elizabeth's death, the Council is recorded as meeting most frequently at Greenwich, Richmond, and Whitehall. It sat besides but far less frequently in the Star Chamber, at Ely House, Oatlands, Nonsuch, Westminster, Wimbledon, Oxford Palce, Cecil House, Somerset House, Hampton Court, Hackney, Wimbledon, the Lord Treasurer's house in the Strand, the Lord Treasurer's chamber at St. James', Mr. Sheriff Saltingstall's, Mr. Sheriff Lowe's, Mr. Sheriff Holliday's house, the Lord Mayor's house in London, the Lord Keeper's (York House, Strand), at Mr. Chancellor's chamber in the Garden at Greenwich, at "the Little Council Chamber," at Lord Buckhurst's house in Fleet Street, Salisbury Court, at Basing House, Hampshire; and at Reading, Putney, and Highgate. (2)

It is thus abundantly clear from the Register that the Privy Council of the Tudors was a migratory body. The fact that fifteenth and sixteenth century monarchs were less on the move than earlier kings, and confined their wanderings within narrower limits, does not prevent this Council with the King from being the real consultative Council, and it is very hard to accept the view, or to find proof in support of it, that the Statute of Retainers in 1503, and the Ordinances of 1526 concerning the Council (3), established a newly-formed branch of the historic Council, namely, that attending upon the King's person, and that it is particularly the stationary Court of Star Chamber at Westminster which is to be regarded as the institutional continuation of the original medieval Council (4). In 1343 a new chamber, the "star chamber," called so almost from the first, was erected at Westminster (5) and set apart for the specific purpose of holding Council meetings; henceforth only the "Judicial Council," the "Council in the Star Chamber," sat habitually at Westminster. No doubt it met there because in the nature of things a judicial tribunal is best held in a fixed place. The real purpose of the measures of 1503 and 1526 was to prevent the increasing absorption of the time of the primary and original Council by judicial business, transacted in the Star Chamber at Westminster. This interfered sorely with its essential and primary function of attending on the King to give him advice. It was this specialised council at Westminster, not the Council with the King, which was the newer body of the two.

During Henry VIII.'s reign the Council appeared to divide, but it never split definitely into two bodies with separate and distinct functions, although, when the King was out of town, part of the Council remained in London to direct such public business as must of necessity be transacted there. The greater part of the members, however, were in constant attendance upon the Sovereign; they resided at Court and accompanied

(1) A.P.C., XI.—XVII.
(2) A.P.C., XVIII.—XXXII., passim.
(3) "Ordinances of the Royal Household," pp. 159—60.
(4) Baldwin: "King's Council," 442, 444, 446, and passim.
(5) Tout, in review of Baldwin's "King's Council," E.H.R., Jan., 1915.

him wherever he went. During Henry VIII.'s reign, so far as we can judge, the Council attendant upon the King usually consisted of the great officers of the Household, a Bishop, and one of the Principal Secretaries. The other, with the Lord Chancellor, the Archbishop of Canterbury, and a few official personages, remained in town. Individual members of the Privy Council, however, moved freely from one to the other, and when the King returned they became once more a single body; at other times they were engaged in close correspondence. (1) The functions of that part of the Council which was left behind in London while the rest was with the King were never defined, and to state with certainty, as has been done (2), that the Council with the King was the advisory body, while that remaining at Westminster was freer and better fitted to deal with the bulk of administrative and judicial business, is misleading.

The Council with the King was of chief importance, and it transacted business with nearly the same punctuality whilst accompanying him on his journeys as when the Court was at Windsor, Hampton Court, or any other of the usual residences. It is not true that " it was not conceived to be a body superior to the other, except as it acquired an advantage by closer contact with the King." (3) In 1520 the Council left in England wrote most humbly to the King in France: they reported on the health of the Princess Mary, on the estate of the realm, and thus concluded, "And we, ensuing your commandment according to our duties, daily assemble and continue in your Council, and have had afore us some causes and matters to be punished and reformed after your laws, as well from far places as from other nigh in these parts, to the ordering thereof we trust we do endeavour us, as shall be to the contentacion of your said Highness "(4). In 1532 Lord Audley wrote to Cromwell to know if the Council in London might open letters that came from Scotland.

When the Privy Council divided into two bodies, that remaining in London deferred in all matters to that with the King. The " Council at Court " sent instructions to the one in London concerning its proceedings (5), and transacted all the real business, nor was it confined to non-judicial matters (6). On the other hand, the Council in London reported everything to the Council at Court and even sent up examinations of prisoners (7). In 1544, when the King went over to France, he appointed five of his Privy Councillors to form a Council of Regency in his absence; the rest went with him. Either the Chancellor or Hertford was ordered to be always in residence at the Court; if neither could be there, the Archbishop of Canterbury or Petre was to remain with the Queen, but, when convenient, all five were to attend her (8). It is significant, too, that throughout the Tudor period, the extant Council Register records almost invariably only the proceedings of the Council with the Sovereign (9).

(1) A.P.C., passim.   (2) Baldwin: 462.
(3) Ibid.: 448.
(4) P. and O., VII. Appendix, p. 337, 13th June, 1520.
(5) L. and P., XVI. 168, 1246.
(6) P. and O., VII. passim; A.P.C., I. passim.
(7) L. and P., XVI. 1047, 1261.   (8) L. and P., XIX. 864.
(9) For exceptions to this below, chap. 10.

The Council with the King had naturally the Stamp and Signet. 9th June, 1543, there is a letter from the Council at Court to the Council in London. In order that the Council in London may expedite matters, " the King commands me, the Lord Privy Seal, to send to you, my Lord Chamberlain, his Signet, to be returned soon by a trusty messenger, because it is here necessary both for his Majesty's causes and also for private suits and matters of his Signet " (1). It would seem that the Council " with the King," or " at Court " (they are interchangeable phrases), was superior in every way to that part of the Privy Council which sat in London.

During the reigns of Edward, Mary, and Elizabeth, little is heard of a " Council in London " (2), probably because they never left town for long periods, and certainly never crossed the Channel. Edward writes in his diary, 10th July, 1552: " It was appointed here, that if the Emperor's Ambassador did move for help or aid, the answer should be sent him by two of my Council, that this progress time my Council was dispersed; I would move by their advice, and he must tarry till the matter is concluded and their opinions had " (3). It would seem that when Edward went on progress few of his Councillors attended him. The rest were taking a holiday, and business had to wait until the King returned.

Mary's Council was too large, and Philip reduced it for working purposes to six or eight. But the deliberations of this inner ring, like those of Cabinet meetings to-day, were not recorded, and the Council meetings entered in the Register of her reign were almost invariably well attended. This would be quite possible, as Mary's Council never sat very far from London.

Under Elizabeth the Council followed the Queen as usual, but her progresses never extended over any considerable length of time. When she left London, one or two of her Councillors may have remained behind to transact any pressing business, but this seems to have been left generally to the Clerks of the Council, who were clever and able men, and quite competent to deal with such ordinary matters as arose in the Council's short absences (4).

Of the forms of summons to the Council we know practically nothing. The Councillors were the advisers of the Sovereign, and he summoned them individually just when and how he pleased. It was the duty of each Councillor to give his advice when asked for it, and of each Minister to execute within the limits of his office all lawful commands the King might issue. There are few instances in the Register, if we may rely upon the names recorded of those present, of a meeting of the full Council. An instance of the whole of the Privy Council being convened occurred in September, 1536, and Sir Ralph Sadler, in a letter to Cromwell, thus states the cause: " After supper His Grace returned into his Chamber and immediately called me to him, saying that he had digested and revolved in his breast the contents of your letters ,and, perceiving how the plague had reigned in Westminster and in the Abbey itself, his Grace said that he stood in a suspense

(1) L. and P., XVIII. Pt. I. 675.
(2) In Mary's reign a committee was appointed " to appoint a Council to attend and remain in London." A.P.C., IV., 23rd Feb., 1554.
(3) " The Journal of King Edward's Reign." Clarendon Hist. Soc. Reprints.
(4) A.P.C., VII.—XXXII. passim.

whether it were best to put off the time of the Coronation (1) for a season. ' Wherefore,' quote he, ' it were good that all my Council were assembled here, that we might consult and determine upon every thing touching the same accordingly. And so,' quoth he, ' write to my Lord Privy Seal, and send unto him word that my Lord Admiral is here, Master Comptroller and the Bishop of Hereford be here, and pray him also,' quoth he, ' to come hither indelayedly; and then,' quoth he, ' we shall soon be at a point. And,' quoth he, ' in case my Lord Chancellor be near London and all that be there of the Privy Council, pray my Lord Privy Seal to bring them with him.' " (2) In November and December, 1540, while the King was absent at Woking, Oatlands, and Hampton Court, Sir Thomas Wriothesley, one of the Secretaries, remained with the Comptroller at Windsor. "The Lords of the Council being departed to their own houses, and yet assembling together at Westminster for the King's affairs at sundry times as they had advertisement of the same from his Highness. And especially they assembled together at one time at the Duke of Suffolk's house, and to them resorted the said Secretary by special commandment of the King's Majesty the 13th December, the Lord Chancellor, the Duke of Norfolk, the Duke of Suffolk Great Chamberlain, the Earl of Hertford, the Bishop of Durham, Sir Thomas Wriothesley Secretary, the Chancellor of the Augmentations " (3). Thus the King seems to have summoned his Councillors whenever he considered it necessary, and to have ordered the presence of whichever of them he pleased. The letters of summons were probably written and sent by one of the Secretaries.

Besides these special sessions convened by the Sovereign, the Council had its general meetings governed by standing orders. Of the arrangements for these sessions for formal or legal business little is known except what can be gleaned from the Council Register. The Council met whenever they considered it necessary, or whenever important business had to be transacted at once. Marillac wrote to Francis I. that every three or four days news came from Germany; the Council then met and reported to the King (4). Probably when the business was of a special nature only those members who were familiar with that particular kind of business would be summoned (5). Chapuys relates how, on 5th November, 1541, the Lord Chancellor and Norfolk were suddenly sent for to Hampton Court where the rest of the Council were sitting, and that on the 6th they returned to London and stayed nearly all night deliberating in the King's apartments. They were dealing then with Katherine Howard's case (6). During the most strenuous years of the Reformation, in the midst of difficulties at home and abroad, the Council was held continuously for six months (7).

The same events led to a degree of caution and secrecy such as had hardly been necessary before. Letters in cipher had long been received and sent, but there were now conferences behind locked doors from which even the clerk was excluded. For the hearing of Lord Dacre's case in 1541, seventeen of the Council met in the Star Chamber to hold a secret conference. But they talked so loudly, relates Paget, that he was able to hear

(1) Of Jane Seymour.
(2) P. and O., VII. p. 10.
(3) P. and O., VII. p. 89.
(4) L. and P., XVI. 762, 27th April, 1541.
(5) L. and P., II. 3271. Hatfield Papers, X., 24th Oct., 1600.
(6) Ibid., XVI. 1328.
(7) Ibid., XVI. 763, 1332.

everything through two closed doors. On 25th November, 1553, there was an order that
" the clerks of the Council shall from henceforth see that none be present in the Council
Chamber (the Council sitting), but only such as be of the Council, and such as shall be
called." (1) Evidently this ruling had become very necessary for, as early as 1539 Marillac
writes that nothing was debated or resolved upon in the Privy Council but people heard
of it. (2)

Occasionally the Council ordered that its meetings should be held on certain days
in the week. On 28th June, 1556, it was resolved that " for the better entreating of
matters of estate," the Council was to sit from henceforth on Mondays, Wednesdays, and
Fridays by nine of the clock in the morning and no other matters to be moved in the
meantime." If the succeeding dates in the Register are any proof, the change was certainly not effected, if it was desired to restrict the meetings of the Council to these days.
It was, indeed, impossible to restrict the Council to certain days so long as the business
to be transacted by it was so multifarious. On 31st December, 1558, it was decided that
the Council should sit every Monday in the afternoon, and every Tuesday, Thursday, and
Saturday both morning and afternoon. By 1565 Tuesdays, Thursdays, and Saturdays in
the afternoon were the regular Council days. On 11th December, 1565, it was decided to
sit in the morning instead of in the afternoon, beginning at nine o'clock ; the Councillors
would then decide if they would sit in the afternoon also. It is impossible to tell from the
Register what were the regular days for the meetings of the Council, for it seems to have
assembled whenever necessary, and often more than twice a day. (3)

Towards the end of Elizabeth's reign the Register becomes more and more of a
letter book and less and less of a minute book. The names of the Privy Councillors who
signed the letters are given, but it is not stated whether a Council was held or not.
When the Council Register begins to take on the appearance of a letter book in 1590,
the Council begins to meet almost every Sunday. Between 2nd October, 1590, and 29th
March, 1591, there were twenty-five Sundays : on twenty-three of these meetings of the
Council are recorded, the only omissions being 14th February and 28th March. (4) Sunday meetings had not been unusual before this time, but they were never held so regularly
as towards the end of Elizabeth's reign. Every kind of business, even judicial, was
transacted at them.

These Sunday meetings were generally held at one of the royal manors, such as
Richmond, Greenwich, or Wimbledon, and are nearly always recorded in the Register as
being held " at the court at . . . ." It is the same with some of the Councils held
on other days in the week. Thus, 27th March, 1592, " at the Court at Whitehall," but
on 28th March, 1592, " at Whitehall." (5) Was this difference in phraseology due to the
Clerks, or might it not be conjectured that this was the method used of recording the
Queen's presence ? Or that the Councils held " at the Court " were the special sessions
of the Council with the Sovereign, and that the others were the ordinary general sessions
of the whole Council or of as many members as were able to attend? The Council
frequently met more than once on Sunday, in the morning and afternoon. It met also
occasionally on Holy Days, even on Good Friday and Easter Monday. (6)

(1) A.P.C., IV. 25th Nov., 1553.
(2) L. and P., XIV. 1261. 13th July, 1539.
(3) A.P.C., passim.   (4) A.P.C., XX.
(5) A.P.C., XXII.
(6) A.P.C., XXVIII., 14th April, 1598 ; XXIV., 16th April, 1593.

Very often the Council met in the Star Chamber, but it did so on no particular days, nor was its business in any way different from that transacted by the Council when sitting elsewhere; it certainly was not wholly judicial. (1)   When the Council referred cases to the Court of Star Chamber, the suitors are generally told to appear on Fridays before the Lords in the Star Chamber. (2)   By 1579 Wednesday is also referred to as a Star Chamber day. (3)   The fact that Wednesdays and Fridays were Star Chamber days had evidently had much to do with the alteration in the Council days at Elizabeth's accession from Mondays, Wednesday, and Fridays, to Tuesdays, Thursdays, and Saturdays.   Towards the end of Elizabeth's reign the Council sat frequently in the Star Chamber both on Wednesdays and Fridays, but the business recorded in the Register on those days is never purely judicial.   In November, 1590, it sat in the Star Chamber every Friday in the month, 6th, 13th, 20th, 27th, and on Wednesdays 11th and 25th. (4) In October and November, 1591, it was the same.   In December, 1591, the Council did not sit in the Star Chamber at all, but it met there again in January and June, 1592. (5) From 20th September, 1597, to 31st July, 1598, it never sat in the Star Chamber at all, or the Register has no record of its doing so.

The Star Chamber was a favourite place for holding conferences: on 17th October, 1596, the Council desired a conference with certain gentlemen of Gloucestershire "concerning some matters appertaining to the county."   They were appointed to meet in the dining-room at the Star Chamber.   On 27th April, 1600, the Governor and three others of the Company of Merchant Adventurers were to attend on the following Wednesday, 30th April, "at the dining chamber near the Star Chamber immediately after dinner," to confer with the Council concerning their petition against the restrictions on the export of cloth. (6)   The Journals of the House of Commons record that, on 7th March, 1553, the King's Council and others are to meet in the Star Chamber at seven o'colck to consult for a subsidy.

The Council was supposed to meet at nine o'clock on ordinary days, but very often it summoned men to appear before that hour.   On 5th October, 1540, the Chamberlain and Comptroller of Prince Edward's household were sent for to appear the following day at eight in the morning, and on 26th December of the same year the Comptroller was again ordered to present himself, this time by seven in the morning, and to bring with him the book of the Household. (7)   On 3rd April, 1552, a letter was sent commanding the Treasurer and the Chancellor of the Augmentations to be with the Council on the following day at seven, bringing with them a note of the money remaining in the Treasurer's charge.(8)   After this time the Council apparently adhered to its nine o'clock rule. Very often the Council assembled in the morning and sat until nine or ten at night, debating subjects on which the Councillors could not agree. (9)   In 1538 John Hussey writes to Lady Lisle: "No news but that the Council sit most of the day." (10)   In 1541 the " Book of Expenses for the Diets of the King's Council at Westminster in the Council Chamber " gives details of the dinners for each day upon which the Council sat, and shows it to have met two or three times a week during the four law terms. (10)   Sometimes the Council

(1) Ibid., I., III., IV., VI., passim.

(2) Ibid., IV. 12th November, 1553.

(3) Ibid., XI., 6th November, 1579.

(4) A.P.C., XX.

(5) Ibid., XXII.

(6) Ibid., XXVI., XXX.

(7) P. and O., VII.

(8) A.P.C., IV.

(9) L. and P., XIII., 14th October, 1538.

(10) Ibid., XVI., 1481.

Register records no meetings for days together; e.g. no meeting of the Council is recorded between 29th Dec., 1549, and 2nd Jan., 1550, none between 4th Jan. and Jan. 11th, and none between Jan. 16th and Jan. 19th. (1) As the Tudor period drew to a close, the Council seemed to find it necessary to sit nearly every day, but important meetings and the transaction of important business are seldom recorded in the Register.

The names of the Privy Councillors present at Henry VIII.'s Council meetings during the latter part of his reign, for which the Register is extant, vary in number from three to seventeen. (2) It is of little use to attach importance to the names of Councillors recorded as present at Council meetings. Very often the number varied according to the movements of the Court. Mary had a large Council and its meetings were very well attended, but we know there was an inner working Council. Elizabeth's Council was small, but increased in size towards her death, when the Council Register became a letter book and recorded the presence of members at the Board far more frequently on Sunday than on any other day in the week. There was generally almost a full Council every Sunday; on other days the Clerk often contented himself with recording merely the names of those Councillors who signed the letters written.

Much doubt has been thrown upon the reliability of the Register as regards the record of the names of the Privy Councillors present at each meeting, and there are proofs that the Register is here of small value. On 25th August, 1542, Norfolk is recorded as present at the Council Board, yet on that same day he wrote from Chisworth, Sussex, to the Council. (3) Lord Ferrers is recorded as attending a Council meeting on 16th Jan., 1550, but he was not sworn of the Council until 26th Jan. (4) From 6th June, 1547, to 3rd Jan., 1548, there are only seven signatures to the Acts of the Privy Council, and they are always the same signatures without variation. (5) Members are also recorded as present who do not append their signatures to the minutes (6) From 3rd January, 1548, to 17th January, 1549, with one exception, there are no signatures at all. During the proceedings against Lord Seymour of Sudely nearly all the Councillors sign, Jan.-Feb., 1549, while again there are none March-Oct., 1549, until the Councillors assembled to depose Somerset. With the exceptions mentioned, the signatures of both Secretaries never appear, though one was Paget, Somerset's most intimate counsellor. The State Papers throughout Edward's reign were signed by Councillors whose signatures never appear in the Register. (7) One of the MS. volumes of the Register which Burnet used in his History of the Reformation contained the Council's order, on 30th June, 1548, committing Gardiner to the Tower and signed: E. Somerset, T. Cant., W. St. John, J. Russell, and T. Cheyne. Burnet detected the fact that Russell originally signed as

(1) A.P.C., II.
(2) The average attendance works out at about eleven.
(3) A.P.C., I. L. and P., XVII. 719.
(4) A.P.C., II.
(5) A.P.C., III. Somerset, Cranmer, St. John, Northampton, Sir Anthony Browne, Sir Anthony Wingfield, and Sir Edward North.
(6) A.P.C., III., June 8th, 10th, 13th, 1550.
(7) C.f. Domestic Calendar and A.P.C., passim.

" J. Bedford," and Dasent says St. John signed " W. Wiltshire," though neither Russell nor St. John received an earldom till January, 1550. Obviously this minute was not signed until after that date, and probably not till the time of Gardiner's trial in December and January, 1550-1. Bedford and Wiltshire then signed with the signatures which had become familiar, but, wishing for some reason to give the impression that their signatures were affixed some two and a half years before their real date, they altered them to the style they bore in 1548. The possibility of such a proceeding greatly impairs the value of the signatures. (1) Not only are the signatures of Councillors present omitted, but the Register also contains the signatures of Councillors not present at the proceedings which they sign. Somerset's signature appears on September 4th, 20th, 25th, and October 2nd, 1547, when all the time he was in Scotland, and an examination of the Register shows that blanks were left for his signature, which he filled in on his return. (2) In Elizabeth's reign letters are recorded as " signed by " or " signed apart by " certain Councillors, but it seems improbable that the Register contains the original signatures, since Burghley would hardly have signed himself " Lord Treasurer," or Whitgift " the Lord Archbishop." (3) The Clerk may have written the signatures in the Register occasionally, as he certainly did in a letter which was sent from the Privy Council to Sir Thomas Finch on 21st March, 1560. The seven signatures to the letter are not autograph, but imitations of the originals, apparently by the Clerk of the Council. (4) Thus it would seem that the Register is hardly to be trusted for an accurate record of the names of the Privy Councillors in attendance at the Board.

Of the procedure of the Council at its meetings there is little evidence, although, to the end of Mary's reign, finance was apparently dealt with first of all. There are no rules extant as to the order in which the Council dealt with the business before it, nor do certain days appear to be set apart for special business, except, indeed, for Ireland occasionally. (5)

The Council dealt with judicial and administrative, petty and important business all at the same meeting. It was, indeed, sometimes so busy that the Councillors declared " they had hardly leisure to eat or drink." (6) Dinner, however, very often came first and business second (7), and the Council ate at the public expense. Their dinners, judging from the accounts in the State papers, were very elaborate affairs, and that the Council appreciated the culinary art was evident from the favour shown to Sir Owen Hopton's cook. On Sunday, 16th August, 1590: "A letter to the Lord Mayor that, at the Council's request, he would grant and bestow on one Richard Large, long the cook of Sir Owen Hopton, late Lieutenant of the Tower, the freedom of some company in that city." (8) The Council's own cook, John Lawrence, petitioned for an annuity in 1535; he declared that he had been their cook for over twenty-three years at only two shillings and fourpence a day, and was therefore deserving. (9)

(1) Pollard, in review of A.P.C., XX.—XXVII., in E.H.R., vol. XVIII.
(2) Pollard: " Somerset," 77—78.
(3) A.P.C., XXVI.
(4) H.M.C., 14 Report—Appendix, Pt. VIII. Finch MSS., p. 5.
(5) A.P.C., VII., 1st Feb., 1559.
(6) L. and P., XVII., 1224; 21st December, 1542.
(7) Ibid., XVIII., 710. 15th June, 1543.
(8) A.P.C., XIX.
(9) L. and P., IX. 1119.

Towards the end of the Tudor period there was apparently a good deal of "red tape" about the Council's procedure. In 1598 Juan de Castro wrote to the Earl of Essex to the effect that, in December of the previous year, he had desired access to Essex to reveal "a business of no little moment." Essex was ill, so Castro thought of approaching Cecil instead. Being unknown to him, however, he went first to Sir Antony Mildmay, whom he had known in France. He, by Cecil's orders, sent Castro to Sir John Stanhope. Castro obeyed, although amazed at such an order being taken in "a matter of such moment and secrecy." Finally Sir John by the Queen's command bade him tell all to "a certain Privy Secretary of the Royal Council called Mr. Waad, at whose will I wrote all these secrets out with my own hand in Spanish, and delivered them to him, as I had before done in Latin to Sir John Stanhope." (1)

The quorum of the Council necessary for business was nominally six (2), although throughout the Register the attendances recorded are very often fewer than that: from 1581 to 1590 five is the average attendance. In 1551 the King wrote to Lord Chancellor Rich desiring to know why the execution of the commission for the trials of the Bishops of Worcester and Chichester had been so long delayed, for "what the King directs by the advice of his Council, though less than eight in number, is of sufficient authority." (3)

Henry VIII., as has been seen, issued directions in 1526 for the transaction by his Councillors of the business which came before the Board, and in 1549 Edward drew up some very similar rules for his Council. He began by ordering the Council to love each other as brethren or dear friends, and to honour each other. None was to be content to hear evil spoken of another, and if he did hear such, he was to report it to the Council Board—a pious and unnecessary adjuration to Edward's factious Council. Six at least of the Council were to be always in attendance at court. Of these six, the Chancellor and Treasurer, or Great Master, or Privy Seal, or Chamberlain, were to be two, and one of the Secretaries a third. In the absence of the rest, these six might suffice, but their proceedings were to be confirmed by the others when convenient. The Council attendant at Court was to assemble on Tuesdays, Fridays, and Saturdays for business, and oftener if necessary. They were to assemble in the Council Chamber at eight o'clock in the morning and sit till dinner time; in the afternoon they were to sit from two till four. For private suits they were to assemble on Sunday after dinner at two until four. All letters were to be received by the Secretary and brought to the Council Board at the hours of meeting, unless they required a "very hasty expedition." All petitions to the King or Council were to be delivered to the Master of Requests, who was to deliver to the Lord President all containing such matters as could be settled only by the King or his Privy Council. The Lord President was then to exhibit them to the Council on the Sunday. The supplicants were to receive the answer decided upon at the hands of the Lord President or such other Minister as he appointed for the business. (4) Suits of the King's servants were to be preferred only by one of the six lords attendant upon the

(1) Hatfield Papers, VIII., 19th May, 1598.

(2) A.P.C., XVI., 12th December, 1588.

(3) Dom. Cal., 1st Oct., 1551.

(4) This sheds some light upon the duties of the Lord President. The scrutiny of petitions might be his particular care, or they might be delivered to him as the most dignified Councillor, if indeed he was accounted such.

King's person, of "them of the outward chambers" by the Lord Chamberlain or Vice-Chamberlain. Finally, the Secretary was to look to the keeping of the Secretary's (1) record of letters to and from the King or the Council, and others matters treated by the Council. And none of the King's Privy Council was to speak for his friends in a matter of justice between party and party, "nor in any other matters above one ime, for that the request of a counsellor is in a manner a commandment." This document is endorsed: "The remembrance given by my master to my Lord Paget 26th May, 1549." (2) It is impossible to discover whether these rules were ever put into force. Edward was keenly interested in business, and there are many memoranda in his hand of matters to be looked into by his Council. On 3rd March, 1552, he drew up more rules for the Council, "for the more orderly and speedy dispatch of causes," in which private suits were to be heard on Mondays only, and not "intermeddled with great affairs." There was to be no assembly in Council unless four were present, and no business should be dispatched by fewer than six, while "no warrant for reward above £40, or business or affairs above £100, pass but under the King's signet." (3)

In Mary's reign the Council's method of doing business was thus described by the Venetian ambassador, Soranzo: "The leading members are lodged in the palace where her Majesty resides, some of them sleeping there, according to ancient custom, so that she may never be alone. They meet very early in the morning, and, provided the chiefs are present (although they may not be more than six or seven) the Council is understood to be assembled, and the President (4) proposes the matters for discussion—though at present the Bishop of Winchester has the management of everything—and each member present is at liberty to give his opinion by word of mouth, the decision of the majority being presented for approval to the Queen, who, deferring in everything to the Council, approves accordingly." (5)

The business of the Council increased so greatly during the Tudor period that there were constant delegations of work to committees. Committees were appointed 2nd February, 1547, to consider Edward VI.'s Coronation, Henry VIII.'s funeral, and various claims. (6) On 31st October, 1549, several committees were appointed to deal with business connected with Boulogne; Calais and its marches; Ireland, the North; Alderney and Scilly; the Isle of Wight and Portsmouth; "the foresight for money" and "the order of the Mint." (7) In March, 1552, also, the young King divided his Council into committees for different matters; some were to hear suits which had usually been brought before "the whole table," others to send matters of justice to their proper courts, to deny such suits as were not reasonable, to certify which were met to be granted, and afterwards to dispatch the parties. Others, again, were to consider the penal laws and proclamations

(1) This probably means the Clerk.
(2) Egerton MSS. (Brit. Mus.), 2603, f. 33.
(3) "A Complete History of England, comprising Hayward's Life and Reign of Edward VI."
(4) Was this the duty of the Lord President?
(5) Venetian Calendar, 18th August, 1554.
(6) A.P.C., II.
(7) Tytler: "Edward VI. and Mary," I. p. 273.

in force, and look to their speedy execution. These were first to consider which were most necessary; then to inquire how they were obeyed; to punish the greatest offenders and proceed against the rest; and finally to inquire into disorders in every shire, punish the offenders, or report what they had accomplished. Other Councillors were to attend to affairs of State generally, and with these the King sat once a week to hear the most important matters discussed. Others were to look into the King's revenue, and cut down expenses, and to inquire into debts owing to the Crown. Others again were to inquire into needless fortifications and have them demolished. (1) On 11th May, 1550, a finance committee had been appointed, but none of these seem to have been permanent." (2)

Mary's Council was so large that of necessity committees were constantly appointed, being generally very small. (3) 23rd February, 1554, order was taken for the formation of eleven committees to deal with debts, the provisioning of Calais, Berwick, Ireland, etc., the Navy, victuals for Calais, etc., for laws to be passed by Parliament and appointment of men to draft them, for the examination of prisoners, to consider what lands should be sold to moderate expenses, to consider patents and annuities, to appoint a Council to attend and remain in London, to order the furnishing and victualling of the Tower. (4) The question of the restoration of Church property was referred by the Queen to a committee in 1556 (5), and on 10th August, 1554, a committee was appointed to inquire into the state of Ireland. (6)

The record of the Council held at Winchester, 27th uly, 1554, is prefaced by these words: " Anno primo et secundo Philippi et Marie Regis et Regine." This change in style is further emphasized by the first entry in the proceedings, which relates that for the use and information of the King, a note in Latin or Spanish should for the future be taken of all business transacted by the Council; that the King and Queen both should sign all important documents, and that a new stamp bearing both their names should be made for use on papers of lesser moment. At a later date, 20th May, 1555, a new seal was commanded to be made for the use of the Council, " with these letters P. and M. with a crown over the same." It was to be committed to the custody of the senior Clerk of the Council. (7)

On Elizabeth's accession several committees of the Council were appointed. On 28th December, 1558, one was established " to understand what lands have been granted from the Crown in the late Queen's time," another " for the care of the North parts towards Scotland and Berwick," a third " to survey the office of the Treasurer of the Chamber and to assign order for payment," a fourth " for Portsmouth and the Isle of Wight," and a fifth " for consideration of all things necessary for Parliament." (8) Throughout her reign the practice of appointing committees was continued.

Scaramelli thus described the way in which the Councillors sat at the Board. He had asked an audience on pressing business with some or all of the Council, which was

(1) J. G. Nichols: " Literary Remains of Edward VI.," 498—499.
(2) A.P.C., III.
(3) Ibid., IV., V., VI., passim.
(4) Ibid., IV., 23rd February, 1554.
(5) Hinds: " The Making of the England of Elizabeth," p. 120.
(6) A.P.C., V.
(7) Ibid.
(8) A.P.C., VII. Strype's Annals, p. 24. Dom. Cal. IX., addenda.

granted. On going down to the Palace at Richmond he was admitted into the Council Chamber and found, " sitting on long benches on each side of a table, the Lord Chancellor, the Lord Treasurer, the High Admiral, the Equerry, the Lord Chief Justice of England, the Treasurer and Comptroller of the royal Household, the Chancellor of the Exchequer, and others not peers, but knights." There were eleven in all, none missing except the Primate, who was President of the Council. "These lords of the Council behave like so many Kings," but he was treated with respect, made to sit on a brocaded chair at the head of the table, and had a gracious and friendly hearing. (1) Very little beyond this is known of the order in which the Council sat around the Board or the way in which their debates were conducted, save for the information afforded us by " An Act for the placing of Lords in the King's Council," 31 H. VIII., c. 10.

(1) Venetian Calendar, 7th April, 1603.

VI. THE SOVEREIGN AND THE PRIVY COUNCIL.

———— :o: ————

THE COMMONS ceased from 1422 onwards to demand the nomination in Parliament of the King's Council. It is not possible to state when the Council ceased to be appointed for a year only and began to hold office during the King's pleasure, nor when they ceased to be paid for their services. Probably the Council of Regency which managed affairs during the minority of Henry VI. set the example of an indefinite tenure of office, and the great lords who composed the later Lancastrian Councils were able to take care of themselves without payment. (1) When the Tudors began to fill the Council with middle-class men holding administrative offices, such Councillors would naturally receive salaries as officials and not as Councillors. With the exception of a few great unpaid magnates, the Council of the later Tudors was a Council of salaried Ministers, not very dissimilar from a modern Cabinet.

Throughout the Tudor period the history of the Council is the history of the monarchy. The power of the Government was greater than ever before, but its strength lay in the royal prerogative. The Tudors had no standing army; a few yeomen of the guard added to the dignity but not to the might of the Crown. They relied on their own abilities and their insight into the national character to preserve them from organised rebellion. In such a system the royal will is the central and driving force, and the personal characteristics of the Sovereign are vitally important. The Crown possessed the power to pry into all matters, great and small, and to crush any individual, however great, who might dare to oppose a royal mandate; and the burden of the exercise of these vast and far-reaching powers was cast upon the Council. A change was inevitable in the constitution of the body which was to carry out this work of government, and the Council, though outwardly unchanged, was gradually transformed from an independent body which had been a bridle upon the royal authority, into a mere corps of officials subject to the King's will and direction. The arbitrary powers exercised by the Tudor Council arose less from the personal character of the reigning monarch, congenial as despotism was to him, than from a gradual encroachment on the liberties of the subject and a corresponding extension of the royal prerogative during the fifteenth century. Parliamentary government had proved a failure. By means of the Council the Tudors re-established a strong government. Their system was " admirably calculated to be either the support of order against anarchy, or of despotism against individual and national liberty."

When the Council Register again appears in 1540, after a break of eighty years, another Council, the Concilium Ordinarium, is seen to be in existence. The time was now ripe for a recognition of the distinction between the " ordinary councillor " and the " privy councillor." The anomalous usages of the past, when men of the utmost diversity of rank were sworn according to the same formula and retained for various kinds of service, had made any such classification impossible. Under the Tudors, however, for the

(1) Anson: II. Pt. 1., 74.

first time in many years, the monarchy was served by a strong body of men, capable of
filling the highest offices and of acting regularly appointed to and sworn of the Council
but were not given to full rank of Privy Councillors, a certain status was now given.
The Concilium Ordinarium is obscure both in origin and composition, but the accounts
of it suggest that the Ordinary Councillors were chosen mainly for legal and judicial
work. (1)) Most assuredly it was not the same body as the Privy Council. The latter
varied in many ways during the Tudor reigns. We have seen it sometimes divided into
two, one section attending the King on progress in the country, the other transacting
business in London—sometimes divided into committees, to each of which some department
of executive business was assigned. But outside this body of Privy Councillors were persons not habitually summoned to meetings recorded as meetings of the Privy Council,
but nevertheless " sworn of the Council," (i.e., the Ordinary Council). Henry VIII. in
November, 1541, ordered his Chancellor to summon his " counsellors of all sorts, Spiritual
and Temporal, with the judges and learned men of his Council " to hear of the misconduct
of Katherine Howard. (2) In 1535 Sir Robert Wingfield protested: " I have been sworn
of his Council above twenty years, and of his Privy Council above fourteen years." (3)
Among the Ordinary Councillors were men of rank and dignity, such as in 1540 Lords St.
John and Windsor, and the Bishops of London and Rochester. There seemed to be also a
survival of the feeling that men might be sworn of the Council to ensure their faithful-
ness in any important service. In 1534 Cromwell proposed " to appoint the most assured
and substantial gentlemen in every shire to be sworn of the King's Council, with orders
to apprehend all who speak or preach in favour of the Pope's authority." (4) Such a
large number of men was apparently sworn of this Ordinary Council that one might
be led to conclude that all engaged in the King's service were his sworn Councillors.(5)
31st October, 1540, Robert Southwell and Dr. Petre are referred to as " being of the
King's Ordinary Council," and are sent down into Surrey to examine into certain riots
which had taken place there. 27th February, 1541, Dr. Tregonwell, " one of the King's
Highness' Ordinary Council," was sent to Plymouth with two others to inquire into the
wrecking of a Portugese ship off that part of the coast. In the reign of Mary, Dr.
Boxall, Warden of Winchester College, was " sworn and admitted one of the King's
and Queen's Majesty's Council-at-large and as one of the Masters of Requests and a
Councillor at that Court," 23rd September, 1556. He was a proto-type of the modern
K.C. (6) On 21st December of the same year he was admitted and sworn of the Privy
Council. (7) As may be noticed in the case of Boxall, William Petre, Lord St. John,
and many others, promotion to the higher rank of Privy Councillor was easily obtained.

The duties of these ordinary Councillors were important, but of a technical kind
such as had always devolved on men of this type. They received petitions, conducted
examinations, and assisted at trials.(8 At sessions of the Star Chamber and Court of Re-

(1) Anson: II. Pt. I., 65.
(2) Nicholas: VII., p. xix.
(3) L. and P., VIII., 225.
(4) Ibid: VII., 420.
(5) Such as, for instance:—John Veysey, Dean of the Chapel of the
Household and the " King's Counsellor," L. and P. II., pt. I., 4297;
Thomas Magnus, Surveyor and Receiver of Lands of King's Wards,
Ibid III., pt. I., 10 36; Thomas Englefield, Ibid IV., pt. I., 1297;
Sir Robert Bowes, Ibid XIX., 278.
(6) A.P.C., V.
(7) A.P.C., VI.
(8) Baldwin: 451.

quests, much of the routine business could safely be left in their hands. In 1540 the Vice-Chamberlains and other servants of the King and Queen were ordered not to molest the King himself with suits, but to put their complaints in writing and deliver them to the Ordinary Council which was " appointed for such purposes."(1) Further, members served on committees and made reports. In 1520 and 1532 they signed letters sent from the Council in London to the King, but it is significant that important letters were signed by the Privy Councillors only. (2) The names of the Ordinary Councillors were never placed with the others upon the Privy Council minutes, and presumably they did not have the right to vote. On 4th August, 1589, Thomas Wilkes, one of the clerks of the Privy Council, is mentioned in the Register of the Council as " Clerk of the Council in Ordinary," though the exact meaning of the title is not clear. (3)

Council Ordinance of H8 ?

It is impossible, however, to dogmatise about the constitution at any given time of Councils whose existence was never defined by statute, and whose composition was mainly determined by practical convenience. It was convenient, during the Tudor period, that the legal and judicial element in the Council should be strengthened by the addition to the King's Council of men whose legal advice might be advantageous, but who were not needed for general matters of State. It is remarkable that a doubt, whether the King's Ordinary Councillors who sat as Judges of the Court of Requests were Privy Councillors, was entertained in the latter part of the reign of Queen Elizabeth. Sir Julius Cæsar tried to prove that the title " Privy Councillor " was identical with that of " Privy Councillor," (4) but neither his facts nor his arguments are very conclusive. After the close of the Tudor period we hear no more of the Ordinary Councillors save in the later description of Hale. (5)

Henry VII. discovered that under a strong King the Privy Council was no check upon the Sovereign, who could appoint and dismiss it and who was not obliged to take or even to ask its advice. It has been seen that Henry's Council exercised very little real influence upon him, and that either he did not bring the most weighty matters before it at all or did not do so until he had made up his own mind, the Council then merely registering foregone conclusions. It was but an assembly of the King's servants exercising powers which were the King's powers, and which he himself might exercise if and when he pleased.

Henry VIII. continued his father's policy as regards the Privy Council. As administrative officials were needed, they were simply provided from the royal household. Scarcely any man held an office of importance who was not familiarly known to the King. Howards, Brandons, Jerninghams, Sydneys, Plantagenets, Sherbornes, Fitzwilliams, Marneys—all had been squires, or Knights of the Body, or Gentlemen of the Chamber, because the King's patronage naturally flowed in this direction. All the great and important offices, whether naval, military, or civil, were filled by men in personal attendance upon the King. The exclusive road to promotion was this personal service to the King. No Minister dispensed or even shared the patronage of the Crown. (6) After the victory

(1) L. and P., XVI. 127.
(2) Nicholas: P. and O., VII. pp. 337, 343, 350, 351.
(3) A.P.C., XVIII.
(4) Leadam: Court of Requests, p. xxxii. Selden Soc. Publications, Vol. 12, 1898.
(5) " Jurisdiction of the Lords," pp. 5—7.
(6) L. and P., I., p. cii.

of the House of York the tendency was entirely in favour of the royal authority. The successors of the Yorkists were wise in making no change in this respect. The Council made the necessary grants for expenditure and determined payments for service, but grants of favours were jealously withheld from its control. While this rule held, the monarchy was not in danger of falling again under conciliar misrule. (1)

All this had changed the King's position and vastly increased his power. Ministers under the Tudors, taken from a lower rank of society, looked up to the Crown and to the extension of its authority as a support for their own. They were the King's servants, an epithet which the ancient nobility would have rejected with disdain. It is clear from the answer made by Henry VIII. to the rebels of Yorkshire in 1536 that the appointment of Privy Councillors was entirely dependent on the King's pleasure. (2) Under Elizabeth, Cecil in 1568 apparently did not know whom the Queen would appoint to the Privy Council, and he speculates in a letter to a friend concerning the choice to be made. (3)

By 1519 Henry had become increasingly vigilant even in the details of administration. In the year he drew up a " remembrance of such things " as he required the Cardinal to " put into effectual execution." These are twenty-one in number and range over every variety of subject. There were five points which the King would debate with his Council: the administration of justice, the reform of the exchequer, Ireland, the employment of idle people, and the maintenance of the frontiers. (4) When once questions of domestic interest had become paramount and the Sovereign and nation were engrossed in religious discussion, Wolsey's genius was no longer required and his fall was inevitable. Hitherto the King's mind had been employed with other things: now " the King has gone beyond me " expressed Wolsey's profound conviction of the real cause of his disgrace and the impossibility of his restoration. (5) He had certainly had great power: he acted without the knowledge of the other Councillors, calling them in only when negotiations were concluded, and we hear of the King writing a letter " according to the minutes " sent him by Wolsey. (6) In 1521 he appears to be taking the place of a Secretary. (7) But both Henry and he often conducted business together without consulting the other Councillors: in July, 1518, the King wrote, " Two things there be which be so secret that they cause me at this time to write to you myself." (8)

Henry, however, was always his own first minister both before and after Wolsey's fall. As Paget told the Admiral of France in 1542, the King could see as far as all his Councillors, and was President of his own Council. (9) Charles Brandon Duke of Suffolk was supposed to have great influence with Henry in the early part of his reign, but he was greatly the King's inferior in intelligence, and after his marriage with Mary was

(1) Baldwin: 457.
(2) L. and P., XI. 957.
(3) " Scrinia Ceciliana " (London, 1663). Letter to Sir H. Norris, 8th April, 1568.
(4) L. and P., III. 576.
(5) L. and P., I., lxxxviii.
(6) Ibid., II. Pt. I. 4438, 4124.
(7) Ibid., III. Pt. I. 1292.
(8) Ibid., II. Pt. I. 4275, 4124. Pt. II. 2500.
(9) Ibid., XVII. 400.

forced to espouse Wolsey's cause in order to keep in the King's favour. The greater part of Henry's Council was said to be "vox et praeterea nihil." Yet Henry often consulted his Council (1); again, on the other hand, he often acted alone (2): 5th April, 1540, Henry wrote to Wallop desiring him to visit the Queen of Navarre again, and elicit information about certain matters. A postscript is then added that, these affairs being mere overtures, the King has not "opened" them to his Council; therefore Wallop's answer must be addressed either to Henry or the Lord Privy Seal.

The Council was always associated with the King in commands given by the latter (3), and letters were almost invariably addressed to the "King and Council," (4) but Government measures by no means invariably proceeded from the Council nor were they all deliberated upon in the Council. Important measures of foreign policy proceeded from the King himself through the pens of his Secretaries, and often through those of others. In confidential matters he wrote in his own hand and read all letters himself. Wolsey and Cromwell were his principal advisers while they remained in power. After the fall of the latter Henry addressed his orders sometimes to one minister, sometimes to another. This view of Henry's character is completely borne out by the State Papers of his time; there were some occasions on which he did not even consult Wolsey. It may be inferred *a fortiori* there were more on which he acted without the advice of his Council. (5)

Since we have no official reports of the debates which took place at the Council Board, it is difficult to decide how far the King's will was disputed or disputable. In 1536 Chapuys reported to Charles V. that, on Wednesday in Easter week, the King's whole Council assembled for three or four hours, and "as Cromwell informed me, there was not one of them but remained long on his knees before the King to beg him, for the honour of God, not to lose so good an opportunity of establishing a friendship so necessary and advantageous; but they had not been able to change his opinion." (6) Henry figures largely in all the instructions and letters sent from the Privy Council to Norfolk in the North of England in 1536—7: e.g. 8th April, 1537, the Council writes to Norfolk to inform him of the King's resolution concerning Norfolk's request for an audience, and of the King's resolution concerning the borders. Further, the King desires to hear Norfolk's opinion concerning the same, and considers that certain matters "must be boulted out," in spite of what Norfolk had written. (7) The hand and will of a strong and independent ruler are everywhere apparent.

But Henry certainly met with occasional opposition from his Council, although it was seldom that the Council had its way. In 1545 both Charles V. and the German Protestants offered mediation in the war between Henry and Francis I., but the latter would not acquiesce in the loss of Boulogne and the former would not restore it. In this matter Henry was opposed by nearly all his Council, but his will prevailed. An

(1) L. and P., II. Pt. I. 3973. IV. Pt. I. 474. XIV. Pt. I. 365.
(2) Ibid., XI. 210. XIII. Pt. I. 1320. XV. 459 (5th April, 1540).
(3) Ibid., XIV. Pt. I. 691, 741, 828, 907.
(4) Ibid., XVII. 856, 1220.
(5) Nicholas: P. and O., VII. xii.
(6) L. and P., X. 699, 21st April, 1536.
(7) Ibid., XII. 864.

advisory body with no independent authority, the Council had constitutionally no status apart from the monarchy. When a Tudor cared to assert his will, no minister could withstand it; Henry VIII. was a Sovereign who determined the policy of his ministers. The evidence goes to show that, till 1520, at any rate, Henry cared little for public affairs and was absorbed in personal amusements; ambassadors complained that he would not read their despatches, and that " agere cum rege est nihil agere." (1) But even Wolsey could only carry out a policy which the King himself imposed, or at best lead him out of it gradually by following it up and showing him other objects. Cromwell's declaration of what he considered to be the true function of a statesmen is very enlightening: it was to endeavour to discover the object that his Sovereign had most at heart, and, whenever he saw it clearly, to throw conscience completely aside and apply all his wits to carry it out. This method is a perfectly sufficient explanation of his whole career. (2) Henry deceived or trusted his Council just so far as suited his purpose, and it appears to have been subservient enough. Henry's personal attendants, however, do not seem to have acted always with the same degree of humbleness; in 1527 a pardon was granted for some offence unspecified to Sir William Compton, with a licence to keep his hat on in the King's presence. (3)

The Council Register, which remains to us for part of Henry's reign, 1540-47, never records the presence of the King, but we know from other sources that Henry often sat at the Council Board. At the beginning of his reign his Councillors are said to have " travailed in such prudent sort with him, that they got him to be present with them when they sat in Council." (4) Moreover, they " daily acquainted him with the political affairs of the realm, that by little and little he of his own accord applied himself to rule and govern, the which at the first he seemed utterly to abhor." (5) In 1519 he drew up a list of matters which he wished to debate with his Council (6), although in 1541 Marillac, the French ambassador, wrote that the Lords had been in Council concerning Catherine Howard's misconduct, with " the King assisting, which he is not wont to do."(7) When he was not present, however, all business transacted seems to have been reported to him. (8)

Henry's frequent absences from the Council may account for the re-appearance of the office of Lord President of the Council, concerning which little is heard during the early part of the reign. Under Elizabeth there was apparently some speculation as to the origin of the office. Sir William Cordell, Master of the Rolls, wrote to Burghley in 1577 that he could find no record that the office of Lord President of the Council had ever been granted by Patent. By the Statute 3 H. VI., he said, it would seem the office was then non-existent, but, by 21 H. VIII., the Lord President had been joined with the

(1) Pollard, in review of L. and P. XX. E.H.R. XXII. p. 361.
(2) Gairdner, in review of " Life and Letters of Thomas Cromwell," by Merriman, E.H.R. XVII.
(3) L. and P., IV. 2927 (22).
(4) Holinshed's Chronicle, III. p. 799.
(5) Grafton's Chronicle, p. 235.
(6) L. and P., III. Pt. I. 576.
(7) Ibid., XVI. 1332.
(8) A.P.C., I. 10th June, 1543.

Lord Treasurer and the Lord Chancellor in naming sheriffs, etc. He then cited other Statutes, but declared he did not remember that Charles Duke of Suffolk, in the reign of Henry VIII., or the Dukes of Somerset and Northumberland, under Edward VI., or the Earl of Arundel, under Mary, had held the office. If they had, it had not been by proper grant. "The Prince by his prerogative published and declared him by his word to be Lord President of the Council." In this way the Sovereign might create the Lord Steward of the Household. When Charles Brandon Duke of Suffolk held the latter office (which was later changed to that of Grand Master), it was without patent, and continued to be so until, in 4 Edward VI., it was given by patent to the Earl of Warwick for life, a thing which had never been done before or since. The first to hold the office was Sir Thomas Neville at the beginning of Henry's reign (1)

Henry treated his Councillors with consideration, allowing them wide discretion in the exercise of their duties, and extending toleration to contrary opinions. To the end of his days he valued a councillor who would honestly maintain the opposite of what he himself desired. He was never impatient of advice, even when it conflicted with his own views, and it has been asserted: "No man was ever advanced to political power in Henry's reign merely because he pandered to the King's vanity or to his vices." (2) But was Sir Thomas More thinking of his own country when he wrote, in Utopia, of the arbitrary rule of monarchs bent on their own aggrandisement and careless of the improvement of their people, and of disputes among their Councillors, agreed on one point only, to flatter and mislead their sovereign? (3) Henry told Francis I. in 1533 that he governed, and was not governed by his Council, otherwise the Council would be King and not he. He desired their opinions, but decided for himself, as every King ought to do (4).

Henry had complete power over his Councillors, for he alone appointed and dismissed them. In 1512 Wolsey wrote to the Bishop of Winchester that the Lord Treasurer [Surrey] had left the Court, "being discountenanced by the King," (5) and in 1538 Henry snubbed Cromwell and sent for Norfolk, telling the former that "he was a good manager, but not fit to intermeddle in the affairs of kings." (6) Yet in 1541 he was reproaching his Council for Cromwell's death, declaring that, upon "light pretences and false accusations," they had caused him to put to death the most faithful servant he had ever had (7). In September, 1539, the Council had named the Lord Chancellor and five other Privy Councillors to accompany the King to Windsor, but the King declared he would have "no more save my lord of Suffolk to accompany him, and my Lord Chancellor, naming of himself Mr. Treasurer" (8). On 26th October, 1541, Chapuys wrote that he had given his principal Privy Councillors permission to go to their country houses for a change of air (9).

We hear very little of corruption among Henry's Councillors, though Chapuys wrote to Charles V., in 1535, that Cromwell had told him he had himself refused a large pension from France, and intended to pass an Act at the first Parliament that no English-

(1) Hatfield Papers, II. 4th January, 1577, p. 437.
(2) Pollard: Henry VIII., p. 241. What of Cromwell and Cranmer?
(3) L. and P., II., p. 278.
(4) L. and P., VI., 1479.
(5) Ibid., I., 3443.
(6) Ibid., XIII., Pt. I., 995.
(7) Ibid., XVI., 1328.
(8) Ibid., XIV., Pt. II., 183.
(9) L. and P., XVI., 1292.

man of the King's Council, on pain of his life, should take a pension from any foreign Prince (1) Norfolk, Suffolk, and several others appear to have been drawing French pensions (2) We hear little, too, of disloyalty to Henry in the Council, but, as Chapuys said in 1542, they were " well grounded in dissimulation " (3) Early in 1541, however, there was a conspiracy in Lincolnshire under Sir John Neville, and about the same time there were signs that the Council itself could not be immediately steadied after the violent disturbance of the previous year. Sir John Wallop, Sir Thomas Wyatt, and his Secretary, Sir John Mason, were sent to the Tower, and both Wriothesley and Sadler, Cromwell's former henchmen, seem to have incurred suspicion. The three prisoners were soon released, and Wriothesley and Sadler regained favour by abjuring their former religious opinions (4).

The spirit of the age during the sixteenth century was one of governmental action in every sphere of national life, nor is it clear that the activity of rulers was generally unpopular. Certainly it was not so in the reign of Henry VIII. and his son. Among Edward's papers there is a curious illustration of the sentiment of his time. In an essay on government he sets out measures which he conceives to be needed for the reformation of various abuses. It is valuable as summarising the theories of the age, and is a eulogy of paternal government, alluding with evident approval to interference with the undesirable activities of individuals (5). Edward, however, did not live long enough to put his theories into practice, though Somerset went a long way in this direction.

The Councillors very soon found Somerset's domination very little to their liking, and on 8th May, 1549, Paget wrote to him, remonstrating on his angry and abrupt demeanour towards those of the Council who differed from him and ventured to express their own sentiments (6). The Protector governened on Henrician lines, for despotic power had been placed in his hands, and the other Councillors were at first entirely under his influence. The Admiral, Somerset's own brother, is reported to have said to the Council one day that as he was uncle of the King it was only fitting he should marry honourably. He had formerly been married to the Queen Dowager, and he considered he deserved more than anyone else the hand of the Princess Elizabeth. He was told in reply that he had better speak to the Protector about it, but that the Councillors would offer no objection (7). By September, 1549, the Imperial ambassador, Van der Delft, expressed to Charles V. his disgust with Somerset's government, declaring that everything was going to rack and ruin, and that the Protector would not be able to stand much longer. On 14th October he sent the news of the latter's arrest, and how the King, " looking astonished," had entered London with the Councillors and nobility, for Somerset had told Edward previously that the other members of the Council meant to do harm to his person (8).

It was Warwick's turn now to become all powerful in the government and to dominate the young King. This latter he accomplished " by giving him money, recommending him to make presents, acquainting him with public business, and choosing to

(1) Ibid., VIII. 429.

(2) Ibid., X. 357, XI. 40.

(3) Ibid., XVII. 1241.

(4) Pollard: Henry VIII., p. 402.

(5) Dicey: 110.

(6) Dom. Cal., 8th May, 1549.

(7) " Chronicle of King Henry VIII." (ed. Hume), p. 162.

(8) Spanish Calendar, 23rd Sept., 1549.

have his opinion so that his commands might be executed without delay. But although his Majesty seemed much satisfied with this proceeding on the part of the Duke, yet such was the excellence of his natural disposition that he would never do any act, either of grace or justice, without the approval of his Council, by which means he became so popular with his Councillors and the whole country, that there is perhaps no instance on record of any other King of that age being more beloved, or who gave greater promise."(1) Warwick was all powerful till the end of the reign. On 13th September, 1550, the Council sent a letter to him enclosing a proclamation which " the Lords have penned according to their opinions," and which they pray him to peruse and " amend it as he shall see cause, and then return it " (2). On 29th July of the following year, his opinion is desired as to an execution which had been deferred. (3) Evidently the Council did not act without Northumberland (as he now was), even in trivial matters.

Edward was keenly interested in State business, judging from the memoranda he has left. He probably sat in Council twice or three times a week. In March, 1552, he wrote, " I will sit with them (4) once a week [upon Tuesday at afternoon both to hear the certificate of things passed and] (5) to hear the debating of things of most importance " (6). We know little else of Edward and his relations with his Council, except that on 10th November, 1551, order was taken that bills, which had in the past been signed by six of the Privy Council as well as the King, were in future to pass the Signet and be signed no longer by the Privy Councillors, since they considered it derogatory to the King's honour. For those, however, who preferred " any manner of bill to the signature," it was ordered that all those bills, which received the signature, were to be put " in a docquet or codicill," and signed by the Council's hands, as a witness that the same had been signed by His Majesty (7). Apparently the signatures of the Privy Councillors as yet carried more weight than that of the King.

Before Mary became Queen the Council showed itself not at all humble in its dealing with her, nor, indeed, was it very subservient after she ascended the Throne. On 7th December, 1550, Mary wrote to the Council concerning her chaplain, against whom the sheriff wished to proceed; the Council, however, sent back her messenger saying they would reply in two or three days when they had leisure (8). But in her quarrel with them concerning the Mass, Mary decidedly worsted both the King and Council, reminding them that they had promised, in a letter to the Emperor, to allow her to hear Mass, and that " though you esteem little the Emperor, yet should you show more favour to me for my father's sake, who made the more part of you almost of nothing " (9). After such a characteristically Tudor reply, Mary heard little more from Edward's Privy Council.

(1) Venetian Calendar, 18th Aug., 1554.
(2) A.P.C., III.
(3) Ibid., under date.
(4) i.e. " the committee of the Council appointed for matters of State."
(5) This has been struck through.
(6) Literary Remains of Edward VI., p. 499, Roxburghe Club.
(7) A.P.C., III.
(8) A.P.C., III.
(9) A.P.C., III. 29th August, 1551.

Mary was not unpopular at the beginning of her reign. Relying on the loyalty of the country, she might with a little energy and talent have ruled the Council instead of being ruled by them. She might have formed what never existed in her reign—a body of trustworthy and obedient counsellors and officials who would have relieved her from the necessity of relying on those who had their personal ends in view (1). Soranzo, the Venetian Ambassador, wrote in 1554, "As according to the custom of the country one of the Councillors is always superior to the rest, and what pleases him seems nearly always to please the others also. The present Prime Minister, as aforesaid, is the Bishop of Winchester, and next to him those most in the Queen's favour are the Earl of Arundel, Lord Paget, and Secretary Petre; but Paget, both because he is a very experienced statesman as also from having been the person who negotiated the marriage with the Prince of Spain, took precedence of all of them until now, when, as an acknowledged anti-Catholic, he is out of favour with Her Majesty. The Bishop of Winchester on the contrary, who at the commencement opposed the marriage and ran great risk of disgrace, until, being convinced of the Queen's firm intention, he deligently aided its accomplishment, is now paramount to everybody." (2) In the same dispatch the Queen was said to rise at daybreak, and to transact business incessantly until after midnight. She gave audience not only to all the members of her Privy Council and heard from them every detail of public business, but also she was accessible to all persons who desired to speak with her. Her countenance was said to show great mercy, which was not belied by her conduct, for, although her enemies were condemned to death, had the executions depended on the Queen's will they would not have been carried out, "but, deferring to her Council in everything, she in this matter likewise complied with the wishes of others than with her own" (3). The Council had its will also over the non-restoration of the Church property, but Mary would not give way in the matter of her marriage. From the very beginning of her reign the Councilors were spies upon her actions. She might receive no one whose business with her was not made public to her advisers, and whose reception they did not sanction: even Renard was excluded for a time, and the Queen was so anxious to see him that she suggested he should come in disguise (4).

After the marriage of Mary and Philip, however, the Council was said to be devoted to the King, "owing to the great rewards they have had from him, for when last here he spent and gave a considerable quantity of money, and distributed vast revenues in Spain and Flanders to propitiate the people here; and he found by experience that what my father used to say of this kingdom was perfectly true, that all, from first to last, are venal and do anything for money. The Count de Feria told me that the King had taken these grandees in such a way, that he can do what he will with them and the realm" (5). This dispatch amply illustrates the corruption rife among the Councillors of Mary. Philip certainly appointed a small Council for business purposes, and there was constant correspondence between the King and this "Select Council" (6). There are

(1) Friedmann: "Some New Facts in the History of Queen Mary."—Macmillan's Mag., XIX., p. 7.
(2) Venetian Calendar, 18th Aug., 1554.
(3) Ibid.
(4) Froude, V., p. 234.
(5) Venetian Calendar, 3rd April, 1557.
(6) See Domestic Calendar for the reign.

memoranda on important matters transacted in the Council in August and September, 1555, during the King's absence in Flanders, which have been annotated in the margin by the King's authority. This Select Council, however, was not always subservient to the King: on 18th December, 1555, they wrote to Philip, stating their objection to a certain licence being granted to Antony Guaras. On 26th February, 1556, concerning some proposition of Philip touching his and the Queen's titles, the Councillors wrote that they could not accede to the proposition, and were sending over the Lord Privy Seal and the Bishop of Ely to Philip (1). Moreover, Badoer, the Venetian ambassador, wrote in October, 1555, that he had it on good authority that Philip had written to Mary that he would not return to England, because he had to live there in a manner unbecoming to his dignity, "which requires him to take part in the affairs of the realm, though with her counsel and that of her Councillors," whereas in Spain he was accustomed to rule absolutely (2). In 1579 it was said, that when Philip was King of England he was never able to appoint any one of his own people to the Council (3).

The Queen was little more than a puppet in the hands of her Councillors. We have no record of her presence at the Council Board. They grumbled, and not without reason, that Pole carried on business behind their backs. After the death of Gardiner, he stood in close relations with the Queen, and both Philip and Mary, as has been seen, placed great confidence in him.

Towards the end of the reign, Paget's influence in the Council was very great. Little business of real importance was transacted without consulting him, and he was consulted by letter when absent on such points as the conditions on which licences should be granted in the wine trade, and the strength of the winter garrisons in the North (4). His opinion upon the negotiations for peace between France and England was considered so valuable that he was entreated to come to his house in London, if his health permitted, that his colleagues might confer with him on the subject—a course actually taken when his opinion was required upon the sending of money to Ireland (5).

The rank of Privy Councillor was said to have been conferred by Mary on all those from whom she had anything to hope or fear, in order to keep them under obligation to her (6). This was very different from the usual Tudor practice, by which the Council was "usually chosen from amongst the chief nobility, though not from obligation oor of necessity, but by the King's will, though it is presupposed that the principal charges and offices of the realm and of the Court can only be conferred on great personages, and above all on such as are in the confidence of the Sovereign, who, never limiting himself to any certain number, also admits others into it, regardless of nobility or ignobility, either of ecclesiastical or secular grade—such persons in short as are most to his taste; and in this matter likewise, fortune and favour often prevail over merit. By these individuals the kingdom is governed in all circumstances under the pleasure of the King " (7).

(1) Dom. Cal., 26th February, 1556.
(2) Ventian Calendar, 13th October, 1555.
(3) Ibid., VII. 761 (1579).
(4) A.P.C., VI. 12th September, 1558; 30th September, 1558.
(5) Ibid., 24th September, 1558; 27th October, 1558.
(6) Venetian Calendar, 3rd April, 1557.
(7) Venetian Calendar, 13th May, 1557.

Elizabeth followed out the customary Tudor policy in choosing her Councillors, and at her first reception held at Hatfield, 20th November, 1558, she declared that she required of her councillors "nothing more but faithful hearts in such service as, from time to time, shall be in your powers towards the preservation of me and this Commonwealth. And for counsel and advice, I shall accept you of my nobility and such others of you the rest, as in consultation I shall think meet and shortly appoint; to the which also I will join to their aid, and for ease of their burden, others meet for my service. And they which I shall not appoint, let them not think the same for any disability in them, but for that I consider a multitude doth make rather discord and confusion than good counsel" (1). She made Cecil Secretary and a member of her Privy Council because, as she said, "This judgment I have of you, that you will not be corrupted with any manner of gifts, and that you will be faithful to the State; and that, without respect of my private will, you will give me that counsel you think best, and if you shall know anything to be necessary to be declared unto me of secrecy, you shall show it to myself only; and assure yourself I will not fail to keep taciturnity therein" (2). Cecil's career shows how faithfully he performed his charge.

The Queen treated her Council so well that "she was never obnoxious to any of them, and they were all devoted and addicted to her"(3). In 1588 they were said to be raising a thousand horse at their own cost as a guard for her person, the Earl of Leicester contributing three hundred and the other Councillors a hundred each (4). But there was undoubtedly some corruption in Elizabeth's Council, and Sir James Crofts, the Comptroller, seems to have been the worst in this respect (5). Philip wrote to Mendoza in 1582, "As one of the most powerful levers may be to give a sum of money to some of the Councillors and Ministers, a customary thing in that country, you may open the way by promising presents to such as you think fit, if they will arrange for the Queen to intervene and aid in the settlement of a fair peace with my rebel States" (6).

Elizabeth's treatment of her Councillors as individuals, however, often left much to be desired. By 1576 Burghley was said to be the only one of her ministers whom she treated with anything approaching respect. Walsingham was the object of her vulgar abuse; Leicester she alternately petted and insulted; Hatton and Heneage were treated in a similar fashion but with even less consideration (7). She had a fancy, too, for giving nicknames or familiar titles to those about her. Burghley was her "spirit," Hatton her "eyelids," Whitgift her "moon"; there are copies of two letters extant in which she adressed Lord Mountjoy, when her Deputy in Ireland, as "mistress kitchen-

(1) Froude, VI., 120. Dom. Cal., 20th Nov., 1558, does not give the words, but only a reference to the occasion.
(2) Ibid., VI., 121.
(3) "Annals of the First Four Years of Elizabeth."—Camden Soc., 1840, p. 12.
(4) Spanish Calendar, 17th July, 1588.
(5) Spanish Calendar, 3rd May, 1579; 13th Sept., 1579.
(6) Ibid., 20th May, 1582.
(7) Hume: "Burghley," 310.

maid " '1\. She was very hard to please, and sometimes so " impatient and testy, . . . none of the Council but the Secretary [Robert Cecil] dare come in her presence " (. .

The Queen and her Council worked on the whole very well together: Elizabeth was not as a rule impervious to remonstrance. But it was said, " The principal note of her reign will be that she ruled much by faction and parties which her self both made, upheld, and weakened, as her own great judgment advised: for I dissent from the common received that my Lord of Leicester was absolute and above all in her grace. . . . I know it from assured intelligence that it was not so." Walsingham is described by the same authority as the best linguist of the time, but he " knew best how to use his own tongue, whereby he came to be employed in the chiefest affairs of state "; Sir Nicholas Bacon was an " an archpiece of wit and wisdom," and Christopher Hatton " a mere vegetable of the Court which sprung up at night and sunk again in his noon " (3). As a judge of character, Elizabeth excelled, and the men of greatest influence with her and who influenced national policy, were Burghley, the Marquis of Winchester, Leicester, Walsingham, and Robert Cecil. Leicester was the only worthless one amongst them. In 1569 Leicester and Cecil were said entirely to govern the Queen (4). When Bacon wrote he clearly recognised the practice of having Cabinet Councils. He spoke of the inconveniences of a Council, and the remedies for the same. The inconveniences are three; first " the revealing of affairs, whereby they became less secret; secondly, the weakening of the authority of Princes; thirdly, the danger of being unfaithfully counselled. For which inconveniences, the doctrine of Italy and the practice of France in some King's time hath introduced Cabinet Counsels; a remedy worse than the disease." He asserts that " Princes are not bound to communicate all matters with all Councillors, but may extract and select. Neither it is necessary, that he, that consulteth what he should do, should declare what he will do." Bacon was voicing the policy of the Tudors, and he himself shows French influence in his introduction, when he dictates his essays to the Bishop of Winchester, " Counsellor of *Estate* to her Majesty " (5). *dedicates*

But Elizabeth was quite capable of negotiating and transacting business without consulting her Council. With her Councillors, as with foreign states, her line of conduct was as Machiavellian and as replete with dissimulation as that of Henry VII. It is said in 1578, when Alençon's messengers came to Audley End, that the object of their mission was still a secret unknown to most of the Councillors (6), and the Council Register throws little light on such secretly conducted negotiations. In 1586 Secretary Walsing-

(1) " Letters of Elizabeth and James VI."—Cam. Soc., 1849, p. 11.

(2) Dom. Cal., 9th March, 1603. But this was in old age and illness.

(3) " Memoirs of Robert Carey and Fragmenta Regalia," pp. 178, 223, 230, 248.

(4) Spanish Calendar, 25th September, 1569.

(5) Bacon: Essay on Counsel.

(6) A.P.C., X., p. 15.

ham wrote to Leicester in the Low Countries, who had been grumbling that the Council wrote to him so seldom: "They answer, as it is troth, that Her Majesty retaining the whole direction of the causes of that country [the Netherlands] to herself and such advice as she receiveth underhand, they know not what to write or advise. She can by no means, as I have heretofore written unto your Lordship, endure that the causes of that country should be subject to any debate in Council, otherwise than she herself shall direct, and therefore men forbear to do that which otherwise they would " (1). Evidently the Council was subservient to Elizabeth in this matter. But in 1568, when Mary of Scotland arrived in England, the Council over-ruled the Queen concerning her treatment: "her views did not prevail, as a majority of the Council was of a different opinion," and the Duke of Norfolk, with the Earls of Arundel and Leicester, were ordered to be summoned so that a full Council might decide what was to be done (2). Elizabeth seemed chary of acting entirely on her own responsibility. In 1595, for example, Thomas Smith, Clerk of the Council, wrote at her command to Robert Cecil concerning the punishment of one Wood. The Queen thought it right that the first part of his sentence should be remitted, but, for the second part, that the order of the Star Chamber should be proceeded with. Cecil was to acquaint the Lord Treasurer and Lord Keeper of this decision. Then, in a postscript, "In all this (above written) she referreth herself to my Lord Keeper and my Lord Treasurer, that they may do herein as they shall think meet." (3)

Little is known of Elizabeth's presence at the Council Board. At the beginning of her reign she appears to have sat there every day except when travelling (4). Towards the end of her reign the formal meetings of the Council seem to have been held on Sundays only wherever the Queen was. Business of all kinds was transacted then. There were mid-week meetings also, but the Register reveals little of the Council's proceedings at the same, often merely recording the letters which were written, and the names of those Councillors who signed them. In 1601 Lord Hunsdon wrote to Cecil concerning a matter about which he had already complained to the Lord Treasurer, but nothing had been done, so "I do entreat that upon Sunday you will recommend the consideration hereof to their Lordships at the Council Table " (5).

The Queen was not privy to all judicial complaints, however. The Council wrote to Lord Stafford touching his behaviour towards his tenants, that " if Her Majesty were informed thereof, it were like that such displeasure would ensue towards him as he would be loth to sustain "(6). Nor did she hear of all the business that came before the Council Board (7). It was impossible for her to do so, for the mass of work increased daily. The

(1) " Correspondence of the Earl of Leicester." (Camden Soc. 1844), No. 86.

(2) Spanish Calendar, 22nd May, 1568.

(3) Hatfield Papers V., 5th December, 1595.

(4) Strype: "Annals of the Reformation," p. 10.

(5) Hatfield Papers VI., 21st August, 1601.

(6) A.P.C., XI. 3rd August, 1579.

(7) A.P.C., XVII. 15th June, 1589; XXVI. 11th August, 1596.

Secretaries were too busy to do anything but Government business, and we have just seen Elizabeth employing a clerk to write her letters. Before 1580 she had her own private secretary, Thomas Windebank.

The Privy Councillors under the Tudors enjoyed many privileges. Their dinners when they sat at Westminster were a public charge (1). Occasionally they dined with the Sovereign (2). They were the recipients of many fees and annuities (3), and obtained grants of licences and monopolies (4). At Henry VIII.'s death, many acquired higher titles, owing to Paget's convenient memory, and during the reign of Edward VI. they obtained on easy terms grants of the lands which had been appropriated by the Crown (5). In August, 1553, soon after Mary's accession, the Council passed a self-denying ordinance which reveals what had been taking place in the last reign. The Council advised that no further grants of lands or fee farms should be made, excessive salaries should not be attached to old offices, illegal licences to trade were not to be given, leases were not to be granted for more than twenty years, and then only upon sufficient rents, while grants of annuities and pensions were discouraged (7). This ordinance applied to the general public as well as to the Privy Council. The keynote of the entries in the Register of the Council under Edward VI. is rapacity. Nor had their character improved in the reign of Elizabeth, for in 1569 the Duke of Alva described them as "always on the look out for their own interests" (6).

Their increasing importance was recognised by Parliament as early as 1487. 3 H. 7, c. 14 is entitled "An act concerning those conspiring to destroy the King or any Lord Chancellor or great officer." It enacted that to destroy or murder the King, or any lord of this Realm, or any other person sworn of the King's Council, Steward, Treasurer or Comptroller of the King's Household was felony. The offender was to be tried by the Steward, Treasurer or Comptroller of the King's Household, or one of them, with twelve "sad and discreet men of the Chequer Roll of the King's most honourable Household." By 11 H. 7, c. 25, perjury committed before the King's Council was to be punished at the discretion of the Lord Chancellor, the Treasurer, both the Chief Justices, and the Clerk of the Rolls. The statute 21 H. 8, c. 13, allowed certain persons to have chaplains to serve them in their houses, amongst them those of the King's honourable Council. Another statute, 3 and 4 Ed. 6, c. 5 made it high treason for twelve or more persons to assemble to attempt to kill or imprison any of the King's Council.

In conclusion, the comparison between an Elizabethan Privy Council and a Victorian Cabinet, a committee of the unwieldly modern Privy Council, naturally suggests itself. In reality, however, there is more of contrast than of comparison, despite a delusive superficial resemblance. Both are small bodies consisting mainly of administrators with a sprinkling of persons included for their political influence, experience, or importance, apart from administrative ability. In both an "inner ring" exists. Both possess advisory and administrative functions, but the modern Cabinet has, of course, no judicial

(1) A.P.C., XIII. 854.
(2) Ibid., II. Pt. I. 2736.
(3) Ibid., IV. 961.
(4) A.P.C., II. 18; III. 15, 16.
(5) A.P.C., IV. p. 387.
(6) Spanish Calendar, 13th June, 1569.

duties. As a Cabinet, indeed, it has no powers or functions of any kind, for whereas Elizabeth's Privy Council is a body whose powers and functions were well known to the law and the constitution, the Cabinet has still no legal existence. The Sovereign generally sat in the Tudor Privy Council; his appearance at a modern Cabinet meeting would constitute a constitutional revolution. Records of Privy Council meetings were kept, carefully if somewhat eclectically, whereas minuting at a Cabinet meeting is, if not absolutely inhibited, at least highly informal and unofficial.

VII. THE PRIVY COUNCIL AND ITS WORK.

——————:o:——————

THE TUDORS were essentially men of action. One finds in them an intensity, an impatience of control, and a power of will, which have hardly their equal in English history. All this was reflected in their Privy Council, and at no other period is the national executive more deeply coloured by the personality of the Crown.

The powers of the Council in its corporate capacity were so wide and multifarious that anything like a full description of them would require a separate treatise. It has been rightly said that the period of the Tudors was the period of government by Council, for it was in and through the Council that absolute monarchy performed its work. The authority wielded by this body, representing the Sovereign who was always supposed to be present in Council, embraced not only every department of administration proper but also comprised what now would be considered exclusively legislative or judicial functions.

A.—JUDICIAL.

The Norman Curia Regis had been a Court of prelates and barons, and it is not until the days of Henry II. that a smaller group of professional judges is found doing the ordinary and rapidly increasing work of the Curia Regis. During the thirteenth century there came into being a distinction between this permanent Council and the Great Council of the Realm—the Concilium Regis as opposed to the Commune Consilium Regis. Its members were *magnates de concilio*, and comprised the justiciar chancellor and treasurer, some or all of the judges of the royal curia, a number of bishops, barons, and others who in default of any other title were known as councillors. They took an oath to give advice, to protect the King's interests, to do justice honestly, and to take no gifts.

But the relations of the King's Council to the Great Council of the Realm were still indefinite. In either of these two assemblies the King could do justice; under Edward I. the machinery of government worked so easily and there was (except in 1297) so little opposition to the King, that men were not very careful to distinguish between the two bodies. This was noticeable as regards legislation; the contrast between statute and ordinance was not emphasized. But especially was it so as regards justice. Under Edward I.'s steady rule all worked well; there was no need to distinguish between the jurisdiction of a permanent group of advisers and that of an occasional assembly of prelates and magnates.

The evolution of definite judicial bodies such as the Courts of King's Bench, Common Pleas, and Exchequer had not exhausted the fount of royal justice, and if all other courts failed the King might still do justice in his Council or in his Parliament. Errors of all inferior courts might be brought in the last resort for correction before the King in Parliament or before the King in Council. During the reign of Edward I. the Council still exercised a jurisdiction which it was somewhat difficult to distinguish from that of Parliament. The two worked together so harmoniously that the Council seemed at times a standing committee of the Parliament, or the Parliament a particularly full and solemn meeting of the Council meeting of the Council. This harmony was soon dispelled, however; there was constant friction between the Council and Parliament nearly all through the fourteenth century. Time after time the latter sought to limit the judicial functions of the former, but with indefinite success.

Three species of jurisdiction exercised by the Council may be distinguished. First, the power to correct errors or ordinary errors of ordinary courts. Second, an original criminal jurisdiction. Third, an original civil jurisdiction. The first of these has the shortest history, for the function of correcting errors in law becomes definitely the work of Parliament, but is exercised only by the House of Lords. This the Council had to forego. The Statute of 4 Hen. IV., c 23, makes it clear that the Council had been calling in question the judgments of the ordinary courts, and therefore provides that after judgment given the parties should be in peace until the judgment be reversed by attaint or by error. Throughout the Tudor period, however, the Council exercised an appellate jurisdiction. Though not interfering with judgments already given, it had a wide field of action open to it. (1)

The original civil jurisdiction of the Council soon came to be exercised by the Chancellor in the Court of Chancery. The series of fourteenth century statutes directed against the jurisdiction of the Council seems to have been directed as much against its interference in civil litigation (2) as against its claim to a wide criminal jurisdiction. It was then the view of Parliament that the courts of common law were sufficient. Gradually, in the fifteenth century, the Council seems to have abandoned the attempt to interfere with cases which common law courts could decide, but it soon became apparent that there were cases in which, although no relief at all could be got from these courts, yet, according to the ideas of the time, relief was due. By this time, too, it was becoming the practice of the King's Council to refer all petitions relating to civil cases to the Chancellor, the King's chief legal adviser, so that petitioners who wanted relief no longer addressed their complaints to the King but to the Chancellor, and he seems commonly to have dealt with them instead of bringing them before the King and his Council.

(1) Maitland states there is hardly a case of error before the House of Lords between Henry IV. and Elizabeth. He attributes this partly to the Council's having "assumed" a very wide power of jurisdiction (p. 245). Since the Council exercised only the jurisdiction which was inherent in the Crown, it is surely hardly correct to term that same jurisdiction "assumed."

(2) 5 Ed. III. c. 9; 25 Ed. III. stat. 5 c. 4; 28 Ed. III. c. 3; 37 Ed. III. c. 18; 38 Ed. III. c. 9; 42 Ed. III. c. 3.

It has been, however, over the jurisdiction of the Council as a court of first instance in criminal cases that controversy has raged. It is of great constitutional importance, and, as Bacon said, the supreme jurisdiction of the King in Council was always
received through all the changes and development of the judicial system. The series of
fourteenth century statutes which tried to put a stop to legal proceedings other than
those in the ordinary courts of law has already been mentioned. But none of the Acts
thus passed seems to have had much immediate effect, and under Henry IV. and Henry
V. Parliament is still petitioning against the jurisdiction of the Council. Their petitions
were not granted; at last they became silent, and it would seem that the control which
Parliament obtained over the Council under the constitutional rule of the Lancastrians
modified this jealousy. Throughout the whole of the Tudor period this series of hostile
statutes remains disregarded but unrepealed, and they were of vast importance later on
as the basis for the erroneous contention that the Star Chamber was no legal tribunal.

The Council, however, was not bound down to formal procedure like the common
law courts, and Parliament admitted that it had a certain sphere of jurisdiction. In
1351 Parliament began its anti-Roman legislation, and it was provided by statute in 1363
that offences against the statutes of Provisors and Praemunire should be dealt with by
Council (1). In 1388 another Act provided that Justices of the Peace who neglected to
hold their sessions should be punished at the discretion of the King's Council. Other
Acts conferred upon the Council authority to punish riots, and in 1453 these powers were
extended to cover other misdemeanours (2).

It is hard to say if the remainder of the criminal jurisdiction of the Council was,
at Henry VII.'s accession, legal or illegal. Unrepealed statutes condemned it entirely,
but Parliament and the great mass of the nation, including probably the judges, regarded
it as legal. It was admitted that the Council could punish offences which the common
law courts were unable to punish, and it was felt that there were "over-mighty subjects" too powerful for any court but the Council—men who bribed jurors and even judges.
Sometimes trial by jury ensured the maximum of injustice, and there were men whom no
jury would convict. This was admitted, and a remedy was found in the reserve of justice
to be found, as of old, in the King and its immediate advisers; a justice which would
strike once and need not strike again. This jurisdiction was a necessary consequence of
the great principle of our law and constitution, that it is the first duty of the Sovereign
to see that justice is administered to all his subjects. Hence the jurisdiction of "the
King in Council" (3).

The most frequent cause of the failure of justice was the absence of sufficient
power to enforce it. Especially had this been the case throughout the century preceding
the accession of the first Tudor, and it was the work of this dynasty to bring order out
of chaos in judicial matters. The necessary power could be derived only from the Crown,
and that power, until an age when law had become supreme, was exercised by the King
through his Council. This jurisdiction of the King in Council was never *in its nature*
directly judicial and original or even appellate, but rather only protective, corrective,

(1) 38 Ed. III., stat. 2 c. 2.
(2) 13 Hen. IV., c. 7; 2 Hen. V., stat. 1 c. 8 (confirmed by 19 Hen. VII.
c. 13); 31 Hen. VI., c. 2.
(3 Finlason: "The Judicial Committee of the Privy Council," p. 1.

and restrictive (1), and on this score one can generally find excuses for the apparently arbitrary exercise of jurisdiction by the Council under the Tudors. It was very necessary and it was very salutary; that is the best defence of Tudor rule in every direction. Numbers of suitors found in the Council a Court where the law's delays and counsel's fees were minimised, and where justice was rarely denied because it happened to be illegal. The Council worked to prevent the failure of justice in the ordinary courts by fraud or violence, corruption or intimidation, and especially by combination or conspiracy to obstruct or prevent the course of law.

No regular appellate jurisdiction was vested in the "King in Council" as to suits arising within the realm, except so far as the power and right to do justice is inherent in the Crown. When under Henry VIII. the appellate jurisdiction of the Pope was abolished it was provided by Statute that appeals should go not to the King in Council but to the King in Chancery (2). The oldest form of the Council's appellate jurisdiction is probably to be found in the case of the Admiralty. In the fifteenth century apeals from that court went to delegates or special commissioners appointed by the Crown ad hoc (3). The Channel Islands at all times addressed their appeals to the King in Council, as did Calais. Under Elizabeth this jurisdiction was questioned and confirmed: an Order in Council in 1565, referring to the appeals from the Channel Isles, directed that "no appeals should be made for any sentence or judgment given in the same isles hither, but only according to the words of their charter, *au Roy et a son conseil*, which agreeth, as Sir Hugh Paulet allegeth, with such order and form as hath heretofore been accustomed "(4).

Its claim to an original jurisdiction in criminal cases gave to the Council its most dreaded authority, and during the reign of Henry VIII. this was extended to ecclesiastical causes. In theory the Sovereign is the fount of all justice and the supreme judge, and in judicial as well as other matters, the presumption is always in favour of the royal prerogative, unless there is a statute or ancient custom to the contrary. Moreover, in cases where the law is not explicit the doubt is always interpreted in favour of the Crown. Throughout the Tudor period the Council exercised a jurisdiction which can only be justified on the ground that, besides being necessary, it was the jurisdiction inherent in the Sovereign. It is indisputable that there was a necessity for some such court of justice under the conditions of government in the sixteenth century. The opportunities of breaking the peace enjoyed by powerful subjects were very extensive; the government had no standing army or police to support it; the criminal jurisdiction of the courts leet of the Hundred and Manor had largely broken down, and these courts were at all times peculiarly liable to intimidation from local magnates. The Council was subject to no such influence; moreover, it afforded to poor suitors the further invaluable boon of speedy procedure (5).

(1) Finlason, p. 6.

(2) 25 H. VIII., c. 19.

(3) Carter: "History of English Legal Institutions," p. 175.

(4) A.P.C., VII. Hearn: "Government of England," p. 317.

(5) Although petitions which came before it were not always speedily dispatched. Kingsford's Chronicle, p. 225.

Tudor Parliaments many times recognised the judicial powers of the Council. The statute 3 Hen. VII., c. 1 has already been mentioned. This Act empowered the Chancellor, Treasurer, and the Keeper of the Privy Seal, with a spiritual and a temporal lord of the King's Council, together with the two chief justices or other two in their absence, to call before them persons accused of such common offences as riots, unlawful assemblies, perjury, bribery of jurors, misconduct as sheriffs, and to examine and punish them. The object of this Act was to delegate to a statutory committee of the Ordinary Council part of the judicial work of the Privy Council in order to relieve the latter body; it was rather declaratory than absolutely necessary. The misdemeanours mentioned were very prevalent at the time, and only the Council was strong and independent enough to deal with them. The statute merely emphasised the Council's control over such offences. Whether the committee ever sat and tried cases by virtue of the statute is exceedingly doubtful. The statute 33 Hen. VII., c. 20 speaks of people accused of treason, who, after being examined by the King's Majesty's Council and confessing their crime, then feign madness. In the same statute, c. 23 enacts that persons suspected of treason and murder and sent to be examined before the King's Highness' Counil so that conviction might speedily ensue, were nevertheless to be tried by common law, if found guilty by the Council, in the place where the offence had been committed. Again, the statute 37 Hen. VIII., c. 10 declared that any person who made " any writing confessing that another hath spoken high treason, and shall cast the said writing in an open place where it may be found, and shall not subscribe a name to the same, and within twelve days shall not personally appear before the King and his Council and affirm the contents of the same to be true, he shall then be adjudged a felon." Yet another Act, 1 Edw. VI., 12, mentions the Privy Council in connection with high treason, providing that every accusation of high treason must be made to one of the King's Council or to one of the Justices of Assize, or a Justice of the Peace being of the quorum (1). The Council examined persons accused of treason but never tried the offence.

Other judicial functions pertaining to the Council were also recognised by the statute 33 Hen. VII., c. 39, which provides that in certain cases of legal extortion the offenders " shall suffer such imprisonment as is adjudged by the King or his most honourable Council daily attendant upon his Highness' most royal person." The statute 2 and 3 Edw. VI., c. 6, providing that the Admiral of England an dhis officers should not exact any sums of money for licence to travel to Ireland, was made " because of the great complaints there of and information brought yearly to the King's Majesty's most honourable Council."

The Council did not cease throughout the Tudor period to exercise its criminal jurisdiction, but it is very noticeable that after Elizabeth ascended the throne the Council Register, which had hitherto recorded recognisances at almost every sitting of the Council, is now practically entirely free from them. This was probably because the Court of Star Chamber was relieving the Council of the greater part of its judicial work, and especially towards the end of the reign the Council refers many of the cases before it to the Court, or binds an offender to appear before the Lords of the Council in the Star Chamber. There is once a suggestion of jealousy on the part of the Council. Sir William Paulet, whose case had been deferred that he might formulate his charge, transferred it to the Star Chamber. The Council ordered that a matter brought before their table should not be removed to another Court without their authority, and requested Paulet with all speed to exhibit his bill of complaint before them (1). It is very clear from the Council Register that the Council and the Court of Star Chamber were two separate and distinct courts both exercising inquisitorial and judicial powers, the former being the superior, and making use of the latter. At this time, too, the Council begins to delegate its ecclesiastical jurisdiction to the Commissioners for causes ecclesiastical. Its relations with the Courts of Star Chamber and High Commission will be dealt with later.

Very little is known of the Council's procedure when trying the cases which came before it, because only the result of its judicial work, and not its method of taking evidence or passing sentence is recorded in the Register. A case in 1553 throws some light upon the matter, however. One Edward Underhill was brought before the Council for a ballad he had lately printed. He was committed to Newgate, where he remained for a month, until the Council could deal further with the him. All the Privy Councillors seem to have questioned him in turn; there was nothing formal in the the procedure, and it was like an interview before a committee. There were practically no witnesses, and the Council decided by a majority into which prison he should be thrown (2). Unlike the Court of Star Chamber, it was a secret court; on 1st June, 1578, a letter was directed to the Attorney-General that a certain case before the Council had been found to contain " very foul matter " against the accused, whose " lewdness was considered by their Lordships as deserving of open punishment." He was therefore requested to lay an information against him in the Star Chamber that the matter might be ordered there " according to justice "(3). Moreover, it was the duty of the Councillors and part of their oath to observe secrecy. In April, 1555, Michiel, the Venetian Ambassador, reported that the Lords of the Council were proceeding to the examination of certain prisoners suspected of conspiracy at Cambridge. Fresh arrests were made daily, " but, as usual with them, everything is done very privily, no one daring to speak about it, so that with difficulty can the truth be ascertained save at the end, when on a sudden we shall witness either the punishment or the acquittal " (4). Sir John Hussey wrote on 22nd June, 1539, to Lord Lisle that certain prisoners had been brought before the Council, but no one was admitted. Two of the men had been sent to the Fleet, and two to the Gatehouse (5). In 1602 there were brought before the Council " certain bold fellows that lay high matters to the Lords' charge; as Arthur Hall who accuses the Lord Keeper, one Atkinson who accuses the Lord Treasurer, and two others Mr. Secretary. They were heard in great secrecy and sent to the Gatehouse. Their cause will thrive ill when their adverse party is judge et partie " (6).

(1) A.P.C., VII. p. 405.

(2) Narratives of the Reformation," Camden Society, 1859.

(3) A.P.C., X.

(4) Venetian Calendar, 26th March, 1555.

(5) L. and P., XIV. 1144.

(6) Dom. Cal., 5th Jan., 1602.

Evidence before the Council was taken upon oath, for perjury before the King's Council was made a statutory offence (11 Hen. VII., c. 25). The summons to appear before the Council in its judicial capacity took various forms. Summons "by Writ or by Privy Seal" was provided by the Statute "Pro Camera Stellata" in the case of the court it set up. It was probably in this way that men had been called before the Council too, and this method was usual throughout the Tudor period. In 1496 a correspondent wrote to Sir Robert Plumpton, "There was a Bill put into the Parliament a little before Christmas that no privy seal should go against no man but if the suer thereof would find surety to yield the parties defendants their damages, and after that intent, it is said, the lords of the counsell behave themselves" (1). The Act of 1504, "De Retentionibus Illicitis," enacted that the Lord Chancellor or Keeper of the Great Seal or "Counseill," had full power and authority by the Statute to send by "writ, subpœna, privy seal, warrant, or otherwise by their discretions" for persons offending or doing contrary to the premises (2) without any suit or information laid before them; to examine the same by oath or otherwise at their discretion, and to judge all persons found guilty in the premises by verdict, confession, examination, proofs, or otherwise "in the said forfeiture and pains as the case shall require," as though they were condemned therein after the course of the common law," and to commit such offenders to ward and to award execution accordingly " (3). On 26th June and 3rd July, 1551, is recorded the appearance of two men summoned by Privy Seal to appear before the Council, and in 1520 Surrey wrote to Wolsey requesting the speedy settlement of a suit between the towns of Ross and Waterford, in which letters of Privy Seal summoning them to appear had been delivered to the burgesses of Ross.

Pursuivants delivered the orders of the Council and brought men before it: 19th July, 1576, Sir George Puttenham, who had not paid a certain sum to his wife as ordered by the Archbishop of Canterbury, was commanded by the Council to do so "or appear before it in the company of the bearer hereof, one of the Queen's Majesty's Pursuivants." In its judicial work the Council depended very largely upon informers. This class of men, although unorganised, was the nearest approach to a police force that the Tudors had, and they took care to encourage them. The Council had never been so freely open to hear informers and to receive charges often of the most trivial kind; enemies and critics of the Government were pursued remorselessly. Arrests were carried out on the word of an informer, and in 1504 the Act against Retainers already noticed provided that the informer should have "such reward of that that by his complaint shall grow to the King as shall be thought reasonable," as well as his costs. In October, 1542, ordinances were drawn up for the instruction of the garrison at Hull. In one of these the men were exhorted to observe their oath, which was as follows: To be true to King Henry VIII. and his heirs, and to reveal to the Privy Council anything he learnt which was prejudicial to the King, Realm, or the safety of the fortress (4). The Council saw to it that in-

(1) Plumpton Correspondence, p. 114. According to Pollard, the Bill did not pass and is not mentioned on the Rotuli Parliamentorum, although the statute 11 Hen. VII. c. 15 provided against similar abuses in the county courts.

(2) I.e., prohibitions of livery, signs, tokens, etc.

(3) 19 Hen. VII., c. 14.

(4) L. and P., XVII. 140.

formers were suitably rewarded. In 1574 information was laid before them that the Steelyard, which was under a statutory obligation to import a certain number of bowstaves every year, had not been fulfilling its obligation. The Council, however, could not then afford to offend the Steelyard, and so it remitted the forfeiture of £6,000 which was due and claimed by the informer, but the Steelyard was ordered to recompense the informer for his loss (1). In 1575 the clothiers of the West were ordered by the Council to contribute to a fund for the compensation of an informer, who had incurred heavy costs in order to prosecute fraudulent clothworkers, and who had lost the penalties which would have come to him had the cases gone to court, because a General Pardon had been issued (2). Again, one Hinder an informer was allowed as a reward to transport eight hundred quarters of grain (3). But the lot of the informer who laid a charge and then failed to substantiate it was not a happy one. Often he was imprisoned for his pains (4). On 23rd June, 1578, it is recorded that Thomas Weriet had been committed to prison for delivering to the Queen's Majesty a "very slanderous bill" against Sir John Perrot; he was re-committed to the Marshalsea, because on examination he could not prove it. On 26th December, 1579, and 24th April, 1580, certain dishonest informers and defaulting collectors of fines appeared before the Council for punishment. It was not with impunity that the common informer could complain against those in high places; in 1579 one Giles Foster exhibited against the Earl of Rutland a bill in which there were "very uncomely speeches against him which seemed to touch him much in honour and credit." The Council ordered the informer "for his lewd demeanour used towards the Earl being so honourable a personage" to be put in the Marshalsea till further order was taken concerning him (5).

The punishments inflicted by the Council were many and varied. Sometimes it inflicted the statutory punishment provided for the crime in question; at other times the penalty was greater than any law warranted. Mere caprice lightened or aggravated it, and abject submission was the best road to the Council's favour. The penalties most commonly inflicted were fine or imprisonment or both. Those implicated in Wyatt's rebellion were imprisoned, and then heavily fined and bound in a recognisance to appear before the Council at certain times stipulated by the latter (6). In 1601 those connected with Essex's conspiracy and disturbance in London were brought before the Council and very heavily fined; Rutland £30,000. Bedford £20,000, Monteagle £10,000, etc. (7). The punishments inflicted often seem excessive and brutal, but it must be remembered that the enormous fines were habitually reduced, for they were imposed not "secundum qualitatem delicti," but "in terrorem populi." Moreover, the cruelty of the Council was the cruelty of the times rather than its cruelty as a court of Justice. The punishments awarded by statute law or common law were quite as severe (8).

(1) A.P.C., VII., 5th February, 1574.

(2) A.P.C., IX., 2nd September, 1577; X., 9th September, 1577.

(3) A.P.C., XI., 14th July, 1579.   (4) A.P.C., I., 27th April, 1546.

(5) A.P.C., XI., p. 348.   (6) A.P.C., IV., 18th Jan., 1554.

(7) H.M.C., Rutland MS. I., 10th May, 1601.

(8) Occasionally the punishment was made to fit the crime. On 12th July, 1546, a man who had been sent to the Council from Surrey for lewd words was by them sent to Bedlem "for that he seemed to be in a frensy." In 1545 one Richard Reed, a London alderman, refused to contribute to a benevolence for the war with Scotland. The Privy Council wrote to Sir Ralph Evers that since Reed refused "to disburse a little of his substance" in the defence of the Realm and himself, the King thought it would be well for him to do some service with his body. Consequently, he was sent to Sir Ralph Evers to serve as a soldier, and in any enterprise against the enemy he was to ride and do in every way as the soldiers did, so that he might know what pains other poor soldiers had to bear, and might feel the smart of his own folly. (L. and P., XX., 98.) A man who objected on religious grounds to eat swine's flesh was imprisoned and fed on nothing but pork.

deal with those
who inveighed against
& Anglican doctrines

The recusancy laws of Elizabeth often provided alternative penalties of fine or punishment. Recusancy fines in Lancashire had been granted to one Nicholas Annesley. Some recusants, however, chose rather to be imprisoned than to pay, although it was Her Majesty's intention " to terrify the offenders and that the penalty might rather be moderated by some gentle composition with the said Annesley than that the extremity were sought by the entire execution of the statute." Their Lordships considered imprisonment no sufficient punishment, and those refusing to pay were to be sent before the Council (1).

Occasionally the conditions of recognisances into which guilty persons entered before the Council were strange and somewhat arbitrary. In 1541 one Poyner, who appears to have been a " procurer of perjury," and a " great embracer and maintainer of brabbling matters and suits," was ordered by the Council to stand in the pillory at Northampton, Stamford, Oxford, and Aylesbury, wearing a paper declaring his offences. Later, he was bound in five hundred marks not to practise the office of attorney or counsellor in law, nor meddle in any matters concerning law between party and party, nor devise or write any legal instruments without first obtaining the King's licence (2). On On 13th September, 1548, the Earl of Oxford was bound in a recognisance not to sell land or household effects without the Protector's permission or dismiss any of his officers. Again in 1558 Lord Latimer, who appears to have been a rogue of the first water, entered into a recognisance of a thousand marks continually to attend upon the Council and not to leave without the permission of the Lord Chancellor or the rest of the Council. Moreover, he was to " make no part or portion of his land away, neither bestow any of his daughters in marriage without the Queen's Majesty's special licence so to do."

The punishment for lewd or seditious words was as a rule branding, the pillory, whipping, or the stocks, but it is very noticeable throughout the Tudor period that the Council rarely if ever carried out its own punishments; this was entrusted to local officials. In 1541 the Dean of York and others declared two women guilty of " detestable offences " in the North. The Council ordered that the one who had burnt a house was to be indicted and executed according to law, but the Dean was commanded to cause the tongue of the other woman " to be pierced and slit through with a burning iron, to the intent that she might never disclose her vicious and abominable doings " (3). In 1581 the Council interfered and ordered a man to be executed immediately. One Mantell had pretended to be King Edward VI. and had been arraigned for treason accordingly before the Justices of Assize, and condemned. His execution had been respited owing to some point in law which had arisen. Since then he had broken prison, and so, said the Council, " he hath by another law deserved to be punished as a traitor." A frequent punishment for women was the " cucking stool." On 26th August, 1553, Lord Mordaunt and Lord St. John at Bedford were ordered to punish a woman, committed by them for seditious words against the Queen, " with the cucking stool or otherwise, on exami-

(1) A.P.C., XI., 14th April, 1580; XII., 15th July, 1580.

(2) P. and O., VII., pp. 217, 227.

(3) P. and O., VII. 17th July, 1541. See also A.P.C., IV., 7th July, 1552; X., 7th December, 1578.

nation of her qualities." For the same offence in the following year the sheriffs were ordered to give the same punishment to "two wives of Stepney." Occasionally the "dungeon amongst the rats" in the Tower was ordered (1), but sometimes a summons before the Council Board resulted in nothing more dreadful than a "good lesson," or an exhortation "to be friends" with one's enemy (2). Another punishment sometimes inflicted by the Council was that of committal to the galleys. What the galleys really were in the Tudor period seems an insoluble problem. In 1549 the judges were ordered by proclamation to arrest tellers of vain forged tales and commit them to the galleys, there to row during the royal pleasure. In 1545 it was ordered that vagabonds, together with common players, masterless men, and evil disposed persons should serve in the wars in the galleys which would be armed by 1st June of the same year (3). In 1551, however, there was a warrant recorded to Sir Edmund Peckham to pay £231 12s. 0d. and £55 "for the discharging of the galleys"; and two days later a letter was sent to the Lord Admiral to disarm the same two galleys (4). Under Elizabeth the galleys are again mentioned, but not until the end of the reign. In 1593 two "very lewd and loose fellows," who had already been censured in the Star Chamber "for counterfeiting some of our hands to certain warrants," being again found guilty of the same offence, were sent from the Marshalsea to Sir John Hawkins, who was instructed "to cause them forthwith to be placed in the new galleys, and fast tied with chains in such a sure sort as they may not by any means escape, allowing them for their diet under the ordinary allowance for some time, and in any case not to suffer them to be delivered withought the privity of me, the Lord Admiral of England" (5). On 19th June, 1602, the Council sent letters to the Justices of Assize throughout the realm for the reprieving of felons condemned in their circuits. They were, apparently, to serve in the galleys instead unless condemned for rape, burglary, or other notorious offences. Their friends were to contribute £3 a year to their maintenance if possible: otherwise the country was "to be moved" to do so, for by this means it was freed from unprofitable members who would do more mischief to the country than the money would make good. If the men would not do the work required of them in the galleys, they were to be sent back to prison (6).

Under the Tudors the practice of using torture to extract confession was very common. But the rack was rarely, if ever, used for the punishment of crime (7). I have found no instance of it. Occasionally a man was put in the chamber of Little Ease in

(1) A.P.C., X., 17th November, 1577.

(2) A.P.C., IV., 20th Jan., 1554; III., 8th March, 1552.

(3) Steele: "Proclamations," p. 81, 26th May, 1545.

(4) A.P.C., III. 14th Feb., 1551.

(5) A.P.C., XXIV., 26th August, 1593.

(6) Addit. MS. 11404 (Brit. Mus.); A.P.C., XXXII., Appendix. Rymer: II. 17th June, 1602.

(7) P. and O., VII. 16th November, 1540; A.P.C., III. 5th March. 1551; V. 4th December, 1555; VII. 18th January, 1567; XII. 24th Dec., 1580; XIV. 23rd Dec., 1586.

order to stimulate confession. It was not in London only that the Council ordered torture to be used; on 27th January, 1555, the Mayor of Bristol was instructed to put a suspected coiner on the rack, and "to use all other means whereby the truth and whole circumstances thereof may come to light." Torture was practised by the Council's orders in the Tower, Newgate, and King's Bench prisons. The amount necessary was usually left to the gaoler's discretion, or the Council sent its representatives; these then reported the confessions which were the result of the pressure applied. On 8th September, 1588, a letter was sent from the Council to the Lieutenant of the Tower and three others to appoint a day on which they were to examine an Englishman taken in a Spanish ship and presumably a traitor, "using torture to him at their pleasure." The rack was not the only form of torture used. Suspected thieves who refused to confess were put "to the rack and torture of the manacles" (1). In 1597 the ringleaders of a gang of Oxfordshire rioters who had been causing trouble over some enclosed land were ordered to be moved to Bridewell and put to the manacles and torture, "that they may be constrained thereby to utter the whole truth of their mischievous devices and purposes in this wicked and traitorous conspiracy " (2).

In the minds of many investigators into the jurisdiction exercised by the Privy Council during the Tudor period, the jurisdiction of the Court of Star Chamber and that of the Council are indistinguishable, and they find no difference between the judicial functions exercised by the Council as the Council and those exercised by it when sitting as a part of the Star Chamber. It is true that the nature of the jurisdiction of these two courts was identical, but their procedure and composition was very different. The full maturity of the Court of Star Chamber is in the reign of Elizabeth, but throughout the Tudor period the Council, sitting as the King's Privy Council and transacting at the same time administrative and other business, exercised a wide and far-reaching jurisdiction wherever it happened to assemble, i.e. wherever the King was. It is impossible to lay sufficient emphasis upon this point. There was a very real distinction between the King's Privy Council and the Court of Star Chamber, even as courts of justice (3).

The sphere of the Council's jurisdiction was unlimited. There was no question now of what it had a right to do; it was a question of what it did. Under the Tudor Sovereigns the Council interfered in all matters small as well as great. It is impossible to give a complete analysis of the offences punished by it. The Council Register must be studied before the work of the Council, judicial as well as administrative, can be properly appreciated. The issue of proclamations invested it with enormous powers, for it was the executive body which issued them and either the judicial body which punished offences against them, or else the master of the Star Chamber when the latter court enforced them. A few examples of offences actually punished and of its judicial work may give some idea of its enormously wide field of action. It is not possible to draw a distinct line between the offences which the Council punished as the government and those which it punished as a law court. The characteristic feature of the Tudor period is the inseparable combination in the Council of political and judicial authority.

(1) A.P.C., XIX. p. 69; April, 1590.
(2) A.P.C., XXVI. 19th Dec., 1596; also XXVIII., 1st Dec., 1597; 17th April, 1598.
(3) See below, chapter IX.

Innumerable petitions were brought before the Council—some important, some trivial. Much of its judicial work was done at the instance of private suitors, for, in addition to asserting their right to act in every case where the law courts could not interfere, the King and his Council avowedly acted in cases in which other courts could not interfere. Of these cases breach of proclamations was one species, but only one in a thousand (1). The Council exercised an authority also not unlike that of a censor. The age was one of interference, and probably popular feeling invited the intervention of the government. Some of the cases were, no doubt brought before the Council because for various reasons it was impossible to get justice elsewhere. These suits chiefly concerned land, its ownership, inheritance, and occupation. Disturbances and quarrels over enclosures also came before the Council, and recognisances were entered into at the Council Board for such a trivial matter as the damaging of a fence. The rights of tenants were the especial care of the Council, and they were protected against grasping landlords, especially if the latter were powerful men or corporations. A " poor tenant " of the Dean and Chapter of Durham complained that he could not enjoy his tenement in peace. The Council ordered that he was to be relieved at the hands of those " that make profession of religion "(2). The Council also took action on the complaint of Lord Stafford's tenants in Gloucestershire that he was claiming them as villeins, whereas they protested that they were freemen and their ancestors before them. Lord Stafford was ordered to prosecute his right by the law of the realm and not to use " violent proceedings and threatenings " (3). Disputes concerning lands in Ireland came before the Council (4), contracts were enforced by it (5), the fraudulent use of trust money inquired into (6), action taken on behalf of poor debtors, especially those in prison (7), and the payment of a legacy enforced (8). In many ways the Council's jurisdiction approximated very closely to that of a court of equity.

Stronger and purer justice could be obtained at the Council Board than elsewhere; hence the number of cases which came before it. Moreover, the age was litigious. Many suits, too, were brought to the notice of the Council which later were taken before the Court of High Commission. Matrimony, alimony, cases of abduction, and family

(1) A.P.C., III. 22nd Oct., 1551; IX. 3rd Jan., 1576—punishments for refusing to sell at prices fixed by proclamation.

(2) A.P.C., X. 23rd June, 1578; 30th May, 1578; XI. 24th May, 1579.

(3) A.P.C., XIV. 31st March, 1586; 17th July, 1586.

(4) A.P.C., XI. 24th Nov., 1579; 20th March, 1580.

(5) Ibid., XIV. 29th May, 1586.

(6) Ibid., XV. 18th July, 1587.

(7) Ibid., X. 29th June, 1578; XI. 14th June, 1579; XVII. 23rd Jan., 1589.

(8) Ibid., XV. 5th Feb., 1588.

quarrels all came into the Council's purview (1). The victim of a confidence trick appealed for justice to the Council (2); petty private disputes were tried before it, such as the ownership of a horse and the occupation of the office of stewardship of Tamworth (3). It upheld apprenticeship contracts (4), punished a man for forcing the servant of Mr. Comptroller to open his master's letters (5), looked after the interests of government servants when absent on the Queen's service (6), and punished resistance to royal officials. The Council acted, too, as a censor of morals. It ordered the examination of a man concerning the birth of a child, commanded the Archbishop of Canterbury to punish two persons who had brought about a marriage between a boy of fifteen and a woman of twenty-five; a man appeared before it for the ill-treatment of his wife, and "buggery" was punished by it with imprisonment. The Serjeant-Porter sent to the Fleet for marrying near the throne, and the man who had procured the minister for the marriage secretly arrested (7). The designs of a match-making mother were frustrated by the Council on the complaint of the mother of the victim (8), but at last private suits became too much for the Council. "Nothing is more remarkable than the constant devotion with which this comparatively trivial daily work was carried on by those whose whole energies might well have been absorbed in anxious consideration of the dangers which were so closely besetting the country and the Queen. To Burghley and Walsingham, engaged in laboriously unravelling the tangled threads of a skein of conspiracy and murder, the details of the settlement of a quarrel between two Norfolk neighbours must have been supremely uninteresting; but they seldom missed a meeting of the Council " (9).

It was impossible, however, for the Council to try all the suits which came before it, and it constantly delegated the work to others. It would seem that private suits were very often given over to the Masters of Requests for settlement, for in January, 1553, a list of persons is recorded as appointed for hearing all such private suits as are customarily brought before the King or his Council and delivered to the Masters of Requests (10), and on 14th May, 1598, it sent a petition to them, even after the attacks of the Judges upon the Court, with orders to despatch it speedily with such favour as it was agreeable with "equity and good conscience and in your power to yield." On 12th November, 1549, the Council appointed Wednesday afternoon as the time when they would

(1) A.P.C., V. 18th Aug., 1555; XV. 11th April, 1587; IX. 23rd July, 1576 VIII. 14th June, 1575.

(2) Ibid., XV. 6th Sept., 1587.

(3) Ibid., I. 4th Sept., 1542; X. 22nd June, 1578.

(4) Ibid., IX. 27th June, 1576.   (5) Ibid., 4th September, 1578.

(6) Ibid., VIII. 7th Nov., 1574; XI. 18th March, 1580; XVII. 15th June, 1589.

(7) A.P.C., VII. 23rd Aug., 1565; 29th Aug., 1565.

(8) A.P.C., XV. 6th Sept., 1587; XVI. 30th June, 1588; XVIII. 15th March, 1590.

(9) A.P.C., XIV., introduction p. 10.

(10) E.g. A.P.C., III., 6th Oct., 1551.

hear the Masters of Requests " if matter for the King of greater importance did not hinder."

No incident of daily life in England was too trivial to find a place in the Register, but on 15th April, 1582, the Council in self-defence determined that henceforth no private suits which could obtain redress in any of the ordinary Courts were to come before the Council Board "unless they shall concern the preservation of her Majesty's peace, or shall be of some public consequence to touch the government of the Realm." And no letters for the benefit of such private suitors were to be signed by any of the Council unless brought in by one of the clerks attending at the time and signed with his name at the foot (2). Judging from the entries in the Register, this had no effect in diminishing the work of the Council. In 1589 the Council again took order concerning private suits, because it was so " pestered " at the times of assembling for Her Majesty's special services that it could hardly proceed in the causes which concerned Her Majesty and the Realm. Moreover, such private suits ought to be settled in the ordinary Courts of Law, asserted the Council, and the Judges and Justices of those Courts " find cause of offence, as derogating the lawful authority of those said Courts and places of judgment." No private suits which could be heard and determined elsewhere were henceforth to come before the Council. If, later on, the parties complained that they could not get redress in the ordinary courts, " if justice or the usual help is denied unto them," then the Council reserved to itself the right to take action. No man was to be debarred, however, by this order from informing against anyone in cases of treason or conspiracy or any crime concerning the honour and safety of Her Majesty (1). This apparently had little effect, for in 1594 the Privy Council made a fresh order. Every private suit was to go first before a Master of Requests and the Clerk of the Council " then attendant upon hearing of the complaints." These were to report to the Council cases proper for it to deal with, and to reject such as were " not meet for the Privy Council nor the Queen nor any ordinary Court of Justice or Equity." Such rejected persons were not to be admitted by the Queen's Porter (2).

The Council lent a ready ear to charges of treason and sedition, but though it examined cases of treason and decided whether words were treasonable, yet it never tried the cases (3). Lewd and seditious words were punished by it, and it was the sole judge of what amounted to sedition. This sometimes, as under Mary, varied with the disposition of the dominant faction (4). Besides taking cognisance of seditious words against the Sovereign and against itself, the Council punished also similar criticisms of individual members (5). The press was controlled by the Council. It acted as a prize court. Pirates were tried before it or sent to the Admiralty Court. It punished brawls, riots, assaults, and non-payment of forced loans. It was the court for foreign merchants. It decided disputes between trading or other corporations such as the Universities of Oxford

(1) A.P.C., XVIII. 8th Oct., 1589.

(2) Dyson: " Proclamations," f. 326.

(3) L. and P., IX. 37; A.P.C., XXVI. 15th Oct., 1596.

(4) A.P.C., IV. 15th August, 1553.

(5) A.P.C., IV. 12th May, 1553; XVI. 7th Aug., 1588.

and Cambridge (1) and the municipal authorities. Forgery and false coining came before the Board, together with robbery and burglary, wrecking, breaches of proclamations, complaints against monopolists, forestallers and regrators, defaulting subsidy collectors, individuals refusing to supply levies for the army, and persons without licences of various kinds. It ordered the punishment of juries for what it considered unjust verdicts (2), punished quarrels in the Palace precincts, endeavoured to check superstition and the practice of magic ,conjuration, and "prophesyings," the eating of flesh in Lent, and the abuses of purveyance. It acted as a kind of Court-Martial and punished deserters from the Low Countries in 1587 (3), and the captains of those ships which returned, leaving Drake in the lurch in 1589 (4). A case of poisoning came before it in 1598 (5); poachers constantly appeared before the Board, and the Game Laws were enforced by it. Trivial cases, such as the shaving of a dog, ill-treatment of a maid by her mistress, disturbance in a lady's apartments, a man called a liar in the Chamber of Presence—all were cases for the Council (6). It punished the unlicensed painting of the portrait of "Her Majesty's person and visage to Her Majesty's great offence, and disgrace of that beautiful and magnanimous Majesty wherewith God hath blessed her" (7), concerned itself with the quality of bread sold in London (8), the malpractices of Western clothiers with danger to Sir Christopher Hatton's servant (9), and the disputes between Anne of Cleves and her household (10). Those refusing to pay Ship-Money appeared before it (11). The Council, was however, very merciful, and remitted a clergyman "for this once," accused of seditious words, because he was of "no great wit and less learning" (12). Another, accused of "lewd prophesies," was discharged "because he was a very simple honest, man" (13). In 1578 the Council sent certain of the Yeomen of the Guard, suspected of belonging to the "Family of Love," to the Bishop of London. He certified that their religion was sound, and the Council, in thanking him, ordered the Guard, before they returned, "to repair into some street out of the city where they may remain for to take the air for five or six days" (14). In 1548 Lord Thomas Howard was summoned before the Board because, "amongst other young gentlemen of the Court, he had used himself

(1) Strictly speaking, the Universities were not incorporated till much later.

(2) A.P.C., IX. 19th Dec., 1576; I. 28th April, 1543.

(3) A.P.C., XV. passim.

(4) A.P.C., XVII. passim.

(5) A.P.C., XXVIII. 12th April, 1598.

(6) A.P.C., IV. 15th Sept., 1558; IX. 26th May, 1577; VII. 17th Jan., 1564; XI. 18th March, 1580.

(7) A.P.C., XXVI., p. 96.

(8) A.P.C., VIII. 20th March, 1574.

(9) A.P.C., IX. 1577.

(10) A.P.C., V. 17th Sept., 1556.

(11) A.P.C., XVI. 14th July, 1588.

(12) A.P.C., II. 30th March, 1547 (p. 465).

(13) A.P.C., III. 21st May, 1550.

(14) A.P.C., X. 12th October, 1578.

in disputations of Scriptural matters more largely and indiscreetly than good order did permit " (1). The Council saw to it that justice was done to the poor, especially to those who could not afford to pursue a long suit at law (2).

After the breach with Rome, the King, as Supreme Head, exercised supreme ecclesiastical jurisdiction. As a matter of course he acted through his Council, and more business was added to the work already superintended by his over-worked Councillors. Towards the end of Elizabeth's reign the ecclesiastical work of the Council was gradually delegated to the Court of High Commission, although, as will be shown later, before the Court of High Commission existed there had been frequent appointments of Commissioners for causes ecclesiastical, to whom the ecclesiastical work of the Council had been entrusted. But even so the Council transacted much ecclesiastical business of its own. Recusants were dealt with by the Board, assemblies of " Non-Conformists " and " the Family of Love " were suppressed and the ring leaders brought before the Council (3). It enforced the banishment of seminary priests, looked after the collection of tithes, forbad unlicensed preaching, saw to the proper payment of a curate, and imprisoned the " Light of the Faith " in Newgate (4). Those who heard Mass were brought before it, although to hear and celebrate the same was an offence of which the common law courts took cognisance (5). Disputes over livings were referred to the Council and the recusancy laws strictly enforced. The light thrown by the Register on the Council's method of dealing with heretics effectually destroys the fable of the loyalty of the recusants and the services rendered by them at the time of the Armada. Just at that time especially the Register is full of entries concerning them; the laws against them were more rigorously enforced than ever before, and Roman Catholics were forced to sell their arms, by the command of the Council, that the loyal subjects of the Queen might be suitably armed at this time of danger (6). On 27th December, 1589, the Council ordered that a gaoler in Lancashire, who was out of pocket over the lodging and diets of the recusants in his care, was to have a third part of the money accruing to the Queen by recusancy fines in Chesire and Yorkshire. Any trouble occurring over Divine Service came before the Council, heretic bishops were tried before it (7), and on 28th July, 1557, the Council required from the Abbot of Westminster a list of those persons who had taken advantage of the restored right of sanctuary, with a note of the causes compelling them to take the step.

(1) A.P.C., I. 2nd May, 1546.

(2) A.P.C., IX. 10th July, 1576; XI. 25th Feb.; 17th March, 1579; XXXII., p. 268, 10th Oct., 1600.

(3) A.P.C., X. 19th Sept.; 15th Dec., 1578.

(4) A.P.C., IV. 2nd March, 1554.

(5) A.P.C., XI. 1st Jan., 1580.

(6) A.P.C., XV., XVI., XVIII., XIX., passim.

(7) A.P.C., II. 30th June, 1548; III. 28th Sept., 1551; VI. 15th July, 1558.

Much of the Council's judicial work was done by arbitration, the arbitrators being appointed by the Council (1), and many cases were referred by it to be tried elsewhere, e.g., to the Star Chamber(2), to the Lord Mayor of London and his brethren (3), to the Common Law (4), and to the Assizes (5). Occasionally the Council ordered stay of proceedings in another Court (6); in 1589 proceedings in the Court of Delegates were to cease because the case was depending " before their Lordships in the Star Chamber " (7).

The Council is often recorded as consulting the law officers of the Crown before venturing to pronounce sentence (8), and it frequently urged the Justices of the Peace to take action, and kept the sheriffs active in doing their duty.

Occasionally the Council seems to have tried to enforce martial law, or to permit its enforcement in time of peace. In 1547 a letter was sent to the Lord Deputy of Ireland giving the Chancellor authority to make out letters patent under the Great Seal " for the enlargement of the Marshal's authority to do execution upon malefactors by death or otherwise," according to his instructions from the Lord Deputy and Council. Such authority was not to be abused, however; in case of such an event, it was to be " restrained in time lest it escape into any inconvenience " (9). In 1513 Rymer records a commission to Sir Thomas Lovell to hear and determine all murders, treasons, etc., in the absence of the Earl of Surrey, Marshal of England (10). In 1589 Elizabeth, in order to cope with the disorderly soldiers returned from abroad, appointed Provost-Marshals with authority for a limited time to proceed by martial law against those " who shall offend against a proclamation in that behalf published." These officials were found to be very necessary and the time of their appointment was extended. They were supported by contributions from the districts which they supervised, and individuals who criticised them and refused to contribute to their maintenance were called before the Council (11).

(1) A.P.C., X. 12th Oct., 1577; XV. 28th May, 1587.

(2) A.P.C., XI. 10th Jan., 1580.

(3) A.P.C., XV. 4th Nov., 1587; XVII. 26th May, 1589.

(4) A.P.C., III. 29th Aug., 1550; VII. 18th Feb., 1565; XVII. 25th May, 1589.

(5) A.P.C., VIII. 17th and 18th June, 1571; XVIII. 10th Aug., 1589.

(6) A.P.C., VI. 13th Jan., 1557; X. 22nd June, 1578.

(7) A.P.C., 28th Jan., 1589.

(8) P. and O., VII. 29th Jan., 1541; A.P.C., V. 3rd May, 1554; VIII. 15th Dec., 1573.

(9) A.P.C., II. Appendix. Harleian MS., 27th Aug., 1547.

(10) Rymer: Foedera, II. 7th Sept., 1513.

(11) A.P.C., XVIII., 21st Dec., 1589.

The Council's jurisdiction was mostly remedial and corrective. It was appealed to when no satisfaction could be obtained elsewhere (1). Appeals from the Channel Islands went to it. When referring a case to another court, it asked to be informed when justice was impossible or no decision could be arrived at (2). It interfered when justice was delayed, and gave better and fairer decisions (3). Many were the requests to be heard before the Council (4): in 1550 a man was given his choice whether he would be tried by the law or fined by the King with the advice of the Lords, and he chose the latter (5). This, however, may well have taken place on account of the inability of the Council to inflict the death penalty which the common law then provided for so many offences. The Council took cognisance of offences unknown to law (6), ordered trials to be conducted with impartiality (7), and released men and women imprisoned unjustly by other courts (8). In 1579 the College of Physicians was ordered to release a Dutchwoman whom they had caused to be imprisoned for practising physic without a licence, and they were ordered to signify to the Council " what hurt hath been done by her to any of Her Majesty's subjects by her said practice" (9.) Sheriffs (10) and defaulting government servants generally were tried before the Council Board, and this may be regarded as a dangerous experiment in *droit administratif*.

The Council was obliged to recognise some limit to its own judicial powers. In 1511 the Chancellor was directed to send letters to the sheriffs of London to liberate a prisoner in the Counter; the King had previously sent letters for the purpose, but they had been found " not sufficient discharge " (11). In 1590 a Scotchman had been wrecked upon the coast of Norfolk and robbed and spoiled of his goods; he was suing before the Council for restitution. The English ambassador in Scotland was ordered to tell James that the Privy Council in England had not the power of the Privy Council in Scotland in like cases to " take order that the parties interested might have satisfaction of the goods and lands of those that were found guilty, besides the corporal imprisonment "; they in England " had not any authority orderly by any law (as Councillors only of State) to seize any lands and goods of any subject, which proceedings belonged only to judicial courts." They had done what they were allowed to do in such cases; they had committed the party to prison until he complied with their order, and they advised the plaintiff to sue in the Admiralty Court (12). In the thirty-fourth year of Elizabeth the judges resolved that neither King nor Council could commit to prison for more than

(1) L. and P., IV. Pt. I. 106.

(2) L. and P., II. 1915; A.P.C., X. 1st April, 1578.

(3) A.P.C., IX. 16th Dec., 1576.

(4) L. and P., II. Pt. I. 2; 911.

(5) A.P.C., II., 21st Feb., 1550.

(6) A.P.C., VII., 9th June, 1565.

(7) A.P.C., VIII., 25th Jan.. 1575, XV., 7th Dec., 1587.

(8) A.P.C., XIX., 5th July, 1590.

(9) A.P.C., XI., 28th April, 1579.

(10) A.P.C., XXVI., 11th Jan., 1597.

(11) L. and P., I., 1853; A.P.C., XXX., 5th August, 1600.

(12) A.P.C., 27th July; 10th August, 1590.

twenty-four hours unless they assigned cause when demanded by habeas corpus (1). In 1600 the decision of the Council in a controversy between the citizens of London and Newcastle was questioned, and the matter finally referred to the Attorney-General for his decision (2). Magna Charta was certainly discovered before the 17th century, for the Council made use of its authority in 1600 to declare that the use of Venice weights by the silkmen of London was "against the law in the Great Charter, and sundry good statutes " (3).

It would seem that individual Councillors tried disputes and even committed to prison. We have seen that the Clerks of the Council and the Secretary of State were given cases to try, and that their decisions were confirmed by the Council. In 1540 it is recorded in the minute book that a letter had been sent to the Lord Chancellor for a commission to be sent to the Council, " whereby in matters touching the King they and every of them should have authority to take recognisance of such as appear before them " (4). In 1553 is recorded the release of a man who had been a long time in prison in the Porter's Lodge, committed thither by Lord Cobham and Mr. Secretary Petre on suspicion of robbery. He was released because no proof could be brought against him (5). On 28th April, 1588, a letter was sent to the Lord Chief Justice and the rest of Her Majesty's judges, to the effect that of late certain persons had been committed to prison by the Council, when such a course had seemed fit in their opinion. These same prisoners had procured writs of habeas corpus to be delivered out of prison without the knowledge of the Council, and so Judges were admonished to have more respect towards the Council, and, when asked to issue such a writ of habeas corpus, to take order " that such Councillor as did commit the party might be made privy thereunto " (6). This would seem proof enough that individual Councillors did commit to prison. Moreover, when the Council took order in 1589 concerning private suits which came before it, it is recorded that " their Lordships have promised and concluded among themselves that neither they in general, nor any of them in particular, will hereafter, in regard of any private person or cause, contrary to the form of this order, move, require, or do anything that shall impugn or violate the same " (7). Later in the reign we have Anderson's record and the request of the Judges and Barons of the Exchequer to the Lord Chancellor and Lord Treasurer made in 1591. They desired some order to be taken that persons might not be committed to or detained in prison, by the command of any nobleman or councillor, against the laws of the Realm. Some have been imprisoned and suffered great loss for bringing ordinary action at common law and had been compelled to abandon them against their will, although judgment and execution had been obtained. Writs had been directed to

(1) H.M.C., Lonsdale MSS. Notes in Parliament, 15th May, 1626. This is very possibly a dim recollection of Anderson's record, for which see below.

(2) A.P.C., XXX., 29th June, 1600.

(3) A.P.C., XXX., 3rd Feb., 1600. A. F. Pollard asserts that Magna Charta had not been " discovered " at this time. See review of A.P.C. in E.H.R., XV.

(4) P. and O., VII., 2nd Sept., 1540.

(5) A.P.C., IV., 7th Jan., 1553.

(6) A.P.C., XVI.

(7) A.P.C., XVIII., 8th October, 1589.

their gaolers and they had been discharged; but they had been again committed to prison in secret places, so that, on complaint made, the Queen's Court could not learn to whom to direct the writ. Many officers and serjeants of London had been committed for executing writs sued out of the Court at Westminster. Men were sent for to London by pursuivants, and constrained by imprisonment to withdraw their lawful suits and pay the pursuivants great sums of money. The judges consider that in one case only might a man be put in custody by the Council, and not delivered by the courts or judges, viz. when committed " by Her Majesty's commands or by order of the Council for high treason." Even then the judges might award the Queen's writ to bring such persons before them, and if on return thereof the cause of imprisonment was properly shown then the prisoners ought to be remanded and not delivered (1). This was a direct attack on the Council's jurisdiction, which was probably represented in its very worst light by the Common Law judges, impelled as they were by jealousy. Both versions that we have of this answer of the judges are singularly obscure, and perhaps intentionally so, and there is a considerable difference between them. The judges manage to avoid a distinct declaration whether they will or will not bail prisoners when the return to the writ of habeas corpus merely asserts that the prisoner was committed by the command of the King or the command of the Council. Professional feeling was rising, and it is not surprising that the legality of the jurisdiction of the Council was attacked whenever possible.

It would be interesting to know what became of the petitions to Parliament during the Tudor period. Probably in the early fifteenth century Parliament had begun to hand over these petitions to the Privy Council it controlled, for fewer and fewer are recorded on the Rolls, and one may go further and hazard a suggestion that as this practice became more common, and as Parliament grew more discredited and inclined as we have seen, to allow the Council a statutory jurisdiction in some cases, these petitions came to be made directly to the Council.

In 1547 the Council appears to decide a disputed Parliamentary election at Sandwich. The Mayor, at the instigation of the Jurates, had proceeded to a new election, and had dismissed the Town Clerk because he refused to surrender the town seal. The town was ordered to pay £100 to the King for not returning burgesses, and smaller sums to the injured parties (2). In 1597 the Archbishop of York petitioned the Council that Sir John Saville and Sir Thomas Fairfax had carried their election for the shire by " disorderly scenes and partial and unlawful behaviour of the under sheriff." The Justices of the Peace wrote to Sir John Stanhope asking him to request the Queen and the Privy Council that they might not, by violence and practice, have their free election taken from them. One of the knights returned was ordered to appear before the Council, and on 23rd October, 1597, the Register records that Sir John Saville was this day committed to the Fleet by warrant from the Lord Keeper, Lord Buckhurst, and Mr. Secretary (3). On 10th December, 1555, Sir Antony

(1) The reading given by Dicey is " committed by Her Majesty's special commandment, or by order from the Council Board, or for treason touching Her Majesty's person " (p. 116), following Hallam, chap. 5.

(2) A.P.C., II. Appendix, 11th Dec., 1547.

(3) Hatfield Papers, VII. 3rd Oct.; 5 Oct.; 19th Oct., 1597; A.P.C., XXVIII. 23rd Oct., 1597.

Kingston was committed by the Council to the Tower for "contemptuous behaviour and great disorder in the Parliament House."

B.—ADMINISTRATIVE.

Our modern system has been created much more by the administrative action of the King's Privy Council than historians allow. The pivot of Tudor administration was the Privy Council. The records of its everyday working are not exciting reading, but it is only by its everyday working that an institution can be judged. The efficacy and stability of a government do not depend upon its relations with eminent men, but upon its treatment of the millions upon whose lives the most minute biographical research can throw no ray of light. The ordinary citizen was never governed with a more enlightened insight into his real needs and interests than under the Tudors. Thus he was always on the side of the government, and regarded with comparative indifference the fall of Wolsey and Cromwell, the proscription of the Poles and the Howards, the hanging of the monks under Henry, and the burning of the Protestants under Mary (1). The Council Register provides a partial explanation of this phenomenon; it is obvious, from the infinite pains which the Council took to do the right thing even in the most trivial cases, that the government of the Tudor sovereigns was fair and honest in intention. They wielded their extensive prerogative in the legitimate interests of good administration, and not with the ulterior object of enforcing any theory of divine right; they practised what eighteenth century sovereign preached—a paternal despotism. During the Tudor period the resources of the Crown were sufficient to give ample rewards for every kind of service. In respect of the work accomplished, the Council was always a power most vital to the well-being of England. It was free from the vice of formalism; industrious, persistent, and watchful, it was useful less in the way of conspicuous dramatic action than in the constant control and supervision of minor interests. It acted in matters for which Parliament had neither time nor patience nor knowledge; in times of the utmost difficulty and danger it was the only body capable of meeting the emergency, and once at least in the period under review it was instrumental in saving the kingdom from utter destruction.

The time of the Council was occupied, as that of every Government must be, with an infinite number of trivial matters. It had at one moment to settle questions of policy, at another to provide funds by which the administration could be carried on, at another to review minute accounts, to communicate with aliens or merchants, or to interfere for the preservation of the King's peace. With its assistance exclusively the King dealt with those cases, whatever their nature, which belonged to the prerogative only.

The administrative work of the Council is excellently well illustrated by the subject matter of the proclamations issued by it. Under Henry VII. Papal Bulls were promulgated in this way. Other proclamations relate to foreign affairs, war, peace, truces, the expulsion of aliens, preparations against invasion, etc. In 1487 trade with the possessions of Maximilian was restricted, import and export alike being forbidden without special licence under the Great Seal, although by the statute 23 H. VI., c. 5, the practice of licensing had been abolished. By proclamation a staple of metals was incorporated at Southampton in 1492; duties payable by Venetian merchants were raised; trade with Flanders stopped altogether in 1493 with the exception of the wool staple fixed at Calais, until resumed by the Intercursus Magnus in 1496, which latter was confirmed and elucidated by proclamation in 1499. The frequency of proclamations concerning the coinage

(1) Pollard, in review of A.P.C. in E.H.R., XV.

shown that it was a subject of great anxiety to the King and his Council. There are undated proclamations against the exchange and export of precious metals. Another prohibited the introduction of the depreciated Irish coinage into England. Distraint of knighthood was a source of revenue throughout the Tudor period, and was enforced by proclamation. In 1493 a proclamation was issued against vagabonds, the first of a long series throughout the Tudor period. The affairs of Calais formed the subject of several proclamations and the internal troubles of the reign have left their mark on its proclamations in warnings and pardons: Henry's first proclamation was an offer of pardon (1).

The actual government of the country was concentrated in the hands of the Council, either directly as in Central and Southern England, or through Deputies and Councils as in Wales, Ireland, the North and Calais. The reception of Perkin Warbeck in Ireland brought home to Henry VII. the necessity of bringing that country into closer connection with England. Poyning's Law in 1498 provided that every Bill intended for presentation to the Irish Parliament should be drafted by the Irish Privy Council, certified into England under the Great Seal of Ireland, and then considered and approved by the English Privy Council.

The number of proclamations issued by Henry VIII. amounts to two hundred. Only thirty-six of these purport to be made by the advice and consent of the Council, but the greater part of the others are pure mandates. "The King our Sovereign Lord straitly chargeth and commandeth," is a common form. The recurrence of the advice clause in the proclamations of 1541-6 is probably due to the Act of Proclamations in 1539, which gave to proclamations so issued the force of law with certain limitations which are well known.

The share of the Privy Council in the issue of proclamations is not very clear. We have its records for only seven years of Henry's reign, but, of all the proclamations issued in that time, only three are mentioned in the Register: 6th May, 1541, for the one Bible of the greatest volume to be placed in every church; 15th July, 1543 against resort to the Court on account of the plague; 7th July, 1545, for the preservation of game around London. Apparently the Council had power to issue proclamations without the Royal signature: on 20th October, 1540, a proclamation forbidding Londoners to resort to Court was issued under the "Stamp and Signet." Proclamations seem to have been drawn up and sanctioned in very informal fashion. In 1538 Cromwell, referring to the conveyance of coin out of the Realm, asserted "that the King, with the advice of his Council, even if there were no Statute, might, to withstand so great a danger, make proclamations which should be as effective as any Statute" (2). Of the well-known Statute of 31 Hen. VII., c. 8, it need only be noted that the advice of the Council was required for proclamations creating non-statutory offences. That of 34 and 35 Hen. VIII., c. 23, enacted that judgment might be given against offenders by nine of the King's Council. Steele declares it to be a matter for conjecture how the issue of proclamations was proved in a court of law, since they are nowhere on record, except that of 23rd Jan., 1542, of Henry's style as King of Ireland. But he appears to have overlooked the fact that proclamations were not enforced by the courts of law. The Council issued the proclamation; the Star Chamber saw to its enforcement. Statutory powers to issue certain other proclamations had been given, chief amongst them being those relating to the prices of wines, which, according to 28 Hen. VIII., c. 14, were to be fixed by certain of the Council with the help of the two Chief Justices.

(1) Steele: "Proclamations," I., p. 77.
(2) L. and P., VIII., 1042.

There were many proclamations in Henry's reign dealing with the coinage. Others of considerable importance deal with religion. In 1529 a proclamation was directed against the sale of heretical books, a second one included among forbidden books vernacular translations of the Scriptures, and a third promised an authorised translation. In September, 1530, the introduction of Bulls from Rome was forbidden; in 1535 sheriffs were instructed to report to the Council on the obedience of bishops and clergy to the orders of King and Parliament. Many proclamations were issued against printing; in 1538 it was ordered that no book in English should be printed in England until it had first been examined by the King, or one of the Privy Council, or a bishop. In 1546 Henry's religious proclamations were brought to an end by one suppressing all English books printed by Frith, Tyndal, Bull, and others, including Tyndal and Coverdale's New Testament. Other proclamations dealt with enclosures, and in February 1529 one was issued commanding "all enclosed grounds to be laid open and the ditches filled, and the hedges and pales broken down and taken away before Easter next." The prevalence of vagabondage, the price and supply of corn and victuals of all kinds, were all subjects for proclamations. Many were issued enforcing the laws concerning vagabondage (1). Sumptuary regulations also frequently appeared. In 1517 the Council limited the number of dishes to a meal, and enforced its orders by threat of punishment before the Board. There were proclamations against excess in dress, enforcing Acts of Parliament (2), for the encouragement of archery, to put down shooting with cross-bows and hand-guns, and also games of chance and skill. In 1544 a newsbook was ordered by proclamation to be brought in and burnt within twenty-four hours on pain of imprisonment (3). Prices were fixed for wine, sugar, flesh, and arms. Regulations were made affecting wool and kersey-making. Declarations of war and peace, rebellions, the maintenance of Calais and Boulogne, the plague, the preservation of hawks' eggs and game, dispensation from the observation of Lent, and disputes about tithes in London are the other subjects dealt with by Henry's Council through the medium of proclamations.

Under Edward VI. the Statute of Proclamations was repealed. Enclosures and the coinage are the chief subjects of his proclamations. There were vain attempts to check the rise in prices, and proclamations were issued ordering the strict enforcement of the laws against forestallers and for the supply of the markets. One provided a penalty of six months' imprisonment and fine at will, or the pillory with loss of ears, for spreading reports of a further debasement of the coinage. Justices of the Peace were ordered to enforce a proclamation, upon pain of heavy forfeitures, fixing the price of victuals. Many proclamations were made relating to the religious settlement. They provided for the payment of pensions to the religious, checked the unruly behaviour of the London mob to priests in the streets, prohibited irreverent discussion of the Sacrament, forbad unlicensed preaching, suppressed rumours, prohibited the export of victuals and arms, and compelled printers or importers of English books to obtain licenses. On 28th April, 1551, a proclamation was issued "for the reform of vagabonds, tellers of news, sowers of seditious rumours, players and printers without license, and divers other disordered persons." The performance of interludes was forbidden altogether without the license of the King or his Privy Council.

(1) Steele: Nos. 125, 126, 132, 157.

(2) Ibid: Nos. 138, 156.

(3) Ibid: No. 253.

The Council Register and the State Papers witness to the continual activity of the Council in every department of national life under Mary. The Statute of 1 and 2 Philip and Mary, c. 3, s. 11, gave statutory power to the Council to order the arrest of any noble spreading seditious rumours, although he was to be tried by his peers. Most of Mary's proclamations are concerned with the coinage and religion. Obedience to the Legate's orders was enforced by proclamation; the jurisdiction of the Bishops over the circulation of books was affirmed; and the possession of a certain tract was proclaimed to be rebellion, entailing immediate execution by martial law (1). Seditious rumours, vagabonds, the expulsion of the Scots and other foreigners, the war with France, the manning of the Navy, orders to gentlemen to return to their homes in the country, were all subjects of proclamations. Others forbad quarrelling in churches or churchyards, and the wearing of unduly long rapiers; several protected game, and afforested certain areas.

Of the legality of these proclamations at Common Law it is difficult to speak with certainty, but probably no judge would have assented to that of June, 1555, denouncing the penalty of martial law for the possession of a book, even treasonable. Coke later declared that of 30th March, 1558, forbidding the import of French wines to be illegal.

The Privy Council of Elizabeth exercised its extensive powers in every direction. In this reign for the first time we find the Privy Council issuing orders in its own name in the form of proclamations, such as those for the reformation of abuses in dress and for the proper observation of Lent (2). The coinage was regulated by proclamation, and the settlement of religion, and the questions connected with it, were frequent subjects of proclamations. Order was taken in May, 1559, for licensing interludes. Anabaptists were ordered into exile at twenty days' notice, 22nd September, 1560; the importation of controversial treatises against the Reformation settlement was forbidden; bitter attacks on Burghley led to a proclamation against seditious slander in 1573; and another ordered the strictest enforcement of the Act of Uniformity. Stubbs' "Gaping Gulf" was suppressed by proclamation in 1579. The sect and books of the Family of Love were to be suppressed; in 1581 students were recalled from beyond the seas, foreign travel restrained, and the harbouring of Jesuits forbidden. Separatists were often the subject of a proclamation. The Martin Marprelate tracts led to the issue of a proclamation against them, promising pardon to anyone informing the Council of the printers or authors of the same (3). Men suspected of being implicated were tried before the Council Board (4). In 1588 the coming of the Armada was heralded by the Bull of Sixtus V. and a number of controversial tracts, the publication of which was ordered by proclamation to be punished under martial law (5).

Other proclamations dealt with the observance of Lent. They prohibited the eating of flesh in Lent, and were issued together with orders of the Privy Council on the same sumject. The penalties ordained were much greater than those authorised by the Act of Edward VI. The first orders of the Council on this subject which have been preserved date from February, 1589, and after that date they were issued annually. After

(1) Steele: No. 488.
(2) Steele: Nos. 515, 811, etc.
(3) Steele: No. 812.
(4) A.P.C., XVIII., 24th August, 1589.
(5) Steele: No. 802, 1st July, 1588.

1592 the Lords Lieutenant of counties were commanded to prescribe these orders to the Justices of the Peace and the officers of corporate towns, the sheriffs being altogether ignored. Fish-days and the licensing of ale houses were also subjects of proclamations.

Piracy and foreign trade were constant sources of proclamations throughout the reign of Elizabeth. In March, 1572, a stringent order was issued against the Beggars of the Seas, threatening death by martial law to anyone aiding or joining them (1), and from that time piracy appears to have been officially veiled under commissions of reprisals. Many proclamations related to the export of cloth, fish, and grain. Others fixed the price of wines, and one in January, 1564, forbad the importation of any French wine at all. A maximum price was fixed for hops and for provisions at Tilbury Camp and near London (2). The export of grain was frequently restrained, its waste checked, laws for planting hemp enforced, and the growth of woad forbidden. Many proclamations were issued before the unlawful importation of caps was stopped. Social life was dealt with in several proclamations. Sumptuary regulations were issued, fixing the dress of every class of men according to their rank and income (3). The length of rapiers and daggers was limited, and in 1574 the dress of women regulated. The last order issued on such subjects attributed the great decay in hospitality to the expense of dress. "Dags and hand-guns" were several times prohibited, and orders for the "maintenance of artillery" and the keeping up of a supply of horses given. Proclamations adjourned the law courts on account of the plague. The regulation of wages by the Justices of the Peace was made with the authority and approval of the Council. The history of the Great Lottery can be traced in five broadsides, and the turbulence of London apprentices in some very severe proclamations. Regulations for the swans on the river were issued from time to time. Weights and measures form the subject of a proclamation, the monopoly of saltpetre was withdrawn in 1590, regulations for the post-service were made, and the service controlled by the Council.

Many of Elizabeth's proclamations threatened offenders with penalty of martial law (4). Idlers and vagrants in London were to leave at once on pain of death, armed vagabonds were to be executed, rescuers of prisoners punished by death. Two proclamations were issued forbidding building in London (5), on the strength of which very heavy fines were inflicted in the Star Chamber. An order that all discharged pressed men were to be re-engaged by their former masters may be justified on the ground of public policy, but could hardly be enforced in a court of law. A proclamation of June, 1570, is almost the only sanitary measure of the reign. Before Elizabeth's death the mention of the Star Chamber had become an almost invariable sign of an order not enforceable by law (6).

The subjects of Elizabeth's proclamations are typical of the daily work in which the Council was engaged. All the matters mentioned in them give rise to entries in the Register at one time or another. As the Venetian ambassador wrote in 1551, "Matters of importance relating to the Sovereign or the people are referred to the King's Privy Council . . . and whatever they decide there is published by edicts and proclamations which have the vigour and force of laws, provided they do not extend to

(1) Steele: No. 668.
(2) Steele: Nos. 587, 803, 903.
(3) Ibid.: Nos. 515, 891.
(4) Ibid.: Nos. 668, 802, 805, 809, 818, 840, 873, 874, 879, 916.
(5) Ibid.: Nos. 749, 927.
(6) Ibid.: Nos. 638, 818, 871, 927, 932.

capital punishment or to the disinheritance of anyone; or that they be not in effect repugnant to the ancient Statutes. Those who disregard these proclamations are imprisoned, but not for life, and the decrees remain in force at the King's pleasure and during his reign; and this it what relates to the King's royal and absolute power " (1). The Venetian envoys were always well informed, but it is remarkable that so nice a constitutional point as the limitations upon the power of issuing proclamations should have been so clearly understood. It seems that these limitations were well known to all long before the famous dictum of the judges later.

One of the Council's most important duties was that of interviewing foreign ambassadors. Receptions were held before the Council, and the King's communications to ambassadors were commonly given in the same manner. It is from the letters of Spanish, Venetian, and French envoys that the best description of the Council's proceedings are obtained. In 1514 Henry wrote to Leo X. that, after many discussions between his Council and the French ambassadors, they had at last arranged a peace (2). It is recorded on 3rd Aug., 1550, that the young king, in answer to the French ambassador, " referred the answer to the Council." In 1562 the Council is recorded as replying to the French ambassador at the Guildhall (3). In 1572 De Spes was summoned before the Council at Whitehall, told that he had plotted with traitors against the Queen's life and the peace of the country, and would be expelled as Dr. Man, with far less reason, had been expelled from Spain (4). Individual members of the Council were occasionally used on diplomatic missions, and throughout the Tudor period it was quite customary to make use of the Clerks of the Council in this way. Nothing can be learned from the Register of this part of the Council's business; important matters of foreign policy were naturally not recorded in it.

The Council obtained its information from many different sources. Informers were always a power to be reckoned with by defaulting officials or criminals. In 1578 the Council desired information concerning Stukeley's projects in Ireland. As he and his Italians happened to be in Portugal, the Council called upon the Bristol merchants trading to that country to supply information as to his designs. Cromwell in Henry VIII.'s time, and Burghley and Walsingham under Elizabeth had elaborate systems of espionage, as had Essex and Sir Robert Cecil after them. The rival parties in the Council were apparently served by rival organisations of spies. Foreign spies caught in England were brought before the Council and imprisoned by it (5). Information concerning suspected sedition, heresy, or verbal treason must have been procured from spies or informers.

A large part of the public business in which the Council was engaged was naval or military. During the whole of the Tudor period the Privy Council retained, under the Crown, the immediate control of military affairs. The ancient obligation upon every freeman to defend his country still held good in the sixteenth century. Commissions of Array were issued by the authority of the Crown to leading persons in the counties and large towns, and to others possessing military experience, empowering them to make lists of the able-bodied men within their districts, to fix the arms, horses, and equipment to

(1) Venetian Calendar, May, 1551.
(2) L. and P., I. 5319.
(3) Forbes: " A Full View . . .," p. 150.
(4) Hume: " Burghley," p. 263.
(5) A.P.C., VI. 6th Jan., 1558.

be provided by each man, and to drill the forces so raised. These lists were to be sent in to the Privy Council. When required for active service, the forces were called out by means of special letters sent from the Council to the Lords-Lieutenants in the different counties. The entry in the Council Register for 2nd August, 1586, records some of the duties of these Lords-Lieutenants, such as to put in execution the orders appointed for last year for the training of horsemen and footmen in the counties of their Lieutenancies, "touching the provision of petoronells of the Justices," repressing the carriers of news, and looking to the landing of Jesuits, etc. A list follows of the Lieutenants of the various counties. The Crown seems to have appointed these Lieutenants through the medium of the Council, for in February, 1586, the Marquis of Winchester, Lieutenant of Hampshire, is recorded as being appointed to succeed the late Earl of Bedford in Dorsetshire.

The Council attended to every detail of the provisioning of the Army. On 30th August, 1542, it contracted with London brewers to supply beer for the Scottish expedition. On 6th Sept., 1545, it appointed commissariat officers for Boulogne, and in 1553 Muster Masters were appointed and instructions given to them. It gave orders concerning the arming and equipment of the Yeomen of the Guard, the officers of the Household, and other men about the Sovereign's person; they were ordered to provide their own weapons, or the cost would be deducted from their wages (1). All negotiations for supplies of mercenaries passed the Council's hands (2), but it would allow no English subject to enlist abroad without its express permission (3). Maimed soldiers were recommended by it to the charitable, and collections were ordered for their benefit after the sermons at St. Paul's Cross and elsewhere in the City (4). Impressment was ordered by the Council, especially in the case of the "idle and loose persons lurking" in the city of London. In 1588 the press-gang was, by command of the Council, used to complete the complements of the Queen's ships (5). Captains of experience were sent, in December, 1587, into the maritime counties to survey the fortifications and garrisons there; their pay was fixed by six of the Privy Council, the usual quorum for Council business. The victualling of the forces in the Low Countries is the subject of many entries in the Register (6). The payment of the Army was the business of the Council (7); it appointed "warden-generals" (8), ordered the appointment of chaplains paid at the rate of 20s. a day (9), and busied itself with contracts for the equipment of the forces in the Low Countries (10). Everything connected with the defence of the country either by land or water was the special care of the Council.

The navy was manned and equipped on principles similar to those which governed the maintenance of the army. Those who refused to contribute to the levies for the army or to the provision of ships were called before the Council and punished. Naval officials were appointed by it, and in 1557 the Lord Treasurer and the Lord Admiral appear to have been jointly responsible for the Fleet. The former undertook, if present wants were made good, not to spend more than £10,000 a year on the upkeep of the Fleet" (11).

(1) A.P.C., V. 6th Aug., 1556.   (2) A.P.C., VI. 18th Jan., 1558.
(3) A.P.C., VIII. 21st May, 1572; IX. 23rd Oct., 1575.
(4) A.P.C., XIV. 20th Nov., 1586.
(5) A.P.C., XVI. 21st Aug., 1588.
(6) A.P.C., XV.; XVI., passim.
(7) A.P.C., IV. 30th Sept., 1552.
(8) A.P.C., III. 25th Feb., 1551.
(9) Dom. Cal., 21st Sept., 1589.
(10) A.P.C. Dom. Cal., 5th April, 1595.
(11) A.P.C., VI. 8th Jan., 1558.

In Mary's reign, however, the naval forces of the Crown were neglected. The Council Register admirably illustrates the Council's control of the Fleet, especially during Elizabeth's reign and at the time of the Armada. Ammunition, victualling, even strategy were all directed by the Council (1). It gave orders concerning the Spanish prisoners taken (2), provided many precedents for the later Stuart ship-money, and prohibited the export of English commodities in foreign bottoms (3). In time of peril the Council showed itself at its best. When it realised the danger from Spain in 1579, immediate measures were taken. The fortifications at Portsmouth were surveyed, order taken concerning the maintenance of the beacons, arrangements made to supply crews in an emergency, an embargo laid on ships and mariners, seamen impressed, gun-powder imported, and general musters under special Commissioners ordered throughout the country(4). Throughout the Tudor period the Privy Council controlled and directed both military and naval affairs, and, especially towards the end of that time, this purely administrative work occupied most of the atention of the Board (5).

The Council had also ecclesiastical functions, and many of these were recognised by statute. "An Act concerning Peter's Pence and Dispensations," 25 Hen. VIII., c. 21, provided that licences and dispensations hitherto obtained from Rome should henceforth be obtained from the Archbishop of Canterbury. "An Act for the payment of tithes," 27 Hen. VIII., c. 20, provided that application for aid in compelling payment might be made by the ordinary to any of "the King's most honourable Council" or Justices of the Peace. These might imprison the offender until he promised to pay. By 28th Hen. VIII., c. 16, all Bulls, Faculties and Briefs were to be brought by the King's subjects "to such persons of his Council, or of the Masters of his Chancery, as the King's Highness should name and appoint, to be examined by them" before being lawfully re-granted by the Archbishop. The Chantries Act of Edward VI. empowered the King, with the advice of his Council, to convert the revenues of chantries "and other such abuses" to good and godly uses. By the statute 3 and 4 Ed. VI. c. 11, Edward was empowered to name, by the advice of his Council, thirty-two persons to examine the ecclesiastical laws, and compile such as should be thought convenient by him and his Council to be practised in the realm (6).

Recusants, Popish and otherwise, came especially into the Council's purview. It concerned itself with heretic-burning (7). It is often recorded as present at sermons (8). It ordered shrines to be taken down (9), though later, in 1600, it checked a piece of Puritan vandalism in the city (10). The servants of the Royal Household were commanded to attend church (11); the Corporation of Bristol to conform, and not have to be fetched to Divine Service by the Dean and Chapter (12). The Council appointed and deprived bishops, issued

(1) A.P.C. XVI. passim.
(2) A.P.C., XVI. 28th July, 1588.
(3) Ibid.: 25th March, 1588.
(4) A.P.C., XI. passim.
(5) A.P.C., IV., V., XVIII., XXVI., passim.
(6) See also Prothero: "Select Statutes," pp. 185, 206, 241.
(7) A.P.C., V. passim.
(8) "Diary of Henry Machyn," p. 248. Cam. Soc., 1848.
(9) P. and O., 22nd Sept., 1541.
(10) A.P.C., XXX. p. 27.
(11) A.P.C., XII. 7th Aug., 1580.
(12) A.P.C., VI. 24th Aug., 1557.

orders for the observation of Lent (1), and professed to be a judge of what was agreeable to the Christian religion (2). A Bible in Welsh was ordered to be used in Wales. The Council also licenced preaching and insisted upon beneficed clergy preaching; the clergy in the dioceses of Worcester and Hereford " as have many benefices, be non-resident and keep no hospitality, and have not in their churches the sermons required by the laws of Her Majesty's Injunctions," were required to contribute to the repair of a bridge, concerning which the inhabitants of Upton in Worcestershire had petitioned the Council (3). Much of the Council's ecclesiastical work in Elizabeth's reign was carried on by the Ecclesiastical Commission.

Another duty which fell to the Council was that of supervising education in the country. The Crown possessed statutory powers to make regulations for schools and colleges. On 5th June, 1552, a letter was sent to the Chancellor of the Augmentations ordering him to certify what free schools had been erected. In the same month the Deans and Chapters of Westminster, Canterbury and Worcester were bidden to place three children in their schools (4). The Council also interfered on behalf of poor schoolmasters: the Mayor and Corporation of Ludlow were ordered to pay the schoolmaster there £20 per annum, " appointed by their purchase of King Edward VI., for the entertainment of a schoolmaster," or to show the Lords of the Council their reasons for refusing to do so (5). The supervision of the erection and maintenance of schools occupied the attention of the Council (6). It looked to the education of the children of a Roman Catholic (7). It could permit or prohibit the reading of a book (8), and in 1582 there occurs an amusing instance of its educational zeal. One Christopher Ockland petitioned the Council concerning his book " De Anglorum Proeliis," a patriotic compilation which he had published at great expense. He had since added a short appendix on " the peaceable government of the Queen's Majesty." The Council wrote to the Commissioners for Causes Ecclesiastical recommending the book as worthy of being read, " especially in the common schools, where divers heathen poets are ordinarily used and taught, from which the youth of the realm receive rather infection in manners and education than advancement in virtue. In place of which poets their Lordships think fit this book were read and taught in the grammar schools." The Commissioners were ordered to write to all the bishops in the realm recommending that in all grammar and free schools Ockland's book should be read and taught by the schoolmasters, " in some one of their forms in the schools fit for that matter," in the place of such heathen poets as " Ovidi de arte amandi, de tristibus " (9).

Another most important branch of the Council's work was, not only under Edward VI. but in other reigns, its control over national finance. The coinage was its especial care, warrants for payment to the different Treasurers formed a large part of its daily

(1) A.P.C., XI. 13th Jan., 1579, and passim.
(2) Ibid.: 15th Jan., 1579.
(3) A.P.C., IX. 18th April, 1576.
(4) A.P.C., IV. 5th June; 14th June, 1552.
(5) A.P.C., IX. 3rd May, 1576.
(6) A.P.C., XVII. 9th March; 30th June, 1589.
(7) Stafford MSS., p. 193; H.M.C.
(8) L. and P., VII. 571; A.P.C., XIII. 6th Aug.; 9th Sept., 1581.
(9) A.P.C., XIII. 21st April, 1582.

business (1), and it also negotiated foreign loans (2). It administered the royal estates, and also seemed to have charge of the Privy Purse. On December 12th, 1545, a warrant was sent to the Treasurer of the Augmentations to pay £56 in wages to the " keepers of the King's privy boats " (3). On 17th April, 1547, it settled the dress bills of the two Princesses. Under the minor Edward it had full control of the Privy Purse (4). Payments were made by it for the performance of plays before Elizabeth. It issued warrants to the Mint for the Queen's Maundy money (5), the debtors of the Crown came before it, and it carefully watched all the financial rights of the Crown (6). The Statute of 7 Edward VI., c. 1, provided that all collectors of the King's revenue, when required by the Council, should declare in writing the sums due to the King; further, they should render yearly accounts to the King and Privy Council. The Council controlled the wardships of the Crown (7), and forced loans and benevolences were levied with its advice (8). There was no appropriation of supplies by Tudor Parliaments; and the Council spent money as it wished. In April, 1553, a warrant under the sign-manual was sent to William Dansell, Receiver-General of Wards and Liveries, to pay to the Surveyor of Works £500 to be expended as the Privy Council directed. All monies went through the Council's hands, and none was paid out except by the King's order or theirs (9). On 18th Oct., 1558, the Tellers of the Exchequer appeared before the Council, and were ordered to presen to Mr. Secretary a full report of the sums of money in their custody, and, in future, not to " defray " any money without warrant from the Council. Every week henceforth they were to present to the Council an account of the money received and disbursed. The accounts of all ventures in which the Sovereign or the Council was interested were strictly audited by the latter (10).

Besides a censorship of the Press, the Council also exercised similar power over the theatre. It controlled popular amusements. In 1555 a letter was directed to the Lord Warden prohibiting May Games, while in the following year a stage play at Hatfield Braddock in Essex was prohibited, since such assemblies were said to be dangerous owing to the state of men's minds (11). On 28th Sept., 1578, the Cheshire justices were ordered to suppress the wakes, since the people assembled " under pretence of cheering and feasting, terming them wakes, where they do for the most part no good exercise, but fall to intemperate drinking and tippling." The earliest mention of actors in the Register is in 1543, when four players belonging to the Lord Warden were committed to the Counters for playing, contrary to the order of the Lord Mayor. In 1546 five persons, " calling themselves the Earl of Bath's servants," were imprisoned for playing lewd plays in the suburbs; four days later they were liberated upon bonds not to play without the special licence of the Council. A strict censorship over the theatre was exercised by the Coun-

(1) A.P.C., passim.
(2) A.P.C., I. 21st July, 1546.
(3) A.P.C., I.
(4) A.P.C., II.; III. 27th April, 1550.
(5) A.P.C., X. 18th March, 1578.
(6) A.P.C., XXVIII. 27th Dec., 1597.
(7) L. and P., I. 4870.
(8) L. and P., XVII. 193; A.P.C., V. 10th June, 1554.
(9) A.P.C., IV. 14th May, 1552; III. 10th Jan., 1551.
(10) A.P.C., XVII. 18th July, 1589.
(11) A.P.C., V. 24th June, 1555; 14th Feb., 1556.

cil (1). In 1577 the theatres in London and Middlesex were closed by the Council's orders, in order to avoid the plague, and in 1579 they were ordered to be closed during Lent (2). In 1600 the Council issued regulations for the theatres in London; only two houses were to be licensed, one for the use of the Lord Admiral's company, the other—the Globe—for the Lord Chamberlain's company. The rest were to be suppressed and no new houses were to be built. There were to be performances only twice a week, none " on the Sabbath day upon pain of imprisonment and further penalty," and none at all during Lent (3).

It was the Council's special duty to protect aliens, who lived in England only by permission of the Crown, and had no legal status. The insular prejudices of the English were very strong during the Tudor period, and there were constant petitions before the Council for redress of wrongs done to aliens who had settled in the country (4). Complaints of piracy, committed by English subjects against aliens, were dealt with either by the Council or the Admiralty Court, and were innumerable. The chances of redress depended mainly upon the diplomatic situation, and the Council's attitude varied according to foreign relations. The utmost deference, for example, was shown to Spain in 1579 and in 1587, to Denmark in 1588, and to Scotland in 1590 (5).

Much of the Council's time was occupied in regulating trade, fixing prices and wages, and settling trade disputes. The trade in corn, wool, leather, fish, sugar, spices, coal, gun-making, and brewing, all give rise to entries in the Register. The Government fixed prices in arbitrary fashion, and tried to keep them low by taking stern measures against engrossers and forestallers. It encouraged arable farming and the growing of flax and hemp, restricted dairy farming, regulated the soap-boiling trade, ordered that no starch be made from grain, and that sheep were not to eat pease, fixed the price of a Bible that the printer might not be out of pocket (6), and extended to cattle drovers the supervision under which cornfactors carried on their business (7). The Council did as much as possible for companies in which the Crown was interested. Sir Martin Frobisher's worthless Meta Incognita was the source of many entries in the Council Register, and the Council did its best to ensure profit for the Queen at least; the shareholders were ordered to pay in full or appear before the Council (8). The Council granted trading charters, and upheld the monopoly of, and the regulations made by, companies so chartered. It also exercised close control over them (9). In 1556 a company was chartered by the Council to secure the profits of the fisheries of the Bann in Ireland. It was empowered " to take any such convenient ground upon the North parts of their Majesty's realm as by their discretions may seem convenient for their sureties, and the same ground so taken to make strong and fortify, and being fortified to keep and defend it," and " to do certain services in the North parts of the said realm, in places now, without the leave and privity of their Majesties, inhabited with the Scots, not being their natural sub-

(1) A.P.C., VI. 14th June, 11th July, 5th Sept., 6th Sept., 1557.
(2) A.P.C., IX. 1st August, 1577; XI. 13th March, 1579.
(3) A.P.C., XXX. 9th March, 22nd June, 1600; XXXII. 8th Nov., 1601.
(4) P. and O., VII. 7th Oct., 1540; V. 25th Sept., 1556; XXXII. 30th Nov., 1601.
(5) A.P.C., XI., XVI., XIX., passim.
(6) P. and O., VII. 1st May, 1541.
(7) A.P.C., VIII. 15th May, 1575.
(8) A.P.C., X. passim.
(9) A.P.C., XI. 24th May, 14th July, 6th Nov., 1579; XXXII. 12th Oct., 1601.

jects." For these purposes the Government stores of munition were placed at their service, on recognisances being given for their restitution, the sole condition being, apparently, to secure the persons of certain notorious pirates (1). This is a clear precedent for the great modern Chartered Trading Companies with semi-imperial powers. The Council settled disputes between individuals and these trading companies, and aided the latter in their difficulties, for the customs duties they paid were valuable. Restrictions were imposed upon trade by the Council, and transgressors were punished by it. Abuses in manufacture were sharply repressed. Exports and imports were carefully regulated in accordance with the prevailing mercantile theory. Licences had to be obtained to export a cargo of " corrupt and musty wheat " (2), of old shoes, and to transport into Scotland four hundred quarters of beans (3). The Council used its own discretion regarding the temporary suspension of a statute in certain cases. In 1548 it allowed the Merchant Adventurers and Merchants of the Steelyard to ship what quantity of cloth they pleased, provided they paid the proper customs, in spite of a statute of 33 H. VIII. which prohibited the export of cloth when it had reached a certain price (4). There are many similar entries in the Register. The Council saw that its restrictions must be relaxed occasionally, but they persisted in their policy of fixing prices until the very end of the period.

The Council did, however, encourage new industries and inventors, and occasionally subsidised the former (5). Preference in trade was always given to the Crown, and " permission money " to trade was exacted from the trading corporations, besides frequent loans which the companies dared not refuse (6). On 11th May, 1555, a minute in the Council Register records that barge masters on the Thames were forbidden to work on Sundays; they were to go instead to Divine Service. Freedom of trade was restricted in order to maintain a decaying port (7). Trade disputes were sometimes referred for settlement by the Council to commercial men, and it called upon the great companies to contribute to the expenses of Commissioners sent to Denmark to confer on the subject of the passage of the Sound (8). Nothing was too insignificant for the notice of the Council, while with great questions it alone could deal.

During the Tudor period local government was reorganised, partly by statute, and supervised and controlled by the Council. The Justices of the Peace have been aptly styled the Tudor " maids of all work," and rural administration rested almost entirely upon their devoted shoulders. Many statutes authorised the interference of the Government in local affairs. The Act 19 H. VII., c. 18, enacted that all, who professed to have rights to levy tolls upon the Severn, were to prove the same before the King's honourable Council in the Star Chamber. The Act 21 H. VIII., c. 16, confirmed a decree, made in the previous year, by the King with his most honourable Council in his Star Chamber at Westminster, concerning " artificers strangers, what they may do concerning retaining

(1) A.P.C., V. 22nd Sept., 1556.
(2) A.P.C., XI. 27th Feb., 5th March, 1580.
(3) A.P.C., XXX., p. 431.
(4) A.P.C., II. 9th Nov., 1548.
(5) A.P.C., IX. 11th July, 1577; IV. 3rd June, 1553.
(6) A.P.C., V. 27th Aug., 1556.
(7) A.P.C., XVI. 18th Nov., 1588.
(8) A.P.C., XXX. 24th March, 1600.

apprentices, journeymen," etc. By 33 H. VIII., c. 9, one of those innumerable measures "for the maintaining of artillery and the debarring of unlawful games," it was enacted that the Privy Council might send, to towns requiring such, bowyers, fletchers, stringers and arrowhead makers dwelling in London who were not freemen of the City and did not pay scot and lot. By the Statute 2 and 3 Philip and Mary, c. 16, the Mayor and Aldermen of London were empowered to fix the fares charged by watermen rowing between Gravesend and Windsor. A table of fares was first, however, to be brought to the Privy Council for allowance. The J.P.'s, sheriffs, and mayors, assembled at the General Sessions, were empowered by 5 Eliz., c. 4, to fix the wages of "artificers, labourers, servants of husbandry, and apprentices" in the district. These assessments were to be notified to the Privy Council, after being certified into Chancery, and then the Chancellor was to be empowered by the Council to give orders for their proclamation. Sheriffs and J.P.'s had to answer before the Council for any wrong-doing in the exercise of their duties, and the latter are the subject of constant references in the Register. They were urged to take action in certain matters, or to obey more fully and willingly the instructions sent to them. In 1576 the Council ordered the Lord Keeper to put certain persons out of the Commission of the Peace because they did not attend church. The expenses of the Sheriffs were taxed by the Council; on 17th February, 1588, it was recorded in the Register that the Sheriffs were to restrain "their unnecessary expenses in keeping of tables apart, which is done more for ostentation than for reason." After 1597 the Council committed to the Assizes most of the cases of lewd words, scandalous publications, and seditious prophesyings which came before it. It enforced the decisions of local courts. It tried disputes between local bodies and government officials, and controlled the jurisdiction exercised by the Lord Mayor of London.

The appointment and dismissal of municipal officers frequently occupied the attention of the Council. The choice of mayors gives rise to many entries in the Register. In 1543 a certain man was not to be chosen by the inhabitants of Hull, because he had been chosen for the "Customershippe." In June, 1546, the King is recorded as allowing the free election of the Mayor of Chester "only for this time." Similar cases of interference occurred in 1556 at Coventry and Rye, in 1557 at Calais, and in 1567 at Carlisle. In 1576 the Council wrote to the Corporation of Hereford, forbidding them to choose as their mayor a certain man who was likely to "make some innovation in the orders and liberties of the city, and to be a hinderer of the godly proceeding of the present state of religion established in this Realm." In 1577 the Council dictated the choice of the Mayor of Dover; in 1580 the Mayor of Barnstaple was displaced for "notorious crimes," and in 1586 the Jurates of Winchelsea were ordered to choose for their mayor "an able and sufficient man, good and sound in religion and fit to govern there." The Council did not interfere in mayoral elections only. It took order in September, 1586, concerning the displacement of certain "ancient aldermen" in Lincoln. The appointment of a gauger at Chester came before its notice (1), while the constable of Maidstone was to be dismissed in 1576, because a complaint had been made to the Council that he was of "disordered life and behaviour."

The officials of the great trading companies were not exempt from the Council's attention. In 1542 it recommended a certain man to the Merchant Adventurers for their

(1) L. and P., XII. 817.

governor (1), as it did in 1577 to the Company of Spanish Merchants. Such recommendations were practically commands. The actions of these Companies were controlled by the Council (2), and, in 1578, it called upon the representatives of the Merchant Adventurers at Hamburgh to revoke an unjust decision which had been given by them, just as in 1577 it ordered the Lord Mayor to release two men imprisoned by him on suspicion. Occasionally, as at Dartmouth in 1580, the Council compelled men to fill offices to which they had been appointed. At other times, its intervention was necessary to keep a man in an office from which others desired to expel him; in 1586 it ordered the "Common Crier" of Evesham to be retained in office, until "it shall be by due course of law evicted from him." Again the Council sometimes took action in order to obtain an office for some individual. This was the case in June, 1600, when the Council requested the Corporation of Plymouth to admit to the town clerkship a man whom the Council had recommended five or six years previously, when there was no vacancy. It often requested the City of London to admit individuals to the freedom. It interfered in the freedom from arrest of Members of Parliament, in the election of Fellows at Cambridge, and with the College of Physicians.

London came especially under the notice of the Council, and the Register is full of entries recording instructions to the Lord Mayor concerning the proper government of that city, and of rebukes for not carrying out his orders. The Mayor of London was very much at the Council's beck and call. In 1535 Sir John Allen, a "King's Councillor," was ordered by the King's letters to be elected Mayor, and he was accordingly chosen (3). The Council had little confidence in the Mayor in 1578, for during the Queen's absence from the City, in July, it appointed three to assist him in the government of the City, since it was Her Majesty's desire "to have the same in the meantime well governed." He was the Council's tool and mouthpiece; he received constant instructions concerning the cleansing of the city and the avoidance of the plague; he was ordered in July, 1573, to allow Italian musicians in the City, and in 1586 not to admit a suspected heretic to office. The lighting of the City gave rise to an entry in the Register in 1600, and on 10th July, 1601, the Council stooped to administer a rebuke to the Mayor for impressing the servant of a peer. London and its over-population occupied much of the attention of the Council, and many regulations were issued to check building and the letting of tenement houses.

Besides the functions already dealt with the Council had an abundance of such on any and every subject—such functions as naturally fall to a body including all the departments of State in one comprehensive whole. The Register admirably illustrates this necessary but tedious work. Already in 1572 the poor occupied the attention of the Council. Claims to incorporation came before it. It dealt with insurance cases as early as 1570. Wales and Ireland are the subject of many entries in the Register throughout the period. It was left to the Council to take measures against the Plague, to look to the drainage of the Fens, to reward such men as Richard Hakluyt, to appoint heralds, and control all posting arrangements. It granted passports and safe-conducts, issued sumptuary regulations, dealt in summary fashion with vagabonds, masterless men, and gypsies, and regulated alehouses and gambling dens. It was an important factor in de-

(1) L. and P., XVII. 1055.
(2) P. and O., VII. 28th Dec., 1541.
(3) Wriothesley's Chronicle, I., Cam. Soc., 1875.

ciding royal marriages (1), and played a prominent part in such important State trials as those of Anne Boleyn, Katherine Howard, Mary Stuart, and Essex. A dissatisfied Member of Parliament was referred to it (2). It was always busy, and in time of danger supervised everything. It upheld grants of monopolies; letters of marque were not obtainable without its orders; and it granted licences for such objects as the export of blackamoors from England in 1596, for begging, and for acrobatic performances. In 1576 and 1588 it took order concerning the custody of certain public records (3); but its orders were not always obeyed, for, on 3rd July, 1590, a minute was entered in the Register which is practically identical with one of 16th November, 1589. It forbad a duel between Lord Grey and the Earl of Southampton in 1600 (4), it tried to check extortionate charges by innkeepers for oats and horses in 1543, and through it the Crown exercised the dispensing power (5). The State Papers include several memoranda of business showing what multifarious duties were fulfilled by the Council. (See L. and P., XII. 815, 816, 1091.) It cannot be a matter for surprise, if occasionally it seemed dilatory in dealing with matters which came before it (6), when it was occupied with such things as warrants for bear-baiting, for the payment of gardeners' bills, the care of a lunatic, the gowns of prisoners in the Tower, the drains at Guisnes, a letter to a disagreeable father in favour of his son-in-law, the payment of poor mariners, and the provision of carts for transporting Lady Derby's luggage from the Court. It sanctioned collections for the relief of towns destroyed by fire, and for the repair of a road through the Fens. It gave permission for Dr. Smith " with the red head " to visit a prisoner in the Tower, and ordered fodder for the deer in Woodstock Park.

With such matters as these was the Council's time occupied. The entries in the Register, which records most of its daily work, must be studied before a full understanding of the exact meaning of the term Conciliar government can be obtained.

III.—ADVISORY.

The duty of the Council to advise the Crown, and how it was performed, has been treated of previously. But the advice of the Council was also freely sought by individuals, and as freely given. On October 3rd, 1540, the Council's opinion was sought by a Justice of the Peace concerning the bailing of a parish priest brought before him for lewd words, and on 20th November, 1541, the Council was asked to specify the punishment to be inflicted in a similar case. In 1576 its advice was desired as to the removal of certain aliens from Colchester to Holstead, and, on 1st Aug., 1589, the Lord Mayor requested advice as to the treatment of soldiers and sailors returning home from abroad.

Throughout the period the Council's command of, and attention to, detail is extraordinary. The conciliar government of the Tudors was an arbitrary government, but it was for the good of the nation at large. Occasionally conciliar government appears to the twentieth century tyrannical and harsh, but men of the sixteenth century knew well enough what the needs of that age demanded. The Council was all-powerful and all-seeing, because it was dependent for the fulfilment of its orders upon itself alone. A despotic central authority was necessary, if peace and order were to prevail in those troublous times which followed the Wars of the Roses until the defeat of the Armada.

(1) L. and P., II. 226; Hatfield Papers, I. p. 259.
(2) L. and P., XIV. Pt. I., 1152.
(3) Dom. Cal., 9th Jan., 1576; A.P.C., XV. 16th March, 1588.
(4) Hatfield Papers, X. 3rd Aug., 1600.
(5) A.P.C., XXXII. 6th July, 17th July, 10th December, 1601.
(6) Hatfield Papers, X. 26th July, 1600.

VIII. THE PRIVY COUNCIL AND PARLIAMENT— EXECUTIVE AND LEGISLATURE.

————:o:————

FROM 1459 to 1621 there was no impeachment by Parliament, yet the connection between the Council and the two Houses was closer under the Tudors than it had been for many years before. In the House of Lords the dignity of the Council was enhanced by the "Act for the Placing of the Lords," 31 H. VIII., c. 10. The Chancellor Treasurer, President of the Council, and Lord Privy Seal, if peers, were to take their places on the left side of the Parliament Chamber above the highest members of the peerage, except any of the latter who were the King's relatives. The King's Secretary if a bishop or a baron, was to sit above all other bishops and barons. When, however these Councillors were below the rank of baron, and had not in consequence the right to vote, they were to sit in the above order, "upon the highest part of the Sacks in the Parliament Chamber." When two Secretaries had been appointed, both were to attend in the Upper House whenever the King or Speaker was present. Otherwise, they were to attend in turn for a week at a time, one in the Upper House, the other in the Lower, but when very important business was being debated, both were to assist at the proceedings in the Commons.

The Rotuli Parliamentorum of Henry VII.'s reign shed very little light upon the part played by the Privy Council in legislation at that time. They record the names of the Speakers; beyond that, they embody little else but the results of the session, and seldom contain any notice of speeches or debates. Other sources are equally silent, and the total absence of official returns of members to the House of Commons for the reign renders it impossible to examine its composition with regard to the Privy Council.

The control of Parliamentary elections by the Government during the Tudor period has long been the subject of controversy, but the evidence would seem to show that the interference was more on the part of individual members of the Privy Council than on the part of the Government as a whole. Such interference with elections is not recorded in the Council Register, but it certainly was freely practised by individuals. In 1536, Chancellor Audley directed writs to Viscount Lisle, then Governor of Calais, for the return of two burgesses to Parliament. He sent also a letter, ordering the Council of Calais to return one burgess, and the Mayor and his brethren the other, and praying them to elect persons of "gravity, honesty, reputation, and wit" (Chronicle of Calais) The Letters and Papers of Henry VIII. show how unscrupulously the Lower House was packed by Cromwell in 1539 with members elected to do the King's bidding at all costs. Both large and small constituencies received, directly or indirectly, an intimation of the King's pleasure as to how they should vote. Cromwell, writing to the King on 17th March, said he hoped to obtain the election of one Morison, His Majesty's servant, as he would be a serviceable man, with his learning, to answer all objections, and adding

he hoped, with the aid of other "dedicate councillors," to arrange that His
jesty "had never a more tractable Parliament" (1). The Earl of Southampton,
ig a Privy Councillor, knew about the summoning of a Parliament before the issue
he writs. He went down to Guildford in Surrey, and told the townsmen they must
rn two burgesses, but, if they followed his advice, it would cost them little, as he
ld provide able men to fill their places. The townsmen thanked him, and suggested
; a certain David Mudge might be one of their representatives. The choice of the
r was left to the Earl, who reported to Cromwell, asking if the "King will name
of his chamber or other"; otherwise, he would name one of his own servants. At
dray in Sussex he arranged for two of his own nominees to be returned, and also at
tsmouth and Midhurst. With Farnham he declared he could not meddle, as it was
Bishop of Winchester's town. For the county of Southampton he would see that
gsmill and Wriothesley were returned, according to Cromwell's wish (2). Later on, he
urged to do what he could with regard to Farnham, and he sent a list of the best
t in the district that Cromwell might nominate whom he considered most suitable.
mwell objected to Kingsmill as one of the knights for Southampton, because he was
Sheriff and so obviously ineligible. He had, however, promised Kingsmill that he
ild be the burgess of some borough in a county where he was not sheriff, and Kings-
himself suggested Ludgershall, Wilts., which was "in the rule of Mr. Richard
lges," already knight of the shire for Berks., who might return him (3). Meanwhile,
Earl of Southampton put off the shire-day for Southampton until he knew who was
e Wriothesley's colleague. Before the writ was sent to the county of Cornwall Crom-
l wrote settling the election in favour of the son of Sir William Godolphin, although
re the writ came down "there was a great suit made by Sir Piers Edgcumbe, Sir
n Clamond, and John Arundel, son and heir of Sir John Arundel, knight." In Nor-
: Sir Edward Knyvett offered his services, promising to be at Norwich with his friends
the day of election, and to give their voices to whomsoever Cromwell indicated. The
er of thanks in reply intimated that the return of Richard Southwell and Edmund
ndham was desired. The borough of Gatton, consisting of one house, was owned by
Roger Copley. He placed the nomination of burgesses at the disposal of the Lord
niral, who declined to use it, and pressed Christopher More to do so instead. More
mised it to a friend, who had to give way to a nominee of Cromwell; More could only
that this nominee would be content, considering the circumstances of the borough,
take no wages (4). Apparently the elections to the Parliament of 1539 were rather
ensively controlled by Cromwell and his friends.

Throughout the Tudor period similar interference went on. In Edward VI.'s
gn the Privy Council itself is several times recorded as endeavouring to secure the
ctions of individuals whom it favoured. In August, 1547, a letter was written to the
d Warden of the Cinque Ports "to recommend Sir John Baker so to those that have
naming of knights of the shire, as at the next Parliament he may be made knight of
shire of Kent accordingly." Later on, in September, the Council again wrote to the
riff. stating that they had heard that their request had been construed into a com-
ndment, and that they disclaimed any wish to deprive the shire of its freedom of elec-
a, but nevertheless, if the Council's request were granted, they "would take it thank-

(1) L. and P., XIV. 538. (2) Ibid., 520.
(3) Ibid., 662. (4) Ibid., 645.

fully " (1). Baker, though a Privy Councillor, was not, however, elected. On 28th October, 1551, the Lord Chancellor was asked how many members had died since the last Parliament, in order that " grave and wise men might be elected to supply their places, for the avoiding of the disorder that hath been noted in sundry young men and others of small judgment." In January, 1552, letters were written to the electors of Reading, Essex, Hertfordshire, and Surrey commanding the return of candidates recommended, one only being nominated in each case. It is noteworthy that these were in the home counties.

In Mary's reign the Register has little to record concerning elections to Parliament. There was evidently some interference, however, for, on 10th September, 1553, a letter of thanks was written to the gentlemen of Cornwall for their proceedings in the election of the knights for that county, and signifying that the sheriff had been ordered to accept their election, " without further troubling of the county with any other alteration."

Under Mary, governmental interference seems to have been more restricted, but under Elizabeth there was much, either on the part of the Council or of individuals. The practice of her predecessors enabled her to issue general instructions regarding the choice of members, to nominate candidates to a constituency here and there, and to advise particular constituencies to pay attention to the nomination of Privy Councillors. Any greater interference would have gone beyond the example set by Edward, and much beyond any precedent of Mary (2). Strype records in the "Annals" that in January, 1559, letters were dispatched from the Council to Sir Thomas Mildmay, Sheriff of Essex, concerning the choice of knights for that shire, and that such letters, " instructive of the persons to be elected Parliament men for the shires " had not been unusual in former times, at any rate under Mary. There is an entry in the borough book of Wells of the 13th year of Queen Elizabeth of a letter from Sir Hugh Paulet in the Queen's name desiring the burgesses to elect fit persons to Parliament on peril of the Queen's displeasure. A letter from the Council for the same purpose is also recorded (3). In 1586 the Council wrote to the Sheriff of Norfolk concerning a new writ because of the disorder at the last election. The new election was to be " free and not solicited." Nevertheless, their Lordships declared they considered it strange that one should be chosen knight of the shire, who was considered not fit for the Commission of the Peace, and " though Her Majesty hath no meaning to impeach any way their free election, yet she thinketh some regard should have been had to such letters as were sent from hence by her directions." In September of the same year a correspondent wrote to the Earl of Rutland: " Perhaps I shall be elected a knight for a shire in Wales, unless hindered by the direction sent to all sheriffs for preferring such as served in the last Parliament " (4). In 1585 the Council wrote to Lord Cobham, informing him that a Parliament was to be summoned for 2nd November, and requiring him to see that the boroughs in the Cinque Ports returned men who were " not only discreet and sufficient persons, but known to be well affected in religion and towards the present state of this Government." He was urged to take the course which seemed best to him, and either to nominate the burgesses

(5) A.P.C., II. Appendix, 28th Aug.; 28th Sept., 1547.
(6) Bayne: " The first House of Commons of Queen Elizabeth," E.H.R., Vol. XXII.
(7) Merewether and Stephens: " History of the Boroughs and Municipal Corporations," II. p. 1252.
(8) Rutland Papers, I., 16th Sept., 1586.

imself, or see that a " good and especial choice be made " (1). In 1597 a similar letter
as sent to all the sheriffs concerning the election of knights and burgesses. If such men
ere chosen as were not fit for the service, " we shall have occasion to inquire by whose
efault it so happened " (2). In 1600 the Council, foreseeing possible opposition to Sir
homas Leighton as one of the knights of the shire for Worcester, wrote disclaiming any
esire to restrain the liberty of election or to recommend the candidate, since his merits
nd quality were sufficient in themselves. Nevertheless, any favour which was shown to
im would, asserted the Council, be very agreeable to Her Majesty, just as she would be
qually sensible of any evil measure taken towards him. After this veiled threat, the
lectors duly chose the nominee of the Government.

Individual Councillors interfered with elections to a far greater extent than the
overnment, especially in Elizabeth's reign. In 1559 a letter is recorded to the Mayor
f Grimsby, in which he is requested to withdraw the nomination of his brother in favour
f Lord Clinton, a Privy Councillor, and in the confidence of the government. Evidently
overnment lists of candidates were not issued, or Clinton would have taken advantage
f them. He was probably acting unofficially and on his own account. In this same year
rancis Earl of Bedford was allowed to nominate a burgess for Ilfracombe Regis, and,
a return, the borough was relieved of the burden of paying his wages. This was a com-
ion bribe to secure compliance. In the 26th year of Elizabeth, the bailiffs and aldermen
f Colchester, " to serve the Queen's Grace and get rid of all trouble," made the follow-
ag order: " That Sir Francis Walsingham shall have the nomination of both the bur-
esses of the town for the Parliament, for time to come, according to his honour's letters
o the Bailiffs, Aldermen, and Common Council of the time directed " (3). In the fol-
wing year Andover was restored to representation in Parliament, and the Earl of
eicester, Lord Steward of the borough, wrote immediately asking for the nomination
f one member. He also promised that, if the burgesses were anxious to avoid the ex-
enses of having to pay the other member, and would give the nomination to him, he
ould appoint a pay a " sufficient " man   (4). In 1597 Sir Robert Cecil desired the
omination of the burgesses for East Grinstead. The bailiff replied in a very humble and
pologetic tone that the burgesses were already elected; otherwise they would readily sub-
ait to him the choice of both burgesses and are sorry they did not know his wish in
ime (5). Cecil also wrote for the nomination of the two burgesses for Durham, and
he Bishop wrote in reply: " I cannot learn that even any such was allowed of in the
arliament House, though writs sent out in error have been received for the election of
uch " (6). It was nearly a century later before the Palatine County was enfranchised.
Ie was too late in his request for the nomination of one of the burgesses of Colchester in
he same year, and for both the representatives of Stockbridge and Ripon. But, in every
ase, most subservient letters were sent in reply to his demands. The bailiffs of Stock-
ridge wrote: " We hope you will not be displeased with us, being very sorry that at
his time we cannot pleasure you. But hereafter you shall not only request, but shall
ommand anything which we may do " (7). The town of Romney conferred the nomi-

(1) Hatfield Papers, III., 18th Oct., 1584.
(2) Ibid., VII. Sept., 1597.
(3) Merewether and Stephens: II. p. 1346.
(4) Ibid., II. p. 1393.
(5) Hatfield Papers, VII., 20th Sept., 1597.
(6) Ibid., 29th Sept., 1597.
(7) Ibid., 15th Oct., 1597.

nation of one of their burgesses upon Lord Cobham, and he in turn bestowed it upon Cecil. It appeared to be the practice to confer the nomination of one or other of the burgesses of a town upon the Lord Steward of the place, or some other important personage, on the understanding that the constituents were relieved of the burden of paying wages. In 1601 one Edward Lenton complained to Sir Robert Cecil that his name had been given by Sir John Fortescue to the Corporation of Wycombe to be elected one of their burgesses. They had usually granted the nomination of one to Lord Windsor, the Lord Steward, but this time Windsor had written for both. " Wherefore my humble suit is, that you would vouchsafe, by your letters, to give that corporation some encouragement in electing me; for though my Lord Windsor objects in his letters that I am one that doth but follow my Lord Norreys (in whose business I now am), yet I hope your Honour knoweth that I have given myself as a servant to none but you " (1). In September of the same year, Henry Lock and Dr. Christopher Perkins both wrote to Cecil, requesting to be nominated as burgesses for the coming Parliament. This same Dr. Perkins was sworn Latin Secretary to the Queen on 22nd August, 1601. One Trelawney wrote to Cecil in October, 1601, presenting him with two burgess-nominations for the Parliament. Cecil had again asked for the nomination of one of the burgesses of Ripon, and was given it. The Archbishop of York wrote that " My Lord President " had the other one, and that usually the Chancellor had had one also. A fortnight later, on 22nd October, he writes to Cecil commending the latter for his choice of the Dean of Carlisle as one of the burgesses for Ripon. The evidence would seem to prove that there was not much organised control of elections exercised by the government as a whole, although much was done by individual Councillors.

It is difficult to deal with the influence of the Privy Council in Parliament. The epithet " free " when applied to a Tudor Parliament is of course used relatively, for none were free in the modern sense. All included a number of Government officials, privy councillors, subordinate placemen, and members of the court who were instruments of the governmental will, and doubtless guided the deliberations of the assemblies in which they sat. The same is the case ot the present day, though this fact is often overlooked by these who exaggerate the impotence of Tudor parliaments. But there were degrees in the predominance of the Government element, and some Tudor Parliaments were more independent, or rather, perhaps, less subservient than others. In January, 1547, Chapuys wrote, that no man dare open his mouth in Parliament against the will of the King and Council. Most of the Privy Councillors throughout the Tudor period sat in Parliament. In Edward VI.'s first Parliament, of a hundred and eighty-nine members named in the returns extant, one-third either held office about the court, or were closely related to the ministers for the time being, and all the Privy Councillors with very few exceptions had seats. The connection between the Commons and the Council was very close. It has been said also that, throughout the Tudor period,. the Government could always reckon on a majority in its favour in the House of Lords owing to the large proportion of peers holding office. We have seen that the clerks of the Council generally sat in the Commons. The returns to Parliament for the reign of Henry VIII. are in a bad condition, and it is impossible to say how many of his Privy Councillors sat in the Commons. For the Parliament summoned for 1542 three Privy Councillors are mentioned in the returns, Sir Ralph Sadler, Sir Anthony Browne, and Sir John Baker, and probably most of the rest had seats.

(1) Ibid., XI. 30th Sept., 1601.

For Mary's first Parliament six names of Privy Councillors are to be found amongst the returns. Under the Tudors, Privy Councillors and men on the threshold of the Privy Council were persons of immense importance, and it was only natural that they should seek a seat in the deliberative assembly of the realm. They made, also, numerous nominations to Parliament, but that again was no unnatural proceeding. It was customary for any great man who was closely connected with a borough or county to nominate one of the burgesses or knights. Nevertheless, the unofficial element in Parliament was numerically predominant throughout the period. Almost the only traces of interference with elections are of a normal kind: i.e. the pressure exercised by great nobles and local magnates on the constituencies with which they were connected. It is impossible to state with certainty except in a few cases during the Tudor period, whether this pressure had the Government, as a whole, behind it. We have seen Sir Robert Cecil writing for the nomination of burgesses to several boroughs in 1597. This he may have done in his capacity as Secretary, but governmental interference went little further than this.

In the Lower House the Speaker was in much the same position as the Chancellor in the Upper House; he was the manager of business on the part of the Crown, and the nominee either of the King himself or of the Chancellor. "The Speaker is he that doth commend and prefer the Bills exhibited into Parliament, and is the mouth of the Parliament. He is commonly appointed by the King or Queen, though accepted by the assent of the House (1). Henry VIII. used to require the Speaker to be the exponent of his wishes, and on a few occasions ministers of the Crown, not members of the Commons, made unwelcome visits to the Commons House, as in 1514 and 1523. In January, 1553, Northumberland wrote to the Lord Chamberlain, and added as a postscript: "In my poor opinion it is time the King's Majesty's pleasure were known for the Speaker of the House, to the intent he may have secret warning thereof, as always hath been used, because he may better prepare himself towards his proposition; otherwise he shall not be able to do it to the contentation of the hearers " (2). On 2nd March, 1553, the Commons chose as their Speaker one James Dyer, and went from Westminster " to the court and so presented him to the Council " (3). In Elizabeth's first Parliament, Sir Thomas Gargrave, Vice-President of the Council of the North, was nominated by the Treasurer of the Household and elected Speaker. The Commons' Journals record the Treasurer, or some other Household official, as nominating the Speaker in nearly every case, and as early as 1512 the Comptroller of the Household announced the name of the man chosen. In the Parliament of 1562, after the Lord Keeper's opening speech, Mr. Speaker Williams made a speech to the Queen. " In this ingenious speech I strongly suspect Cecil had a great hand. Who, as he was first chosen Speaker himself but got himself excused, so he seems to have been the main instrument of getting Mr. Williams chosen in his room. For when Sir Edward Rogers, Comptroller of the Queen's Household, had recommended him to the House to be their chief Speaker, and Williams had disabled himself, Cecil answered him the House had gravely considered of him as a fit person, and required him to take the place, and so he was seated in the chair (4). Occasionally during the period a Privy Councillor held the office of Speaker. Thomas Lovell, Henry VII.'s Chancellor of the

(1) Sir Thomas Smith: " De Republica Anglorum," p. 154.
(2) Tytler: " England under the reigns of Edward VI. and Mary," p. 160.
(3) Wriothesley's Chronicle.
(4) Strype: " Annals," p. 257.

Exchequer and a Privy Councillor, was Speaker in 1485. In 1487 John Mordaunt was elected to the office: he appears to have been one of Henry's advisers, but he may not have been sworn of the Council until a later date. Reginald Bray, Speaker in 1495, was a Privy Councillor, as was Edmund Dudley in 1504. Of Henry VIII.'s Speaker, Thomas Neville, 1515, Thomas More, 1523, Thomas Audley, 1529, and Richard Rich, 1536, were Privy Councillors. Only one of Edward VI.'s Speakers was of his Privy Council, Sir John Baker, 1547 and 1552. Two of Mary's were Councillors, Clement Heigham in 1554, and William Cordell in 1558, but of all those in Elizabeth's reign who held the office not one was a Privy Councillor.

The Speaker was paid by the Crown. In 1512 a warrant is recorded to the Treasurer of the Chamber to pay £200 to Sir Robert Sheffield for his services as Speaker. In 1523 Wolsey wrote to Henry: "It has been usual, even when the Parliament has been right soon finished, to give the Speaker a reward of £100 for his household, beside the £100 ordinary. The King is aware of the faithful diligence of More in the late Parliament about the subsidy, so that no man could deserve it better. He will therefore cause the sum to be advanced on learning Henry's pleasure" (2). In 1547 the Council Register records an Order for £100, the Speaker's salary for the last session of Parliament, "as customary." In 1548 and 1552 similar orders were entered on the minutes. In the reigns of Mary and Elizabeth these returns no longer occur, but the Speaker still appears to be the nominee of the Crown.

The Clerk of the Parliament also received a salary from the Government, and seems to have been chosen by the Crown. His office, however, was rather dignified, than politically influential. Brian Tuke was appointed Clerk on 23rd April, 1523; he was probably a Privy Councillor later, because he became Treasurer of the Household in 1528. In 1531 Edward North was associated with him in the office, and he, in 1546, was sworn a Privy Councillor. William Paget, a Privy Councillor, was Clerk of the Parliament in July, 1541, and John Mason in December, 1551. On 30th September, 1597, Sir Thomas Smith obtained the office. One Sir Thomas Smith was already Clerk of the Privy Council, and the two appear to have been one and the same man, but it is impossible to make the statement with any certainty, as some confusion has arisen between three (3) men of the same name. It has been said of the Tudor period, and with truth, that "Secretaries of State, Clerks of Parliament, Keepers of Records, and private antiquaries were bred in a common atmosphere and almost in a family circle." (4). In 1597 Sir Thomas Egerton wrote to Sir Robert Cecil: "I am to remind you of the warrant for Parliament if Her Majesty do still continue in her former resolution. A Clerk of the Parliament is also to be thought of. Whoever Her Highness shall make choice of, shall have well to have some convenient time to prepare and enable himself. He is to receive into his charge Rolls and Records appertaining to the place, to acquaint himself with them beforehand, and be informed by as good means as he can of his duty and charge in this service. Here is like to be new Lord Keeper, new Speaker, new Clerk, and all of us newly to learn our duties. I comfort myself for my part with Her Majesty's wonted gracious favour, else I must seek some new covert to hide me in. I fear some will say of us, Ecce nova facta sunt omnia " (5).

(1) L. and P., III. 3267.
(2) Pollard: "The Authenticity of the Lords' Journals." Transactions of the English Historical Society, 1914.
(3) Sir Thomas Smith, statesman and scholar, 1513—77; Sir Thomas Smith, Master of Requests and Latin Secretary, 1556—1609; Sir Thomas Smith, merchant, 1558—1625. The above-mentioned is probably the second of these.
(4) Hatfield Papers, VII. p. 359.
(5) Commons' Journals, 2nd March, 1549; 6th Feb., 1559, and passim.

The Privy Councillors in the Commons took a prominent place there. They were the recognised medium of communication between the Crown and the Commons, and were appointed to sit upon all Parliamentary committees and to take part in conferences (1). They were active in debate, and Government bills were committed in the commons either to Privy Councillors or to the Secretary. One or more of the Privy Councillors were generally included among those members who took up Bills to the Lords; this last appears to have been usually the duty of the Household officials. In February, 1549, a Parliamentary petition was handed over to Mr. Comptroller and Mr. Secretary to be decided with the help of two private members. If this could not be done, the petition was to be sent to the Lord Protector. On 31st March, 1552, the Commons sent a similar petition to be decided by Northumberland; on 5th April they sent it to the Privy Council, and on 7th April the Council returned it, " to be ordered by this House according to the ancient customs of this House." The Privy Councillors evidently had definite seats allotted to them in the Commons, because on 14th November, 1558, it is recorded that a deputation of dignitaries from the House of Lords " came into this House, sitting where the Queen's Privy Council of this House used to sit; and the Lord Chancellor by his oration declared that by necessity for the safeguard of this realm against the French and Scots a subsidy must be had; Mr. Speaker and the Privy Council then sitting from them on the lowest Benches, and after the declaration made the Lords departed." At the opening of Elizabeth's third Parliament held in 1572 the Lord Steward of the Household, or his deputies, administered the oath to the newly elected Commons; he, with Sir Francis Knollys, Sir James Crofts, Sir Walter Mildmay, and Sir Thomas Smith, went to the Commons while the Queen, with the Lords and Bishops, was attending church. It is noteworthy that the Steward, Lord Clinton, was accompanied by men who were all officials and Privy Councillors. In January, 1581, the Speaker, probably at the bidding of Queen or Council, harangued the House on the advantages of concise speech, urging them to dispense with unnecessary motions or superfluous arguments, and not to speak on first readings, as the Parliament would be a short one. On the same date the fast, prayer, and preaching which the House had resolved upon for itself, was ordered to be a public one, and the Privy Councillors in the House were asked to nominate preachers who were " to keep convenient proportion of time, and to meddle with no matter of innovation or unquietness." On 24th January a very sharp message of reproof against such an innovation was brought down by the Vice-Chamberlain from the Queen. Consequently, some of the Privy Councillors were sent to make humble apology for " the rash and inadvised manner of the proceeding of this house, . . tending to innovation, presuming to indict a form of public fast without order, and without Her Majesty's privity intruding upon Her Highness' authority ecclesiastical."

On 9th February, 1542, Parliament was just meeting, and Chapnys wrote to Charles V. that the King and his Council were so busy that they could not hear other affairs. Already in 1535 the Council's control over legislation seemed well established. One of Pole's correspondents told him that, though Henry had withdrawn himself from the Pope's authority, the laws and ceremonies of the Church still stood in full strength and authority: " And so they shall, I dare affirm boldly, until the King and his Council think expedient to abrogate them, and substitute by common assent others more agreeable to this time, and the nature of our men, and more convenient to our whole country " (1). Cromwell reported to the King that he and the Council were busy upon affairs for Parliament, and it has been seen that Edward, Mary, and Elizabeth all appointed committees of their Privy Councils to deal with Parliamentary business. Many Bills must have been prepared by government draftsmen, but it must be borne in mind that a modern Government drafts nine-tenths of the public legislation which is accomplished, and that the scope of the private member is now insignificant in comparison with the Tudor period, when members were really representatives of their constituents.

Licences to be absent from Parliament were granted by the Privy Council to its members and to peers. On 14th December, 1543, the Lord President of the Council was allowed to absent himself the following session and similar permission was given by the Council to the Bishop of Salisbury in August, 1553, on account of age. These licences were recorded in the Register. In September, 1597, Cecil obtained for the Archbishop of York " the Queen's dispensation " to be away from Parliament. In 1601 Viscount Howard of Bindon wrote to Cecil asking to be discharged, on account of indisposition from attending Parliament and as " some towns, having affiance in the care he will take of their well doing, have given him the nomination of their burgesses," he offers the nominations to Cecil (2). The Council wrote on 23rd September, 1601, to the Earl of Rutland, the Earl of Bedford, Lord Sands, and Lord Cromwell, who had all been implicated in Essex's rebellion. They had been pardoned, and the writs of summons to Parliament had been sent to them, but, in spite of that, the Queen ordered them not to attend, because their offences were fresh in memory and would " renew a very displeasant remembrance of the same. A " great and tumultuous disorder " occurred in the county of Denbigh at the election of the knight of the shire in November, 1601, and the Council summoned the offenders before because the Sheriff had been unable to proceed to the election. In October of the same years the Council summoned before it the Sheriffs of Warwickshire and of the county of Southampton, and administered a strong rebuke to them for delaying the elections of the knights of the shire (3). Both these cases would most certainly have been dealt with in Stuart times by the House of Commons.

(1) L. and P., VIII. 218.
(2) Hatfield Papers, VII. 28th Sept., 1597; XI. undated but before Oct., 1601.
(3) A.P.C., XXXII. 23rd Sept.; 7—16th Oct., 1601.

IX. "SUBORDINATE" BODIES, COURTS, AND COMMISSIONS.

——————:o:——————

THE increase in the business dealt with by the Council under the Tudors gave rise to a number of Courts and Councils in different parts of the country. In speaking of them, the usual interpretation of the word "subordinate" must be avoided. The only body which had any control over them at all was the Council; otherwise, they were independent. With the work of these bodies it is not proposed to deal. They are here of interest only in their relations with the central authority.

The Court of Star Chamber can hardly be said to fall within the above category, for it existed long before the Tudor period. Nevertheless it was a Court which relieved the Council of much of its most important judicial work and became, especially under the last of the Tudors, simply the instrument of the government. What traces there are of the Court under Henry VII. are very meagre and somewhat uncertain; and although there are many references to it under Henry VIII. during the season of Wolsey's power after his downfall it again sank into comparative obscurity. References to the Star Chamber during Edward VI.'s reign are of striking scarcity. During the reign of Philip and Mary it is more frequently mentioned, and at the accession of Elizabeth it sprang into that prominence in which it continued until its abolition.

Side by side with the jurisdiction of the Privy Council existed another jurisdiction, that of the Lords of the Council sitting in the Star Chamber, and the jurisdictions exercised by the two were almost indistinguishable. The Court of Star Chamber did not conceive itself as of statutory origin, nor as limited by the Act of 1487 either in respect of its composition or its jurisdiction. The Statute 3 H. VII.. c. 1, was merely an enabling Act, and, from the very beginning, the composition of the Court of Star Chamber differed from it. Nor is there any record of the committee organised by this Statute exercising jurisdiction. One is inclined to assert frankly that the Act of 1487 had nothing whatsoever to do with the Star Chamber. From the beginning of Elizabeth's reign, or, it may be said, as early as the reign of Edward VI., the right of all members of the Privy Council to a seat in the Court was fully recognised. Even during Henry VII.'s reign, the number of judges in the Star Chamber was often fewer than was required by the Statute 3 H. VII., c. 1, and the judges were often absent; yet again the attendance there was often very large, and never composed strictly of the Privy Council alone. These facts shatter Hallam's statement that, during Henry VII.'s reign and a part of Henry VIII.'s, there existed, distinct from the Council, a Court of uniform statutory composition. As early as the reign of Henry VII, there was a clear distinction between the Star Chamber and the Council. The "King's Council in the Star Chamber," the official style of the Court of Star Chamber, included a large legal contingent. It was not only the Privy Council, in the usual meaning of the term, which sat in the Chamber, bu there were also Councillors who were specially sworn in for that particular purpose (1) The Court was re-inforced in legal competence by the swearing in of experts who thence forward ranked as "consiliarii," though not members of the Privy Ciuncil. It migh be said that the Concilium Ordinarium was here discernible. Bacon described the Cour as made up of four elements—Councillors, Peers, Prelates, and Chief Judges. Camde named certain great officers as composing the Court, "et omnes consiliarii status tan ecclesiastici quam laici, et ex baronibus illi quos princeps advocabit " (2). According t Sir Thomas Smith it comprised "the Lords and others of the Privy Council as many a will and other Lords and Barons which be not of the Privy Council, and which will be i the town " (3), while Crompton wrote " Le Court de Star Chamber est Hault Court, tenu avant le Roy et son Conseil et auters " (4). Hudson asserted that the Lords of Parlia ment who were not members of the Privy Council claimed, and in some cases exercised the right to sit and give judgment (5). Acording to Coke, every Privy Councillor had voice and place in the Court of Star Chamber. The Long Parliament was wrong, his torically, in tracing the origin of the Court of Star Chamber to 3 H. VII., c. 1, but ther can be no question that a distinction was drawn between the Star Chamber and the Priv Council as to composition. The relation between the two was very close, but discrimina tion between them, apparent even under Henry VII., was certainly understood by th time that the new Council Register was opened on 10th Aug., 1540. Although th Register shows that the Council used the Star Chamber as a Council Room occasionall under Henry VIII. and Edward VI., and frequently in the reigns of their successors, thi no longer gave rise to any confusion.

The Court of Star Chamber was at no time during the reign of Henry VIII. tribunal limited in membership and jurisdiction according to the usual interpretation c 3 H. VII., c. 1. In both reigns there were special councillors for the work of the Sta Chamber, but apparently the Privy Council did not consider the Council in the Sta Chamber as a body really separate and distinct from itself. The right of all Privy Cour cillors to sit in the Star Chamber, established at least as early as the reign of Edwar VI., was not a development of the middle of the sixteenth century, but was recognise even in the days of the first Tudors, and the dovetailing of the work of the Star Chambe and Council was perhaps more intricate in the days of Henry VIII. than at any late time. The general body of Privy Councillors probably had little or no desire to tak part in the active proceedings of the Court of Star Chamber, for the privilege of tryin cases of misdemeanour without salary was onerous and uninviting. The presence of th legal officers of the Crown, who were then never members of the Privy Council (6), con

(1) Scofield: "Star Chamber," p. 33. Leadam: "Star Chamber," I. p. xlii.

(2) "Britannia," p. 112 (ed. 1594).

(3) "Commonwealth of England," Bk. III. ch. 4.

(4) "Courts de la Royne," pp. 29, 35.

(5) "Treatise of the Court of Star Chamber," Collectanea Juridica, I. 25.

(6) Except Montague, Chief Justice of the Common Pleas, and Bromley, Chief Justice of the King's Bench, appointed of Edward VI.'s Coun- cil in Henry VIII.'s will.

tributed to the growth of a clearer distinction between the Star Chamber and the Council. The Statute of 1529, like that of 1487, gave statutory sanction to a prevailing use which had arisen out of the indefinite jurisdiction traditionally possessed by the Council. By this Statute the Lord President of the Council was associated with the other dignitaries mentioned in the Act of 1487. He had frequently sat and presided in the Court of Star Chamber. The presiding judge of the Court was the Lord Chancellor or the Lord Keeper, and in his absence the Lord Treasurer, Lord President of the Council, or the Lor dPrivy Seal. The chief officer of the Court was the Clerk, who bore the title of " the Clerk of the Council of State " (1).

The Court of Star Chamber exercised much of the indeterminate jurisdiction inherent in the Council of the King. As early as the reign of Henry VII. litigants accepted the Star Chamber's view of its origin, assumed it to be the King's Council, and, notwithstanding the Act of 1487, to be invested with an indeterminate jurisdiction traditionally possessed by that body and generally conceived of as supplementary to common and statute law. The primary object of 3 H. VII. c. 1 was to obtain statutory sanction for the exercise of part of these powers and others, too, by a Committee-Court of the Ordinary Council. Henry VII. had before him the Lancastrian precedent of the expired Act of 1453, which applied to the whole Privy Council. The enumeration of offences in the Act of 1487 was not by way of limitation but to expand by statute the powers conceded to the Privy Council by Parliament in the earlier Act. Such a construction of 3 H. VII. c. 1 furnishes an explanation of the variations from its provisions practised both by litigants and the Court itself. The Court of Star Chamber never entirely absorbed the jurisdiction practised by the Privy Council. Throughout the Tudor period the latter exercised a jurisdiction concurrent with that exercised in the Star Chamber. The Court exercised far wider powers than those conferred by the statute of 1487, and its procedure differed from that of the Council in many ways. In the Privy Council the King's Justices were not present, and other legal experts sat either as assessors or as judges. Moreover, the Star Chamber sat in public an only in term time, while the Council sat in private and all the year round. Its composition, unlike that of the Privy Council, was variable; towards the end of the sixteenth century it seems to have consisted of the Privy Council and the judges, sitting in public for judicial purposes in the Star Chamber. Its jurisdiction extended to cases of forgery, perjury, contempt of proclamations, frauds, duels and other breaches of the peace, and any cases referred by the Privy Council to it.

The Tudor Court of Star Chamber was one of the most powerful instruments of the government. This was realised and it was made full use of accordingly. It soon outgrew statutory restraints, if it had ever had any, but there was never any well marked division between the jurisdictions of the Privy Council and the " Council in the Star Chamber." In September, 1589, a case is recorded in the Register of the Council as depending " before their Lordships, as well at the Council Board as in the Star Chamber." From the beginning of Henry VII.'s reign there are many indications that the Court of Star Chamber was regarded as distinct from the Council, and especially is this recognised in the Acts of the Council itself. The Court was nothing more than the instrument of the Council, by whom it was directed and controlled. Under Henry VII., interchange of business went on between the Council and the Star Chamber, and there was no hard and fast rule as to which should handle suits of a particular nature. This close relationship continued through succeeding reigns. Recognisances for appearance in the Star Chamber

(1) Scofield, p. 62.

were taken in the Council, and decrees of the Court were enforced by it (1). Frequently the Council is recorded in the Register as ordering the Attorney to lay information in the Star Chamber. Suits were dismissed by the Council to come before the Star Chamber (2), and in 1589 the Council ordered a case to be dismissed from the Court of Delegates, because it was depending in " Her Majesty's Court of Star Chamber." In April, 1588, the King of Denmark had complained of English pirates. The Privy Council promised that judicial proceedings should be taken against the marauders, and that, although one of the pirates had been acquitted by two juries, " those who have so acquitted him shall be called in question in the Star Chamber, and proceeded against with that extremity the grave censure of that High Court may lay upon them '(3). In 1579 a man exhibited two bills against one Bowes, one into the Star Chamber, the other " before your Lordships at the Council Table." Proclamations issued by the government were punished by it " at the Star Chamber at the Council Table there." The Court was evidently expensive, for in 1590 the " poor inhabitants " of East Harlings in Norfolk petitioned the Council against the " uncharitable dealings and oppressions " of their lord of the manor, who had moreover sued them to appear in the Star Chamber, " which they fear will be to their utter undoing, being very poor men." The Council ordered a stay of proceedings and an inquiry into the affair, to be made by the Chief Justice of the Queen's Bench and another (4). On the 1st July, 1590, an order in the Register mentions that the Masters of Requests, attendant in the Court of Star Chamber, were ordered to report upon a certain case to their Lordships. The Council was clearly delegating more and more of its criminal jurisdiction to the Star Chamber, because it was as much as it could do to cope with its administrative work. Much of its ecclesiastical work began to be handed over to the Commissioners for Causes Ecclesiastical. Throughout Elizabeth's reign the Council, in its orders recorded in the minutes, identified itself very closely with the Court of Star Chamber. An appearance before the Council apparently excused such before the Court of Star Chamber (5), and probably men bound in recognisances to appear frequently for a certain period before the Star Chamber, appeared out of term time before the Council. In 1570 a suitor was not allowed to overlook the fact that the Star Chamber and the Council were distinct bodies, although so closely bound together. The Council wrote on 21st Dec. to Sir William Paulet complaining that, although the matter between him and John Yonge had been considered by them, and he enjoined to bring in his bill of complaint, yet they saw he meant to prosecute the case in the Star Chamber. " They cannot but find this manner of dealing very strange, and think that he hath therein much forgotten himself, as they mean not to suffer the authority of this Table to be so much prejudiced as to endure that any matter of complaint, brought and dealt with by them, should by the complainant himself be removed to another Court before the same be heard by their Lordships and ordered."

Through the medium of the Star Chamber the Council exercised legislative as well as judicial powers. The Court of Star Chamber not only expounded the law but issued orders and decrees, often very comprehensive, and in some cases these are so closely analogous to orders in Council that they may almost be regarded as such. The statute

(1) A.P.C., V. 28th Dec., 1555; 10th Dec., 1555.
(2) A.P.C., XI. 10th Jan., 1580, passim.
(3) A.P.C., XVI. 1st April, 1588.
(4) A.P.C., XIX. 15th May, 1590.
(5) A.P.C., XXIV. 31st Jan., 1593.

21 H. VIII. c. 16 confirmed a decree made by the King and his Council in the Star Chamber. Powers of this character were assumed and extended the further because, doubtless, the Star Chamber remembered its origin. They were probably in part a survival of those pre-Tudor days, when the Court of Star Chamber was not distinguishable from the Council (1). In 1589 it was recognised as an established Court of Justice. On 8th October of that year, the Council heard a case and found it depending in the Star Chamber. They therefore dismissed the parties, leaving them " to trial in the Star Chamber, or in such other Court of Justice or Conscience where the same is properly to be determined."

The very close connection between the Star Chamber and the Council under the Tudors is borne out, in the reign of Henry VII., by the fact that the Clerk of the Council, Robert Rydon, and after him John Meautys, was also the Clerk of the Star Chamber.

During the reigns of Henry VII. and Henry VIII. the Court of Star Chamber apparently sat more frequently than in after years. At different times under Henry VIII. different days of the week were named as Star Chamber days. In the eighth year of Henry's reign, the Court sat on Monday, Tuesday, Thursday, and Saturday, while Chancery sat on Wednesday and Friday in each week. In the 21st year, Tuesdays, Thursdays, and Saturdays were appointed. In the end the Court sat regularly every Wednesday and Friday during term-time. D'Ewes says that it was in the reign of Elizabeth that Star Chamber days " were first certainly appointed to be on Wednesdays and Fridays." Hence we find Elizabeth's Council changing its regular days of sitting from Monday, Wednesday, and Friday to Tuesday, Thursday, and Saturday. It seems to have been in Elizabeth's reign that the Privy Councillors as a whole began to take an active part in the proceedings of the Court. The meetings of the Council and of the Court, however, were never allowed to clash. It is very clear from the Council Register that when Council business had to be done on Star Chamber days, the Council came and did it in the Star Chamber either before or after that more strictly legal business which was the special province of the Court (2).

During Henry VII.'s reign it would seem that the records of both Star Chamber and Council were entered in the same book, (3), a fact which is scarcely to be wondered at considering the close connection between the two, and that the Clerk of the Council was the same individual as the Clerk of the Court. After the opening of the new Register in 1540, the records of the Star Chamber were no longer included in the Council minute book, except occasionally where they have slipped in, probably by accident. On 2nd Dec., 1541, there is an entry in the Council Register concerning two men discharged of their " recognisance wherein they were bound for their appearance from day to day before the Lord Chancellor and other the Council in the Star Chamber. Entered by Adam, the Clerk of the Star Chamber." Again on 18th September, 1553, the Council is entered as sitting in the Star Chamber; no business is recorded, and the only presence is that of the Lord Chancellor. Evidently this is a record of a proper judicial meeting in the Star Chamber; no proceedings were entered in the Register because Star Chamber, not Privy Council, business was transacted. After 1580 Star Chamber transactions were occasionally inserted between the leaves of the Council Register. They are always on separate

(1) Scofield: p. 49.
(2) A.P.C., XI., XIV., and passim.
(3) Scofield: p. 27.

sheets of paper, generally of a different size from the Register, and often without date.(1).

Springing from the Council and controlled by it, the Court of Star Chamber shared in the powers and labours of the parent body. It was more than a Court. It was, as Bacon said, " an open Council." The publicity of its proceedings led the Council to hand over to it any matter which for any reason ought to have an open rather than a private hearing before the Council Table, and the great power of the Court made it temptingly efficient as a means of giving emphatic utterance to the will of the Crown. The usefulness of the Star Chamber developed with time. At first it was beneficial: private individuals no doubt obtained an impartial hearing. It fell finally into ill-repute owing to the political and financial ends which it was made to serve. In later Tudor days the Courts of Star Chamber and High Commission worked in concert, helping out or supplementing each other.

The measures of Henry VIII. placed the Church under the headship of the Crown. By the Statutes 31 H. VIII., c. 14, and 32 H. VIII., c. 15, the sovereign was empowered to nominate commissions to inquire into and punish heresy. Edward VI. and Mary used this power freely, and, although the ecclesiastical courts continued to exercise their jurisdiction, the Act 1 Eliz., c. 1, empowered the Queen to appoint any number of persons, being natural-born subjects, to exercise under Her Majesty all manner of jurisdiction in any wise touching ecclesiastical matters. The terms of the Act are very wide, and the commissions issued under it became wider and wider. For the first thirty years of their existence the ecclesiastical commissions, from which the Court of High Commission finally arose, were really used by the Privy Council as an arm of the supreme administrative power of the State, and they had relations with other bodies not of themselves but through the Council. Between 1535 and 1540 they were controlled by Cromwell, who was personally responsible to the King; on his fall they began to be dominated by the Privy Council. The latter's disciplinary authority over heretics, however, was by no means exclusively delegated to commissions, and in July, 1542, it ordered the sheriffs and justices of Coventry to return a grand jury to inquire into heresy under the Act of Six Articles. At a Council meeting on 4th May, 1543, even more explicit directions were issued, while in 1546 the Council directed the Bishop of London and the rest of the Commissioners for the Six Articles " to dissolve their assembly till another more commodious time to set about the same." This close supervision and control became even more marked when an adjustment of the more urgent difficulties left the Council free, about 1564, to turn its attention to the general administration of the Church. Until 1580 Commissions for Causes Ecclesiastical were flexible and adaptable instruments, and, though ecclesiastical in name, were entirely controlled and directed by the State. " A commission was a tool, a machine without institutional life or continuity of its own and the elasticity of its composition, its broad indefinite powers, and its discretionary procedure made it an able servant skilled in many tasks (2). Under Elizabeth the Commissions mainly referred only to the province of Canterbury, including Wales; others were granted for Ireland and the province of York. They were composed of prelates, Privy Councillors, and others, and were given wide general powers to enforce the Acts of Supremacy and Uniformity, and for the punishment of immorality and other ecclesiastical or semi-ecclesiastical offences. Wherever they had jurisdiction, however, their action was always under the supervision of the central Council, of which the Commissioners were often

(1) A.P.C., XII., XIII., XIV., introd.
(2) Usher: " The Rise and Fall of the High Commission," p. 47.

members. The Council regularly determined the Commissioners' competence and jurisdiction, and decided in addition whether their powers should be exercised in a particular case and how they should proceed. Such Commissions were issued periodically from 1559, but the Council kept its position as supreme judge in all cases whatsoever, and reserved the right of making any regulations which it thought fit. There was a large conciliar element in these Commissions, and the jurisdiction exercised was none other than that held and exercised by the King in Council.

The Council Register is full of entries illustrating the control of the Council over the Ecclesiastical Commissioners. Usually it commanded expedition in execution or a prompt and full report of proceedings, or a stay of proceedings until further orders. On 20th July, 1574, a letter was sent from the Council to the Archbishop of Canterbury ordering him to revoke a commission given, on behalf of the Ecclesiastical Commissioners, to a person unworthy. It was to go to a more capable man, and the Archbishop was to give his reasons for granting it to the former. Often the Council directed the Commissioners " to examine the truth of the matter, and to proceed according to equity and justice, and in due course of the laws in such cases provided." Frequently it sent cases to them, promising assistance, and then issuing detailed orders as to the settlement of the cases, extending sometimes even to the penalty. In 1578 the Commissioners had imprisoned a man in York, and had then sent him to London to confer with the Dean of St. Paul's. The Council considered he ought not to return home, but should be imprisoned where the Dean thought fit. Bonds were consequently taken of him before the Council, and the Commissioners notified (1). On 23rd November, 1579, the Commissioners were ordered to " cite peremptorily " a Prebendary of Canterbury Cathedral " for certain horrible offences committed by him." In July of that same year the case of a man " considering he is of the ministry," was put definitely into the hands of the Commissioners. They were many times ordered by the Council to imprison this man, fine that, take bonds for appearances, or for further good behaviour. Occasionally they were bidden to look into a case, or the Council directed a stay of proceedings already instituted, the imprisonment of persons without any direct charge, or the liberation of persons held with or without charge; nor was it above appointing a messenger for the Ecclesiastical Commissioners in Lancashire and Cheshire. If its orders were not carried out to its full satisfaction, full reproof was sure to follow. It is clear from the Register and the recurrence of the phrase " warranted by the laws of this realm," that the Council believed the Letters Patent issued to the Commissioners met every possible requirement of statute or other law.

From 1535—80 the Commissioners were allowed little, if any discretion, and were very closely and immediately controlled by the Council. They executed, at the Council's command, far more arbitrary acts than they ever performed later. In later days, as a court, they heard cases referred to them by the Council, as did every other court in the realm, and while the wishes of that body were indirectly made known to the Commissioners in important cases, yet no decision after 1600 was directly dictated by the political powers (2). By 1579 the Council was sending many cases to them, although about this time it is found blaming them for inflicting too heavy penalties, imprisoning men without sufficient reason, or detaining them unwarrantably long. It ordered the mitigation

(1) A.P.C., X. 10th March, 1578.
(2) Usher: p. 50.

of the lot of the prisoners in the Gatehouse in 1581, any order given by the Council itsel " or by the Lord Bishop of London and Commissioners Ecclesiastical to the contrary not withstanding." In 1579 the Council ordered the release of a man without bonds, an "further, not to be vexed or molested . . . for unnecessary causes." The Council in thi way may have been disowning the responsibility for its own commands. Often it wishe a man to be detained for a time, and was unwilling or unable to assign any reason tha could be made public. If the Commissioners imprisoned him, in due time, after petitior ing the Council he could be released with all the éclat accruing to the victim of illega detention, and none but the Commissioners would be discredited (1). Complaints wer brought to the Council of men arrested by the Commissioners' officers and offered their free dom for a sum of money; and of men cited to appear, charged with nothing, but threatene with a fresh summons if money was not paid to the official. At least one such case wa found true by the Council on 29th April, 1580, and the Commissioners were ordered t punish the pursuivant in question.

Cases were referred to the Ecclesiastical Commissioners as a part of the routin work of which the Council was anxious to be rid. The loss of papal and legatine appellat jurisdiction was keenly felt by English litigants. Laity and clergy alike declined t accept the Archbishop's Courts as final, and appealed to the Privy Council by the time honoured process of petition for redress of grievances which normally possessed no judici; remedy. When it was discovered that the Commissioners was quite capable of dealin with such cases, reference to them became a matter of course. The extremely close supe; vision of the Council was somewhat relaxed, except in visitatorial matters of importanc and the number of litigants increased rapidly. Thus a new court came into being t relieve the Privy Council of the burden of dealing with a new class of cases too numerou and petty for its personal attention. The new phase had begun in 1570, but not unt 1586 does the Commission speak of itself as a court in its own official records. Few pr hibitions were issued to the Commission before Elizabeth's death, probably owing to th Council's prompt action in 1579. One Giles, a rector in Devonshire, proceeded again by the Commissioners, had stopped proceedings by securing a prohibition. The Counc summoned him to London, and treated him in such exemplary fashion as apparently 1 cause suitors to reflect before asking for prohibition, other than as provided for by stri precedent (2).

The Court of High Commission had a distinctly statutory origin; there was n ground for questioning its legality. In this instance, too, the common lawyers were fc a time on the side of the Crown. They disliked the prerogative when it interfered wit the course of common law, but they magnified it when it dealt with ecclesiastical ma ters, for they were glad enough to see their old rival, the spiritual jurisdiction, th humbled servant of the temporal power (3). The Court was not responsible for any on of the policies it enforced; it did not take the initiative and choose them as its especi; duties. The State and Church, which controlled the Court of High Commission an decided that Puritan and Roman Catholic should conform, moral jurisdiction over th laity be upheld, and the press censored, must bear the ultimate responsibility. The Stat and Church expressed the general opinion of the western world of the time, and the Stat employed the Ecclesiastical Commissioners to secure conformity to its creed by suc forcible means as they might find necessary.

(1) Ibid., p. 62.
(2) A.P.C., XI. 26th February, 25th March, 1579.
(3) Maitland: " Constitutional History," p. 265.

The Court of Requests, as conceived by Henry VII., was a court for civil cases corresponding to the Court of Star Chamber which took cognisance of criminal matters. Its existence is almost conterminous with Tudor rule, and it is to Henry VIII. that the court undoubtedly owed its constitution as a definite tribunal, and, though it continued some years longer than is generally supposed, its activity and power rapidly succumbed to the hostility of the Common Law Courts after the death of Elizabeth. The Court of Chancery was busy and popular, but one court was not enough to meet the demand for a court with equitable jurisdiction. Hence there came into being the Court of Requests, a court of equity for poor suitors, or for the King's servants specially privileged to sue there. There appears to be no foundation for the view held by Spence and Palgrave that the court dated from an earlier period than Henry VII.'s reign. The records of the court testify to its activity from the eighth year of that reign; thenceforward is judges were nominated by the King. Even them, however, they were no more than a standing committee. This comparative permanence, however, ensured the growth of curial traditions and continuity of practice. These were developed and maintained by the legal assessors who, at first forming but a numerically unimportant portion of the Court, succeeded eventually in absorbing the whole of its jurisdiction.

The Court of Requests was never placed upon a statutory basis. Its natural evolution from the King's Council, and its gradual development from a tribunal of a more or less shifting committee of an itinerant Council into a court with a fixed habitat and permanent and professional judges, preclude the suspicion that its establishment was due to a far-sighted policy of enhancing the royal prerogative (1). It was peculiarly a Tudor institution, and its history is a striking example of Tudor methods of administration. The paternal aspect of the Government is nowhere more apparent than in the proceedings of the Court of Requests, or " Court of poor men's causes."

The name " Court of Requests " is found in 1529: " Hereafter follow the names of such Councillors as be appointed for the hearing of poor men's causes in the King's Court of Requests " (2). It is clear from a list of judges of the court that it was originally either a delegation or an aspect of the Council, similar in character to the early Courts of Chancery and Star Chamber, and deriving its authority from that fact. Its intimate connection with the Council and the Star Chamber is attested by Sir Julius Cæsar (3), who endeavours to show that all the judges in the Star Chamber, from 9 H. VII. down to 3 and 4 Philip and Mary, sat alternis vicibus in the King's Court at Whitehall commonly called the Court of Requests, or wherever the King held his Council for the hearing of private causes between party and party. Wolsey, when Chancellor, established a committee of the Council to sit permanently " in the Whitehall " for the expectation of poor men's causes depending "in the Starred Chamber," and to the same purpose it was provided in the Ordinances for the Royal Household in 1526 that of those members of the Council in constant attendance upon the King, two should sit daily in the Council Chamber at certain hours to hear " poor men's complaints." Before 1529 this " Court of Poor Men's Causes," as it was called, had attended the royal person on the royal progresses, and it was not until about 1497 that its books indicate any difference between term and vacation. When this discrimination was made, it indicates, as Leadam remarks, that a professional element was getting hold of the court. Wolsey's com-

(1) Leadam: " Select Cases in the Court of Requests," p. ix., x., xi.

(2) Ibid., xiv.

(3) Ibid., cvi., cviii.

mittee became finally the Court of Requests, sitting in Whitehall and consisting, before the end of the reign of Henry VIII., of certain members of the Council and some lawyers both civilians and canonists, styled Masters of Requests, who heard matters referred to them by the Privy Council or coming directly before them. The Masters of Requests were sworn of the Privy Council, but, as time went on, they ceased to be reckoned among the Privy Councillors, and, though sworn as Councillors to the King, had no precedence as members of the Privy Council.

The Court dealt with civil cases resting on the suggestion that the suitor was too poor to proceed at Common Law or was a member of the King's Household. In many cases which came before the Court the first line of defence was the plea that the complaints could and should be tried in the common law courts, the inevitable inference being that the ordinary law courts were much more likely than the Court of Request to favour the wealthy defendant, or that their procedure was so dilatory and expensive as to render it impossible for poor men to resort to them. There is here an instance of the Sovereign seeking, by means of his prerogative, to give the poorer classes a protection they could not obtain from the ordinary law courts. Sir Thomas Smith described it as the Court " wherein all suits, made to Her Majesty by ways of supplication or petition are heard and ended, neither should it hold plea of any other matters than such. And this is called the poor man's Court, because there he should have right without paying any money; and it is called also the Court of Conscience. The Judges in this court are the Masters of Requests, one for the common laws, the other for the civil laws " (1) In Elizabeth's reign there were two Masters Ordinary, and two Masters Extraordinary The first followed the Queen in her numerous progresses, the second remained at White hall.

In the later years of the sixteenth century, the Common Law Courts attacked jurisdiction which deprived them of litigants and fees. There may be some connection between the attacks of the judges upon the Court of Requests, and the revival, about this time, of the appellate jurisdiction of the House of Lords in civil cases. The judges in assailing the Court of Requests with writs of prohibition, treated it as a new court created by the early Tudors, with neither statutory authority nor immemorial custom to support its jurisdiction. If it was simply a delegation of the Privy Council it ranked with the Star Chamber as justified by immemorial custom. If its constitution by Henry VII or Wolsey was the establishment of a distinct tribunal, it could plead no justification, as it had no commission under the Great Seal. Whatever its genesis, as a matter of fact and practice, it had become a distinct tribunal. But the attacks upon it were premature and, as late as 1st May, 1600, the Council Register records: " Roger Wilbraham, by He Majesty's command sworn one of the Masters of Requests " (2). Under James I. and Charles I. the court did much business.

The Council of the North was created by Henry VIII. after the Catholic revolt of 1536 without any statutory authority. It was given a criminal jurisdiction in York shire and the other four northern counties in cases of riots, conspiracies, and acts o violence. It had also a civil jurisdiction of an equitable kind, although, in Elizabeth' reign, the judges of the Common Law Courts pronounced this illegal. Their doctrin seems to have been that without Act of Parliament the King might create a new cour to deal with matters known to common law, but that he could not create a new cour

(1) " Commonwealth of England," p. 167.
(2) A.P.C., XXX.

of equity (1). In August, 1523, Surrey wrote to Wolsey from the North, stating the impossibility of bringing wrong-doers to book in the northern counties. He wrote that there were few gentlemen in Northumberland who had not thieves belonging to them, and that the whole country thought that the talk of administering justice there was intended only to frighten them, as no man was appointed to continue among them to see justice administered. "The judges think it is ten times more necessary to have a Council here than in the marches of Wales " (2). Henry VIII. established the President and Council of the North by Letters Patent. Its powers were as ample and its methods as summary as those of the Star Chamber. It was subsidised by the Crown, as were the similar courts of the President and the Council of Wales, and the President and Council in the West, the latter erected by 32 H. VIII., c. 50, and all three having similar powers. The history of the Council of the North has yet to be written. It was set up " for the conservation of those countries in quiet, and the adminstration of common justice," and was directly under the control of the central Council. On his progress through the North in 1541, Henry made proclamation at York on 20th September, that anyone who had failed to receive justice from the Council of the North should have free access to himself and his Council during their stay in those parts. In 1549, when the Earl of Shrewsbury was made President of the Council of the North, he was instructed that doubtful cases in law were to be decided by the majority of the Council in continual attendance, or, if important, were to be referred to the judges or the Privy Council.

The Councils established in the North, in Wales, and at Calais were constituted on the same plan as the Privy Council, but few of their members belonged to that body, though occasionally the Lord Presidents were also Privy Councillors. This is not surprising, for the Tudor Privy Council was appointed for use and not for ornament, and its members would be of little value in their work of advising the Sovereign of their duties kept them away from Court. If their advice was needed they were summoned to London to give it. However, Sir Henry Sidney, Elizabeth's Privy Councillor, is somewhat of an exception. He was President of the Council in Wales from 1559-1586, and thrice Lord-Deputy of Ireland, 1565, 1568, and 1575. Robert Beale, Clerk of the Privy Council, was also a member of the Council in the North in 1597. He was probably sent there by the government and employed on secret service work, or as a spy upon the Lord President and his Council.

In 1545 the Council in the North was ordered to look to the collection of a loan. It is recorded in the Commons' Journals that on 19th February, 1552, the House ordered the Lord Chancellor to direct the King's writ of attachment to the President of the King's Council in the North to arrest two men, upon the complaint of one of the burgesses of Newcastle. The Privy Council Register abounds in directions to these Councils. In 1546 the Privy Council ordered the Council in the North, together with the Justices of Assize, to inquire into a case of burglary. In 1550 the Lord President was instructed to hear a case between the Sheriff of Yorkshire and one William Tyndal. In 1558 the Earl of Shrewsbury, President and a Privy Councillor, together with his Council were directed to see justice done in the case of the murder of a gentleman of Yorkshire, and in 1578 to settle a case in which the Bishop of Durham was concerned, or inform their Lordships. Towards the end of Elizabeth's reign Lord Burghley, President of the Council of the North,

(1) Maitland: " Constitutional History," p. 263.

(2) L. and P., III. 3240.

complained to the Privy Council concerning the Mayor and Bailiffs of Berwick, who refused to appear when summoned before him, alleging that Berwick was out of the jurisdiction of the Council. The matter was committed for consideration to the law officers of the Crown, who were of opinion that there was no reason why Berwick should not obey a process from the Council of the North. Accordingly the Privy Council took order, 2nd July, 1601, that " from henceforward those of the town of Berwick shall be obedient unto the process directed from that Court [of the North] and shall be subject to the jurisdiction of the same in all civil causes as the other parts of the North are." The Council was evidently still allowed to exercise its civil jurisdiction. Between the death of one Lord President, the Earl of Huntingdon, in 1595, and the appointment of Lord Burghley the younger in 1599, the vigour of the Council as an instrument of government seems to have declined somewhat, for the functions of President were discharged for a time by the aged Archbishop of York. Sir Thomas Smith wrote to the Council in the North and that in the Marches of Wales, that they were " as Parliaments in France. But yet if there be any matter of great consequence, the party may move it at the first, or remove it afterwards to Westminster Hall, and to the ordinary Judges of the Realm, or to the Chancellor as the matter is. These two courts do hear matters before them, part after the common law of England, and part after the fashion of the Chancery " (1).

The Court in the Marches of Wales seems to have originated in the authority granted about 1470 to the Prince of Wales' Council, to restore order and good government in the Principality. Such a Council had existed ever since the time of the first Prince of Wales for the purpose of administering his estates. In the ordinary course of things the Council had authority in the Principality only, therefore it was necessary to confer, by commission, special powers in the Marches, the exercise of which was facilitated by the fact that Edward IV., as heir of the Mortimers, was himself chief Marcher lord. Thus the Principality and the Marches were under one rule. It would seem that in Henry VII.'s reign the change took place by which the Council of the Prince became the Council of the Lord President. The Act 34 and 35 H. VIII. c. 26 gave a statutory basis to this body.

The purpose for which the Conucil grew up was to repress disorder in Wales and the Marches, including the four English counties of Gloucester, Worcester, Hereford, and Salop, and to punish the lawlessness with which the Common Law Courts were powerless to deal. This was its work up to the middle of the sixteenth century. During the succeeding half century, it acted both as a judicial and also as an administrative body, the instrument of the Privy Council in Wales and the Marches. During this period the dignity of the Council increased and its organisation became fixed. The cases with which it dealt, however, were less serious than in earlier years, and by the end of the century its decline had begun. The Council was subordinate both to the Privy Council and the Star Chamber, but it exercised a considerable amount of control over local courts and local officials, especially sheriffs and J.P.'s. It was a link between the central and local government, and also facilitated the working of the new institutions created for Wales by Henry VIII. The Privy Council was the body which determined the powers to be exercised by the Council in Wales, for it drew up the instructions received by each Lord President on entering office. Constant supervision was exercised by it over the subordinate body : one of the special duties of the Secretary of State was to acquaint himself with " the power

(1) " Commonwealth of England," p. 83.

and form of proceeding at the Council in the Marches of Wales, and the Council of the North " (1). The Lord President, or his Deputy, was in frequent communication with the Privy Council, and was bound to send up, every Hilary Term, accounts of fines imposed by his Court. The Council of the Marches was a convenient body for the examination of accused persons. In Bishop Lee's time (1534—43), it exercised summary jurisdiction, inflicting even the death penalty. During Elizabeth's reign, however, serious cases were nearly always dealt with by the Privy Council, Star Chamber or ordinary Courts. There are references to the sending up of prisoners to the Privy Council for further hearing or punishment, and trifling cases are sent from the Privy Council to the Council in Wales for decision. Occasionally the jurisdictions clashed, and a man was summoned to appear before both tribunals: in such cases the Council in Wales had to rescind its order. The dignity and efficiency of the Council in Wales was jealously watched over by the superior body. Care was taken, in drawing up instructions and orders, to have the advice of experienced persons, and the payment of respect to the Lord President and his Council was strictly enforced by the central body. At the same time the Privy Council roundly scolded any tendency in the subordinate body to disobey instructions, and at times a reversal of proceedings before it was ordered on the ground of undue severity. But it relieved the Privy Council of many trivial cases, and, especially in its early days, did work that could be done effectively only by local officials. The Council in Wales also carried out the administrative work of the Privy Council. The duties of the Lord President and his colleagues in this direction were very varied; in every way they were expected to strengthen the hands of the Government.

Throughout its history the Council in Wales was closely connected with the Star Chamber. The two courts existed primarily for the same purpose, the repression of disorder with which the Common Law was unable to deal adequately. They were alike in many points of procedure and in the punishments they imposed. In cases with which either Court was competent to deal, it would seem that the Star Chamber exercised jurisdiction where persons of rank were concerned, and the Council in Wales when the litigants were poor men, and when a local hearing was more convenient. Hence offenders were often sent up to the Star Chamber for trial after examination before the Council, and instances of converse proceedings are also to be found.

The Council in Wales exercised a jurisdiction parallel to that exercised by the Council in the North. Both bodies were established to check lawlessness in specially disturbed districts; both did good service at first, and both incurred unpopularity later. Both were under the supervision of the Privy Council and acted according to its instructions. But the Council in Wales was older and more important, with a statutory basis, while the Council of the North was erected in 1536 solely by royal prerogative. The Presidents of the Northern Council were not men of great note or ability as a rule, while their position was weakened by the existence of the office of Warden of the Marches, who performed many of the military duties which in Wales were incumbent upon the Lord President. The powers of the Council of the North were less extensive than those of the Council in Wales. The former could not punish treason, and it had two distinct commissions, one for causes criminal, the other for causes civil. The Council in Wales, on the other hand, was empowered to hear all manner of complaints, civil and criminal, exhibited by poor persons unable to sue at Common Law. The instructions to the Council of the North resemble in tenor those to the Council in Wales, but lay especial stress

(1) Skeel: " Council in the Marches of Wales," p. 272.

on such matters as recusancy and the conversion of tillage to pasture. Had the existence of the Council in Wales come to an end with the sixteenth century, it would probably have been remembered with gratitude (1).

The extension of the power of the Privy Council under the Tudors was obtained by means of the establishment of subordinate councils such as these just mentioned. They were the instruments of the Crown in the different departments of government. Another Court of which the Tudors made full use was the Admiralty. Admiralty Courts existed as early as 1340 and 1357, and crimes committed at sea were, until 28 H. VIII., c. 15, indisputably within their competence, while criminal cases, even capital, were until then habitually tried in the Admiralty, sometimes without a jury. Henry VIII., on his accession, made treaties with France providing for special tribunals to try piracy claims with dispatch. In England the Earl of Surrey Lord High Admiral, Cuthbert Tunstal Master of Requests, and Christopher Middleton, judge of the Admiralty, were appointed judges. No appeal was allowed, except to the Council on bail. Before Henry's reign, the Court of Admiralty exercised both civil and criminal jurisdiction in virtue of the royal prerogative. It was very closely connected with the Privy Council, and was independent of the Common Law. The Statute 28 H. VIII., c., 15, provided that treasons, felonies, robberies, murders, and confederacies, committed within the Admiralty jurisdiction, were to be judged by Common Law before the Admiral or his deputy, and three or four others appointed by the King. By the Act 32 H. VIII., c. 14, the Admiral was granted jurisdiction in certain cases of contract. But by his letters patent the King conferred a far wider jurisdiction. In 1547 it included "any thing, matter, cause whatsoever, done or to be done as well upon the sea as upon sweet waters and rivers, from the first bridges to the sea throughout our realms of England or Ireland or in the dominions of the same." Appeals from the Admiralty went, in the fifteenth century, to delegates and special commissioners appointed by the Crown ad hoc. By the Statute 25 H. VIII., c. 19, however, commissioners called Delegates of Appeals were appointed to hear appeals from the ecclesiastical and admiralty courts (2). Throughout the Tudor period cases of piracy coming before the Council were constantly delegated by it to the Court of Admiralty. On 27th Nov., 1550, the Court of Admiralty is referred to in the Council Register as the highest " Court of Civilians " in England, and on 9th June, 1589, the Council took order, on a motion made by the Lord Admiral, that no letters of assistance should be granted for commissions out of the Admiralty Court, unless signed by the Lord Admiral, or made out at his request. Under the Tudors the Court of Admiralty was directed and controlled by the Privy Council, and the Lord High Admiral was invariably a Privy Councillor.

Local bodies, such as the Council at Calais, the Deputy and Council in Ireland, the three Courts of the Borders, were all the instruments of a gigantic centralised executive, working without haste or rest, and making its authority felt in the furthest corners of the realm. Custom was held to justify the jurisdiction of the Courts of the Counties Palatine and of the Stannaries, while others were erected for special purposes by the Tudors, not by means of the royal prerogative, but by Statute. Such was the Court of Augmentations, set up by the Act 27 H. VIII., c. 27, to deal with the monastic estates already confiscated. The Statute 32 H. VIII., c. 46, erected the Court of Wards, because Henry knew he was being defrauded of " great rents, revenues, and profits " due to him in his character as guardian of wards, of " idiots and fools natural," and " of all women being his Grace's widows." The administration of feudal wardships was, by this

(1) Ibid., p. 274-5.
(2) Carter: " History of English Legal Institutions," p. 169-171.

Act, severed from the Exchequer. The Court of First Fruits and Tenths was established by the Act 32 H. VIII., c. 45, to collect the revenues of the King as Head of the Church, and 33 H. VIII., c. 39, consolidated the authority of the King's officers in certain castles, estates, and districts "as well in England and Wales, as in Calais and the Marches," by creating the Court of Surveyors. This last had jurisdiction over all "possessions, lands, tenements, and other hereditaments, being in any part parcel or member of the Crown." All these Courts were under the control of the Council. The Master of the Court of Wards, and the Chancellors of the Courts of First Fruits, Augmentations, and of the Duchy of Lancaster were generally Privy Councillors. The records of the Courts are full of correspondence with the Privy Council on matters of the smallest detail. The Tudors also erected two courts, with criminal jurisdiction in cases of treason, murder, manslaughter, etc., in royal residences, by the Statutes 3 H. VII., c. 14, and 33 H. VIII., s., 12, namely, the Court of the Lord Steward, Treasurer, and Comptroller of the Household, and the Court of the Lord Steward respectively. Complaints of, or claims to exemption from, the jurisdiction of such Courts were tried before the Council, and the central controlling body aided its assistants in every way, and governed the country with their aid.

The Council, however, did not rule entirely by these Courts and Councils. Numerous commissions were granted by it when its work became too heavy. At different times under the Tudors, commissions were granted to deal with such matters, among others, as Household causes, piracy, or, as they were called, Commissioners for Depredations, Sacrilege, Crown debts, the sale of Crown lands, for receiving Church goods, for Mint matters, for restraint of the export of grain and victuals, for the causes of poor prisoners, for the Musters, for Insurance in London, for the gun trade and the smuggling out of the country of cannon, for "Sir Francis Drake's commodities," for maimed soldiers, and for Border causes. Privy Councillors were not always included in these commissions, but they were granted to men whom the Crown knew and trusted, or to members of the Ordinary Council. These, having taken an oath, were employed in any special or extraordinary work, and if found capable, were often sent to under take local work as one of the members of the regular Councils, eventually perhaps being raised to the dignity of Privy Councillor. The Council, however, exercised a concurrent jurisdiction even over matters which it delegated to those Boards; the justice dispensed by local courts and commissions came straight from the centre, all complaints and appeals against it being made to the Privy Council.

In this way the Tudor Council ruled England. Such a Government, if the country was to retain her independence and freedom, was the only one possible. Its harshness is proverbial, but its other aspect is too little heeded. It was lenient when justice demanded leniency, even in a time of danger and necessity. It is very difficult to understand the peculiar needs of the time, and the meaning of the records of the Council is in danger of obscurity by reason of this very difficulty. Only when the Government was faced with a danger which one can in part realise, is one able to estimate the true greatness of an administration which raised England from the prostration of the Wars of the Roses to a position in which she was able to defeat the overwhelming power of Spain. No country has ever possessed a central government combining such a perfect organisation in every department of administration, with such dauntless courage, boundless energy, and marvellous grasp of detail. A study of the records of the Council, however superficial, confirms still more strongly the conviction that England and the English people owe more to Consiliar government under the Tudors than they will ever realise.

X. RECORDS.

————— :o :—————

IT remains to say a word upon the subject of the official records of the Privy Counci
One is at once confronted by the great gap from 1460 to 1540. Many suggestions hav
been hazarded as to the reason for this absence of the Council Register. It seems mo
probable, not that there was a gap in the records, as Nicholas thinks, but rather a materi:
loss of such once existent. In support of his view, Nicholas mentions that the new Regi
ter was begun a fortnight after the death of Thomas Cromwell, who had accumulated i
his hands many of the offices of state, and that Paget was appointed clerk to record th
acts of that diligent body which, in a manner, took Cromwell's place. For it seemed ɛ
though the Council of Henry, active enough before, contemplated in the near future a
increase of business which would require official regularity and routine (1). When tɦ
new Register book was started in 1540, the Clerk of the Council was ordered to enter an
register all such " decrees, determinations, letters, and other such things as he should ɪ
appointed to enter, in a book to remain always as a ledger, as well for the discharge ɪ
the said Councillors, touching such things as they should pass from time to time, as al:
for a memorial unto them of their own proceedings." A passage almost verbally idei
tical occurs 19th April, 1550, when William Thomas is appointed Clerk. On 2nd Februar:
1547, it was resolved that any Privy Councillor might ask for the copy of any entry in th
Register, and have it delivered to him, with the signature of the Clerk who deliverɪ
it, and the words " concordat ad originali," (sic). Precisely the same duties as tho:
mentioned in 1540 had, however, been performed by the Clerks of the Council in th
reigns of Henry IV., V., and VI., and, moreover, such officers existed in the reigns ɪ
Edward IV. and Henry VII. and VIII. A failure of the records cannot have been dɪ
to an interruption in the activities of the Council itself, because we know from the Stat
Papers that the Council was by no means inoperative during the reigns of the first tw
Tudors. Again, when in 1540 the records of the Council suddenly reappear, it is not i
a feeble tentative way, as though making a beginning, but in full measure and complel
form, as though long continued.

The Liber Intrationum, commencing in the first year of Henry VII.'s reign, hɛ
already been mentioned. The original of this is lost, but copies of it show it to have bee
a Register in which the transactions both of the Star Chamber and the Privy Council wei
entered. The Council Register, a record of the work of the Council, remains to us froɪ

(1) Nicholas: " Proceedings and Ordinances," VII. Introduction.

10th August, 1540, to December, 1601. A valuable document, Brit. Mus., Addit. MSS. 11404, believed to have belonged to Sir Julius Caesar, appears to be brief extracts from the Register from 21st December, 1601, to 19th March, 1603. From 1504 to 1601 there are very large gaps, especially at the beginning of Elizabeth's reign; for example, the Register is missing 12th May, 1559, to 28th May, 1562, 6th Sept., 1562, to Jan., 1563, 23rd Jan. to 10th Aug., 1563, 10th Aug., 1563, to 12th April, 1564, 28th May to 7th Aug., 1564, from 2nd Oct. to 4th Nov., 1564, 31st Oct., 1565, to 8th Oct., 1566, and from 3rd May, 1567, to 24th May, 1570. Such losses as those just mentioned seriously impair the value of the records. Again, in 1553, there are no meetings of the Privy Council recorded in the Register from 17th June until 16th July, and on that date the names of the Privy Councillors present are not recorded, nor is any place of meeting mentioned. No attendances of Privy Councillors are recorded until a meeting on 13th August at the Tower. There are also many blank pages in the Register, and its silence upon nearly all memorable matters is very disappointing. Very frequently meetings are recorded, but none of the business transacted there is mentioned. On 20th March, 1541, there was a full attendance of Councillors, but only one minute of the business done is entered. The small value of the signatures of Councillors in the Register has already been touched upon.

We know from other sources that the Privy Council must have acted more frequently than the Register would lead us to suppose. But the discussions and decisions of the Council were no more committed to writing than are those of the Cabinet to-day. The Council Register sheds no light upon the tortuous diplomacy practised by the Tudors, nor does it help us to determine the nature, variations, and extent of the influence of their various advisers. Differences at the Council Board never intrude upon the Register, and diplomatic relations are referred to only in the absence of this or that Councillor or Clerk from duties at home. When no business is recorded at a Council meeting it may have been that no business was done, but it is more probable that it was not deemed proper to commit it to writing. Occasionally the Council dispensed with the presence of a Clerk, and, unless the business was reported to him afterwards, no record of it appears in the Register beyond the names of those present. It is evident from the terms of appointment of the Clerk of the Council on 10th Aug., 1540, that it was not intended that the whole of the Council's proceedings should be recorded. There are many entries in the Register of meetings occurring on the same date, and this is ground for assuming that the Privy Councillors in daily attendance upon the Queen were called together to do business whenever a messenger arrived. Towards the end of Elizabeth's reign, there frequently appears a marginal note beside the record of a letter, that "this letter was cancelled and another written instead thereof." This second letter, however, is seldom recorded. There are many references, too, in the Register to the Council Chest; minutes of letters which are not entered in the Register are recorded as being placed in the Council Chest, and, judging from the number of documents said to have been put there, the Chest must have been of tremendous capacity. Minutes are also mentioned as "remaining with the Clerks," but they are certainly not recorded in the Register. Again, the Clerks of the Council had letter books, in which they made a rough copy of each letter as it was written, in pursuance of instructions given by the Council. This "Register of Letters" is referred to by name on 28th Jan., 1548. Only one of these has come down to us in its original form. It covers but a short period, 6th February-13th June, 1547. The dates given in the letter book are not always consecutive, and the entries are hastily made. In 1620 Ralph Starkey copied this letter book and another, which is lost to us.

In doing so he appears to have been under the impression that he was reproducing th actual Council Register, and, from a note at the end of his transcript, he evidentl attached the same importance to the two (1). Occasionally the registering Clerk made us of the blank pages at the end of the Register for the purposes of his letter book. Ther were also " warrant books " containing the grants of offices and pensions made by th Privy Council, but they, too, have disappeared.

It has been mentioned that Star Chamber proceedings are interleaved occasior ally with the Council Register, owing to the close connection between the Star Chambe and the Privy Council. In the Journals of the House of Lords (Vol. II. p. 19), imme diately before the proceedings of the Parliament of 1597, is inserted a page of Privy Cour cil proceedings of 39 Eliz. In the original Council Register there are two blank pages a the time. In the manuscript of the Lords' Journals the Privy Council extract occurs i 1572, but in printing the editor placed it at 1597 in order to preserve chronological se quence. It probably existed loose, and was bound up wrongly into 1572, as it still re mains. The most probable explanation of its presence there seems to be as follows: Secretary of State, to use a later term, had a seat in the House of Lords (2). He ma there have given some rough notes of Privy Council proceedings to a clerk, for the makin of a draft preparatory to copying into the Council Register, and a leaf was left by acc dent in the House of Lords, where it might not be recognised as Privy Council busines Towards the end of Elizabeth's reign the Register falls off in importance as regards judici cases, and becomes simply and solely a letter book. About 1575 recognisances in judici cases cease altogether to be entered in the Register, although the clerk, in the absence the Council, still records the appearances of men bound to appear before the Counci These later Registers still record the judicial business of the Council, but they show tha its time, in mid-week at any rate, was taken up almost entirely with administrative worl It is difficult to understand why the names of those signing the letters in the Registe should be placed at the head of the entries recording those letters. Moreover, occasior ally only some of the Privy Councillors recorded as present at a meeting sign the lette drawn up and despatched. Frequently in the letters sent from the Council an order given for a man to appear before the Board, and then the name of an individual Cour cillor is introduced into the letter; e.g., on 4th May, 1600, the Master and Wardens the Company of Stationers in London ordered a ballad to be suppressed, and if anyor refused to give up his copy of the same, the Council's letter stated that he was " to l brought befor me, the Lord Archbishop of Canterbury, to be ordered therein as the shall be cause." Such letters were often sent from the Council Board, ordering a appearance before an individual Councillor. Towards the close of Burghley's life th Register occasionally records that letters were sent to him for his signature, when he wi unable to attend the meetings, before being despatched.

The Council Register is throughout a record of the meetings of the Council atte dant upon the Sovereign, and not of those Councillors who were left in London to transa business which could only be done in town. For a few days in 1553 we have the unusu feature of a double Register, 12th August—19th August. The Queen left the Tower f Richmond on that date, and the record of meetings there were entered in the " Richmor

(1) Harleian MSS., 352.
(2) Sir Thomas Smith: " Commonwealth of England," p. 51.

Register." On Saturday, 19th August, that part of the Council which had been left in London, probably to deal with an outbreak in the city, was transferred to Richmond, where a full meeting was held on Monday, 21st August. Once again, in 1590, we have a double Register for a short time. Vol. VIII. of the Council Office series contains a record of Council business up to and including a meeting 23rd December, 1590. On 20th December, however, a new volume of the Register (Eliz. vol. IX.) had been begun, apparently by the clerk, Daniel Rogers, who signs the list of Privy Councillors given on the first page, and copious minutes are given of Council business transacted on 20th and 21st December at two or more meetings at Richmond, which do not appear in the preceding volume. No place of meeting is given for the business recorded in vol. VIII. on 22nd and 23rd December. The explanation probably is that while the Court was at Richmond some members of the Council remained in London to wind up outstanding business before Christmas, and that the old Register Book was sent up with them. The Clerk of the Council in attendance at Richmond made his entries at the same time in the new book (Eliz. vol. IX.). This was probably the "New Council Book," for which 6s. 8d. was paid to the Keeper of the Council Chest by the Treasurer of the Chamber, 26th December, 1590 (1).

How the Register was compiled is still somewhat of a mystery, and seems likely to remain so. It was the duty of the Clerks of the Council, of which there were always two in attendance after the beginning of Edward VI.'s reign, to look to the entering of Council business in the Register. Paget, appointed Clerk in 1540, appears throughout to have written the minutes recorded until he was sent as ambassador to France, and Sir John Mason appointed in his stead. The Register is, however, written in many different hands, and it is probable that professional copyists were occasionally employed, for the Clerks of the Council had, especially in Elizabeth's reign, many other interests and duties besides that of attendance at the Council Board. They appear, however, to have supervised and corrected the work. It seems improbable that the Clerks were admitted to all Council meetings, and, at those from which they were excluded, the Secretaries seem to have taken notes of the business transacted, and later on to have instructed the clerks what to enter in the Register. There are many notes of business transacted in the Council in Walsingham's hand (2), and records of Council meetings not mentioned in the Register are to be found among Cecil's papers. One Clerk appears to have been more highly paid than the others. He may have been admitted to Council meetings, at which he would be instructed what to have recorded in the Register. One of his juniors might then perform the task of writing up the minutes. Rough and fair copies were certainly made, for occasionally we have both remaining, and are able to elucidate the one from the other. The rough draft was probably submitted for approval to the Secretary, and then copied out fairly into the Register, for in the rough draft many entries are made and crossed out later, *vacat ex mandato Consilia* (sic), before a fair copy was begun. Moreover, the rough copy has often the original signatures of men bound in recognisance before the Council. Many blank pages in the fair copy testify to the willing spirit but weak flesh of the Clerk; occasionally where the rough draft remains these blank pages can be filled in. Between 8th October, 1566, and 3rd May, 1567, intervals between the recorded

(1) A.P.C., XX. p. vii.
(2) Dom. Cal., anno 1574, passim.

meetings of the Council are so long as to provoke the suspicion that the Clerk of the Council had allowed himself to use his own discretion, and omit to record meetings at which the business was considered by him to be unimportant. Occasionally he condensed the record by including two or more Councils under one entry, the successive dates being given in the margin. The Clerk may have made up the Register from day to day, but a minute recorded 4th February, 1551, refers to an occurrence on 6th February, 1551, which date is actually mentioned, thus proving that the minutes were sometimes written up two or three days after the events recorded in them. During Edward's reign the Privy Councillors often signed the Register, but after that time it was left to the Clerks of the Council to record the names of those present and of those who signed letters. In the later volumes of the Register for Elizabeth's reign the chronological sequence is often disregarded: in 1600 the entries for the last portion of June and the first portion of July are inextricably confused. Evidently, when once the clerks had obtained the necessary signatures to the letters written as the result of deliberations at the Council Table, they did not think it necessary to enter them in chronological order in the Register. For the last years of Elizabeth the Register is written in several hurried hands, and we have reason to deplore the ravages of the binder and the disfigurement made by a later scribbler. It is obvious that, to some extent, the clerks worked independently of each other, and that the sheets containing their entries were handed to the binder to be made up into a volume, with as much regard to chronological accuracy as was possible under the circumstances, the result being overlapping dates, and entries which no system of re-arrangement can reduce to order. The dating of the entries is so irregular in places that we can only imagine many entries, especially those of a formal nature, were made in any vacant space in the Register which happened to be fairly near the actual date, (Vol. XIII., p. vii.). In many cases the letters recorded in the Register were not necessarily signed at the meeting of the Council at which they were approved or even on the same day.

The printed edition of the Acts of the Privy Council also leaves much to be desired. In Vol. II. the entry dated 19th August, 1547, is out of chronological order, but is not marked as being so. In Vols. VIII. and X. (pp. 260, 208), "Protestant" is inserted twice in the marginal summaries without warrant from the entries. In Vol. XI. again, a slight entry, such as "To the Lord Treasurer of Ireland, in answer to his touching the advertisement of the preparation of James FitzMaurice, etc., according to the minute in the Chest, etc.," gives rise to the following comment: "As early as the end of April the intelligence as to James FitzMaurice's preparations (for an insurrection), which had been gleaned from Drury's spies, was conveyed to the Council," (p. ix.). Such examples could be multiplied. In 1579 an entry is given under date 34th December, but no wrong date is noted. Again, an entry 20th May, 1579, refers to the case of a Prebendary of Gloucester accused of forgery, but in the introduction to the volume (p. xxi.) the editor refers to him as the Prebendary of Worcester. The statement that Sir John Wolley first appears in Vol. XV. (p. 7) is inconsistent with the references to him in Vol. XIV. In Vol. XXVI. a meeting is recorded as taking place on Sunday, 25th December, and another on Sunday, 26th December, 1596, but the editor has overlooked this. Sunday, 25th December, should be Saturday, 25th Dec. About 1597 lists of Privy Councillors are given in the manuscript Register, some at the head, others at the side, of certain entries. Of these (we do not definitely know which) one group is the list of those present at the meeting, the other of those who signed the letters of which the entry is the minute. The editor has, however, placed all at the head of the entry without indicating which group, in the original, was in the margin, and which at the head. In Vol. XXVIII. the date given after Sunday, 17th April, 1598, is Tuesday, 18th April; that again is not noted.

Whatever its defects, however, the Register of the Privy Council is an extremely fascinating record of an equally fascinating period in the history of England, and amply repays a study of its contents.

APPENDIX I.—TUDOR PRIVY COUNCILLORS.

———— :o: ————

THE following lists have been compiled from various sources, according to the reigns to which they belong:—

HENRY VII.

No complete list of Henry VII.'s Privy Council, assuming such a definitely organised body to have existed, can be compiled for any specific year. Therefore, the list is alphabetical and must be regarded as very conjectural. It covers a reign of twenty-four years, and it is scarcely necessary to observe that all those here given were not Privy Councillors at one and the same time.

John Alcock, Bishop of Worcester.
John Bailey, Canon of Windsor.
Henry Bourchier, Earl of Essex.
Sir Reginald Bray.
Sir John Cheney.
Sir Richard Croft.
Lord Dacre.
Giles Lord Daubney.
John Lord Dynham.
Sir Edmund Dudley.
Sir Richard Edgecombe.
Richard Fitzjames, Bishop of Chichester.
Richard Fox.
Stephen Frion.
Sir Richard Guildford.
Lord Hastings.
Thomas Howard, Earl of Surrey.
Thomas Janne, Bishop of Norwich.
Oliver King.
Sir Thomas Lovell.
Sir John Mordaunt.
John Morton, Bishop of Ely.
George Neville, Lord Bergavenny.
Dr. Peter Panec.
Henry Percy, Earl of Northumberland.
Sir Edward Poynings.

John Ratcliffe, Lord Fitzwalter.
Sir John Risley.
Thomas Ruthal, Bishop of Durham.
Robert Sherborne, Bishop of Chichester.
Sir Charles Somerset, Lord Herbert.
Edward Stafford, Duke of Buckingham.
Thomas Stanley, Earl of Derby.
Sir William Stanley.
Sir Richard Sutton.
George Talbot, Earl of Shrewsbury.
Jasper Tudor, Earl of Bedford.
Sir Richard Tunstal.
John de Vere, Earl of Oxford.
William Warham, Archbishop of Canterbury.
Sir Robert Willoughby, Lord Brooke.
Lord Grey de Wilton.
Sir Henry Wyatt.

HENRY VIII.

The following is a fairly accurate list of the Privy Councillors of Henry VIII. at the end of 1526:—

John Bourchier, Lord Berners, Chancellor of the Exchequer.
Charles Brandon, Duke of Suffolk, Marshal of England.
John Clerk, Bishop of Bath, Master of the Rolls.
Henry Courtenay, Marquis of Exeter.
Walter Devereux, Lord Ferrers.
Sir Thomas Docwra.
Sir William Fitzwilliam, Treasurer of the King's Household.
Richard Fox, Bishop of Winchester.
Thomas Grey, Marquis of Dorset.
Sir Henry Guildford, Comptroller of the Household.
Thomas Howard, Duke of Norfolk, Lord Treasurer.
Sir John Hussey.
John Islip, Abbot of Westminster.
William Knight, Secretary.
John Longland, Bishop of Lincoln.
Sir Thomas More, Chancellor of the Duchy of Lancaster.
Sir William Morgan, Vice-Chamberlain.
Robert Ratcliffe, Earl of Sussex.
William Lord Sandys, Chamberlain of the Household.
George Talbot, Earl of Shrewsbury, Steward of the King's Household.
Cuthbert Tunstall, Bishop of London, Keeper of the Privy Seal.
John de Vere, Earl of Oxford, Lord Chamberlain.
William Warham, Archbishop of Canterbury.
Dr. Richard Wolman.

Thomas Wolsey, Cardinal Archbishop of York, Lord Chancellor.
Sir Henry Wyatt, Comptroller of the Mint and Treasurer of the Chamber.
  Captain of the Guard?
  Dean of the King's Chapel?

The following list of Henry VIII.'s Privy Council at the end of 1540 has bee compiled from Nicholas's Proceedings and Ordinances of the Privy Council, Vol. VII and from Letters and Papers of Henry VIII., Vols. XV. and XVI.:—

Thomas Lord Audley, Lord Chancellor.
Sir John Baker, Chancellor of the Court of First Fruits and Tenths.
Charles Brandon, Duke of Suffolk, Great Master of the King's Household and Presider of the Council.
Sir Anthony Browne, Master of the Horse.
Thomas Cranmer, Archbishop of Canterbury.
Sir Thomas Cheyney, Lord Warden of the Cinque Ports and Treasurer of the Houschok
William Fitzwilliam, Earl of Southampton, Lord Privy Seal.
Sir John Gage, Comptroller of the Household.
Stephen Gardiner, Bishop of Winchester.
Thomas Howard, Duke of Norfolk, Lord Treasurer.
Sir William Petre.
Robert Ratcliffe, Earl of Sussex, Lord Chamberlain.
Sir Richard Rich.
John Lord Russell, Lord High Admiral.
Sir Ralph Sadler, Secretary.
William Lord Sandys, Chamberlain of the Household.
Edward Seymour, Earl of Hertford.
Cuthbert Tunstall, Bishop of Durham.
Sir Anthony Wingfield, Vice-Chamberlain.
Sir Thomas Wriothesley, Secretary.

EDWARD VI.

A complete list of the Privy Council on 21st March, 1547, as constituted by th King by commission. (See A.P.C., Vol. II.):—

Sir John Baker.
Sir Thomas Bromley, Justice of the King's Bench.
Sir Anthony Browne, Master of the Horse.
Thomas Cranmer, Archbishop of Canterbury. ·
Sir Anthony Denny.
John Dudley, Earl of Warwick, Great Chamberlain of England.
Henry Fitzalan, Earl of Arundel, Lord Chamberlain.
Sir John Gage, Comptroller of the Household.
Sir William Herbert.
William Lord St. John, Great Master of the Household and President of the Council.
Sir Edward Montague, Chief Justice of the Common Pleas.
Sir Edward North, Chancellor of the Augmentations.
Sir William Paget, Chief Secretary.
William Parr, Marquis of Northampton.
Sir Edmund Peckham, Cofferer of the Household.
Sir William Petre, Secretary.
Richard Lord Rich.

n Lord Russell. Keeper of the Privy Seal.

Ralph Sadler. Master of the Great Wardrobe.

rard Seymour, Duke of Somerset Lord Protector.

mas Lord Seymour of Sudeley. Lord High Admiral.

Richard Southwell.

hbert Tunstall, Bishop of Durham.

Anthony Wingfield. Vice-Chamberlain.

Edward Wotton.

Nicholas Wotton, Dean of Canterbury and York.

MARY, 1553.

John Baker, Chancellor of the Court of First Fruits and Tenths.

Henry Bedingfield.

Thomas Cheney, Treasurer of the Household and Lord Warden of the Cinque Ports.

Francis Englefield, Master of the Court of Wards.

iry Fitzalan, Earl of Arundel, Lord Steward and Great Master of the Household.

Richard Freston, Cofferer of the Household.

John Gage, Lord Chamberlain.

hen Gardiner, Bishop of Winchester, Lord Chancellor.

Edward Hastings, Master of the Horse.

holas Heath, Bishop of Worcester.

liam Herbert, Earl of Pembroke, President of the Council in the Marches of Wales.

mas Howard, Duke of Norfolk.

liam Howard, Lord Effingham, Lord High Admiral.

John Huddleston.

Henry Jerningham, Vice-Chamberlain of the Household.

John Mason, Master of the Posts.

liam Lord Paget.

liam Paulet, Marquis of Winchester, Lord Treasurer.

William Petre, Principal Secretary, Chancellor of the Court of First Fruits and Tenths.

iry Ratcliffe, Earl of Sussex.

hard Lord Rich.

Robert Rochester, Comptroller of the Household.

ncis Russell, Earl of Bedford, Lord Privy Seal.

Richard Southwell, Master of the Ordnance.

ncis Talbot, Earl of Shrewsbury, President of the Council of the North.

mas Thirlby, Bishop of Ely.

hbert Tunstall, Bishop of Durham.

Edward Waldegrave, Keeper of the Great Wardrobe.

Thomas Wharton.

ELIZABETH.

Within a few weeks of her accession the following (see A.P.C., Vol. VII.) wei sworn of Elizabeth's Privy Council :—

Sir Nicholas Bacon, Lord Keeper.

Sir Ambrose Cave, Chancellor of the Duchy of Lancaster.

Sir William Cecil, Secretary. *(Senior.)*

Sir Thomas Cheney, Lord Warden of the Cinque Ports and Treasurer of the Househok

Edward Lord Clinton, Lord Admiral.

Henry Fitzalan, Earl of Arundel, Lord Steward.

Nicholas Heath, Archbishop of York (soon deprived and dismissed).

William Herbert, Earl of Pembroke, President of the Council in the Marches of Wale

William Lord Howard of Effingham, Lord Chamberlain.

Sir Francis Knollys.

Sir John Mason, Master of the Posts, Treasurer of the Chamber.

Sir Thomas Parry, Comptroller of the Household.

William Paulet, Marquis of Winchester, Lord Treasurer.

Sir William Petre.

Sir Edward Rogers, Vice-Chamberlain of the Household.

Francis Russell, Earl of Bedford, Governor of Berwick.

Sir Richard Sackville.

Sir Ralph Sadler. *Secretary (Junior)*

Francis Talbot, Earl of Shrewsbury, President of the Council of the North.

APPENDIX II.—BIBLIOGRAPHY.

————— :o: —————

I.—MANUSCRIPTS.

. MSS., 4521.
leian MSS., 297. } Liber Intrationum.

h MSS., 4160—Perkin Warbeck's Proclamation.

on, Titus B., I. 123—List of Henry VIII.'s Council.

sdowne, 683, f. 44—Various lists of Privy Councillors of Elizabeth, of Councillors in Marches of Wales, etc.

sdowne, 104, f. 14—Lists of Privy Councillors of Edward and Mary.

rton, 2603, f. 33—Regulations for Edward VI.'s Privy Council.

on, Nero C., X.—Autograph Diary of Edward VI., (printed for the Clarendon Historical Society, 1884; also for the Roxburghe Club, 1837).

. MSS. 14893—Lists of Elizabeth's Privy Council.

ne, 3194—List of the Privy Council in 1485.

II.—PRINTED SOURCES.

A.—ORIGINAL DOCUMENTS AND LETTERS:—

ndar of Letters and Papers, Foreign and Domestic, of the Reign of Henry VIII.

ndar of State Papers—Domestic.

ndar of State Papers—Milanese.

ndar of State Papers—Spanish.

ndar of State Papers—Venetian.

rnals of the House of Commons.

rnals of the House of Lords.

uli Parliamentorum. London, 1767-77.

ner: Foedera. London, 1873.

ort of the Royal Commission on Public Records, Vol. II., Pt. I. London, 1914.

urn of Members of Parliament. 1872.

ceedings and Ordinances of the Privy Council of England, Vol. VII. Ed. Nicholas. London, 1834-7.

s of the Privy Council, Vols. I.-XXXII. Ed. Dasent. London, 1890-1909.

rdinances and Regulations for the Royal Household." Society of Antiquaries. London, 1890.

on: "A Book containing all such Proclamations as were published during the Reign of Queen Elizabeth . . ." London, 1618.

ele: A Bibliography of Royal Proclamations of the Tudor and Stuart Sovereigns, and of others published under authority 1485-1714, with an historical essay on their origin and use by R. R. Steele. 2 Vols. Oxford, 1910.

Pollard: Reign of Henry VII. from Contemporary Sources. 3 Vols. London, 1913-4.

Memorials of Henry VII. Ed. Gairdner. Rolls Series.

Materials for a History of Henry VII. Ed. Campbell. Rolls Series.

Statutes and Constitutional Documents. Ed. Prothero. Oxford, 1906.

Select Cases from the Court of Star Chamber. 2 Vols. Ed. Leadam. Selden Society. 1904.

Select Cases from the Court of Requests. Ed. Leadam. Selden Society. 1898.

Star Chamber Proceedings during the Reigns of Henry VII. and VIII. Ed. for the Somerset Record Society by G. Bradford. 1911.

Calendar of Hatfield MSS., I.—XII.

Calendar of Stafford MSS.

Calendar of Lonsdale MSS.

Calendar of Finch MSS.

Calendar of Middleton MSS.

Calendar of Rye MSS.

Calendar of Hereford MSS.

Calendar of Rutland MSS.

Calendar of Cowper MSS.

Calendar of Queensberry MSS.

} Historical Manuscripts Commission.

Grenville Papers, 4 vols. London, 1853.

Scrinia Ceciliana. London, 1663.

Plumpton Correspondence. Camden Society, 1839.

Letters of Elizabeth and James VI. Camden Society, 1849.

Leicester Correspondence. Camden Society, 1844.

Letters of Cecil to Carew. Camden Society, 1864.

Chamberlain's Letters. Camden Society, 1861.

Egerton Papers. Camden Society, 1840.

Verney Papers. Camden Society, 1853.

Original Letters of Eminent Literary Men. Camden Society, 1843.

Forbes: A Full View of the Public Transactions in the Reign of Queen Elizabeth. 1741.

B.—CONTEMPORARY NARRATIVES:—

Annals of the First Four Years of Queen Elizabeth. Camden Society, 1840.

Chronicle of Calais. Camden Society, 1845.

Baker's Chronicle. London, 1830.

Chronicle of King Henry VII. Ed. Hume. London, 1889.

Chronicles of London. Ed. Kingsford. Oxford, 1905.

London Chronicle. Camden Society, 1859.

Cooper's Chronicle. London, 1565.

Dr. Dee's Diary. Camden Society, 1842.

The Journal of King Edward's Reign, written by his own hand. Clarendon Historical Society Reprints. Edinburgh, 1884-6.

Literary Remains of Edward VI. Ed. Nichols, Roxburghe Club. London, 1857.

Fabyan's Chronicle. London, 1811.

Chronicle of Queen Jane and Queen Mary. Camden Society, 1850.

Grafton's Chronicle. London, 1809.

Greyfriar's Chronicle. Camden Society, 1852.

Hall's Chronicle. London, 1809.

Harding's Chronicle. London, 1812.

Holinshed's Chronicle. London, 1807.

Italian Relation. Camden Society, 1847.

Machyn's Diary. Camden Society, 1848.

Narratives of the Reformation. Camden Society, 1859.

Walsingham's Journal. Camden Society, 1870.

Wriothesley's Chronicle. 2 Vols. Camden Society, 1875-77.

Paston Letters. Ed. Gairdner. London, 1903-4.

Leopold von Wedel: Journey through England and Scotland, 1584-5. Transactions of the Royal Historical Society, 1895.

C.—CONTEMPORARY AUTHORS:—

Bacon's Essays, privately published, 1912.

Bacon's History of Henry VII. Ed. Lumby. London, 1903.

Sir Julius Caesar: Ancient State of the Court of Requests. London, 1597.

Camden: Britannia, 4th ed. London, 1722.

A Discourse of the Commonweal of this Realm of England. First printed 1581, and commonly attributed to W.S. Cambridge, 1893.

Memoirs of Robert Carey, Earl of Monmouth, written by himself (with Fragmenta Regalia). Edinburgh, 1808.

Crompton: L'authoritie et jurisdiction des courts de la Maiestie de la Roygne. London, 1594.

Hudson: Treatise of the Star Chamber, in Collectanea Juridica. Vol. II.

Harleian Miscellany. Vols. I., II., IV.

Naunton: Fragmenta Regalia (with Carey's Memoirs). Edinburgh, 1808.

Skelton: Poetical Works. Ed. Dyce. London, 1843.

Sir Thomas Smith: De Republica Anglorum. Cambridge, 1906.

D.—MODERN WORKS:—

Anson: Law and Custom of the Constitution. 3rd ed. Oxford, 1907.

Bailey: Succession to the English Crown. London, 1879.

Baldwin: King's Council in England during the Middle Ages. Oxford, 1913.

Bayne: The First House of Commons of Queen Elizabeth. English Historical Review. Vols. XXII. and XXIII.

Beatson: Political Index. London, 1806.

Birch: Memoirs of the Reign of Queen Elizabeth. London, 1754.

Brewer: Henry VIII. London, 1884.

Busch: England under the Tudors. London, 1895.

Carter: History of English Legal Institutions. London, 1902.

Cobbett: Parliamentary History. London, 1806.

Dicey: Privy Council. London, 1860.

Doyle's Baronage of England. London, 1886.

Dugdale's Baronage. London, 1675-6.

A Complete History of England (including Herbert of Cherbury's Henry VIII.). London, 1706.

Finlason: The Judicial Committee of the Privy Council. London, 1878.

Fisher: Political History of England. Vol. V. London, 1909.

Hale: Jurisdiction of the Lords. London, 1678.

Friedmann: Anne Boleyn. 2 Vols. London, 1884.

Friedmann: Some New Facts in the History of Queen Mary. Macmillan's Magazine. XIX., November, 1868.

Froude: History of England. London, 1903.

Gairdner: Henry VII. London, 1907.

Gneist: History of the English Constitution. 2nd Edition. London, 1889.

Gretton: King's Government. London, 1913.

Hallam: Constitutional History of England. London, 1826.

Hannis-Taylor: Origin and Growth of the English Constitution. London, 1889.

Hearn: Government of England. 2nd Edition. London, 1887.

Lord Herbert of Cherbury: Life and Reign of King Henry VIII. London, 1706.

Hinds: The Making of the England of Elizabeth. London, 1895.

Holdsworth: History of English Law. London, 1903.

Hornemann: Das " Privy Council " von England zur Zeit der Königin Elizabeth. Hanover, 1912.

Hume: The Great Lord Burghley. London, 1906.

Hume: Treason and Plot. London, 1901.

Innes: England under the Tudors. London, 1911.

McArthur: The Regulation of Wages in the Sixteenth Century. English Historica Review, XV.

Maitland, F. W.: Constitutional History. Cambridge, 1908.

Maitland, S. R.: Essays on Subjects connected with the Reformation. London, 1899

Merewether and Stephens: History of the Boroughs and Municipal Corporations. London 1835.

Le Neve: Fasti Ecclesiae Anglicanae. Oxford, 1854.

Nicholas: Life of William Davison. London, 1823.

Palgrave: Original Authority of the King's Council. London, 1834.

Palmer: The Celt in Power. Transactions of the Royal Historical Society, 1886.

Percy: Privy Council under the Tudors. Oxford, 1907.

Pike: Constitutional History of the House of Lords. London, 1912.

Pike: The Public Records and the Constitution. London, 1907.

Pollard: Authenticity of the Lords' Journals. Transactions of the Royal Historica Society, 1914.

Pollard: Henry VIII. London, 1905.

Pollard: Political History of England. Vol. VI. London, 1910.

Pollard: Protector Somerset. London, 1900.

Read: Walsingham and Burghley in Elizabeth's Privy Council. English Historica Review, XXVIII.

Scofield: Study of the Court of Star Chamber. Chicago, 1900.

Skeel: Council in the Marches of Wales. Girton College Studies, II. 1904.

Strype: Annals of the Reformation. London, 1709.

Strype: Ecclesiastical Memorials. London, 1721.

Stubbs: Constitutional History of England. Oxford, 1878.

Stubbs: Seventeen Lectures on Medieval and Modern History. Oxford, 1886.

Thomas: Historical Notes. London, 1856.

Tytler: England under the Reigns of Edward VI. and Mary. London, 1839.

Usher: Rise and Fall of the High Commission. Oxford, 1913.

2H 26

LIST OF ABBREVIATIONS.

———:o:———

A.P.C.—Acts of the Privy Council. Edited J. R. Dasent.

D.N.B.—Dictionary of National Biography.

Dom. Cal.—Calendar of State Papers Domestic.

E.H.R.—English Historical Review.

L. and P.—Letters and Papers of the Reign of Henry VIII.

P. and O.—Proceedings and Ordinances of the Privy Council.
Edited H. Nicholas.

CPSIA information can be obtained at www.ICGtesting.com
Printed in the USA
BVOW06s1025230714

360217BV00018B/438/P